TEARDOWN

TEARDOWN

Rebuilding Democracy from the Ground Up

DAVE MESLIN

Research
ZACK MEDOW

Illustrations
MARLENA ZUBER

PENGUIN

an imprint of Penguin Canada, a division of Penguin Random House Canada Limited

Canada • USA • UK • Ireland • Australia • New Zealand • India • South Africa • China

First published 2019

www.penguinrandomhouse.ca

LIBRARY AND ARCHIVES CANADA CATALOGUING IN PUBLICATION

Meslin, Dave, author
Teardown : rebuilding democracy from the ground up / Dave Meslin.

Issued in print and electronic formats.
ISBN 978-0-14-319705-8 (softcover).—ISBN 978-0-14-319706-5 (electronic)

1. Democracy—Canada. 2. Political participation—Canada. I. Title.

JL186.5.M47 2018   323'.0420971   C2017-904555-5
                                                    C2017-904556-3

Printed and bound in Canada

10 9 8 7 6 5 4 3 2 1

Penguin
Random House
PENGUIN CANADA

For Pauline, my parents, and Santiago

CONTENTS

RIGGED

"Drain the swamp!"

Sung by hopeful choirs of thousands, this three-word anthem echoed through stadiums across the United States in the autumn of 2016, a tidal wave of rage that swept their unlikely hero into the White House. Donald Trump told his adoring crowds, "Our movement is about replacing a failed and corrupt political establishment with a new government controlled by you, the people." Meanwhile, an almost identical message was reverberating through crowds of equal size, as Bernie Sanders preached rebellion against a system "held in place by corrupt politics." "The only thing that can stop this corrupt machine is you!" proclaimed one. "This is what a political revolution looks like!" echoed the other. Both peppered their speeches with the word "rigged."

The seeds for these radical sermons had been planted years earlier by the Tea Party, a decentralized and leaderless right-wing movement, and Occupy Wall Street, a decentralized and leaderless left-wing movement.

> We came to protest the blatant injustices of our times perpetuated by the economic and political elites.

Born from obscurity, our movement is a spontaneous force shaking the very glass foundation of the oligarchy that rules in our name.

You probably can't tell which of these quotes is from the Tea Party and which is from Occupy. Despite originating at opposite ends of the political spectrum, both of these anti-establishment uprisings were born from the same sentiment: power has become increasingly concentrated in the hands of the few, disempowering ordinary people like us. The two movements spread quickly, attracting tens of thousands of supporters to their marches and rallies, and inspiring the two underdog presidential candidates—both of whom attracted larger crowds than any establishment candidates had seen in decades.

But these two restless movements were just the tip of an iceberg. People's lack of faith in our political system has reached a crisis point, extending far beyond the United States. A recent poll revealed that only 13 percent of Canadians trust politicians. This is consistent with other surveys across Western nations, which regularly rank politicians as one of the least trusted professions, typically placing them higher than only lobbyists and/or psychics. While some people express their cynicism and anger by attending marches and rallies, most simply give up and tune out. For these people, a rapidly growing group, politics has become a spectator sport—a reality show that feels removed from their own lives. While the final hours of the 2016 US election were tense, with Hillary Clinton and Trump in a virtual tie all evening, the real story is that the largest bloc of voters chose neither of them. The largest group stayed home.

DIDN'T VOTE	93 million
CLINTON	66 million votes
TRUMP	63 million votes

In Canada the previous year, there were cheers from political observers celebrating our increased voter turnout, but the truth is we've set the bar so low that we cheer for failure. Even with the highest turnout in two decades, one out of three voters stayed at home. Here, too, the largest voting segment in the entire country was the group who voted for no one.

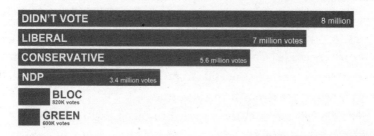

The numbers are even worse when it comes to measuring political engagement *beyond* voting. Between elections, how many people get involved with the decision-making processes that affect their lives, their families and their communities? The answer is almost none. It's hard to blame them. Politics has become a demoralizing farce. Most decisions are made behind closed doors by political insiders, while our legislatures have been reduced to arenas of toxic adversarialism—a childish circus and an embarrassment to our species. But the more we tune out, the more power the insiders have. And the more power they have, the more reason we have to tune out. You can see how quickly this snowball of apathy can grow.

So we find ourselves in a crisis of cynicism, flowing in three directions. First, we have our growing collective cynicism towards politicians. Second, there's a reverse flow: political elites are cynical about us. Unless they're asking for our votes or donations, political leaders seem uninterested in our capacity to participate.

But the third direction of cynicism is the most dangerous: we've lost faith in each other.

Stereotypes abound of a mindless, consumer-driven, self-absorbed society filled with people who are completely uninterested in politics, their community, or the pursuit of the common good. Think of how we've normalized the use of the word "populist" to describe political messages that are self-serving, ignorant or hateful. The actual word simply means "support for the concerns of ordinary people." So the way we're currently using the word endorses the belief that ordinary people are crude by nature and that the elite educated political class needs to operate independently from the desires of the population—to protect citizens from themselves. Ironically, this is exactly the kind of condescension that has propelled so-called populist leaders into power in the first place.

I believe in people. I look around, at my friends, my family, colleagues, neighbours—and I see individuals who are inspiring, caring and open-minded. And sometimes I'll start up a political conversation with a stranger just to make sure I'm not deluding myself from within a social bubble. I tend to do this in the two places that are most conducive to long discussions with complete strangers: taxicabs and barbershops. I'll broach a political topic, and the first response is almost always dismissive or self-deprecating—"Oh, I don't know much about that," or "I don't really care"—accompanied by a shrug. It's as if they're trying to live up to our own cynical clichés of human nature. But if I gently push a little further, like heating up frozen soup, their opinions and ideas begin to thaw and the individual flows outwards. Even if I disagree with their views, I find myself appreciating their thoughtfulness and the complexity of their positions.

So, as a mass culture, we seem to be unplugged, uninterested and self-absorbed. But as individuals, we're curious, passionate and contemplative. How can we resolve the contrast between these two portraits of who we are?

Each person's lived experience provides a unique point of view that has value. As Jason Darrah, Edmonton's director of public communications, once told me: "People have local knowledge. The drainage experts can't beat a citizen who says, 'Every time it rains, it pools right there.'" Whether that knowledge is about pooling water or something more profound such as knowing what it's like to live on minimum wage, to be racially profiled, or struggle with addiction, these perspectives represent an ocean of wisdom and experience. In addition, we each have distinct approaches to problem-solving, unique communication skills and particular ways of exploring our creativity. But in a culture of disengagement, these voices and skills lie dormant behind a wall of apathy.

How do we tear down this wall? The first step is to recognize that human behaviour depends on environment. We can feel restrained or free, based on where we are and what's happening around us. Think of something as simple as singing. Children laugh and sing without restraint, but as we grow older we learn to become more reserved. Most adults don't sing. But there are five interesting exceptions: national anthems, happy birthday, karaoke, prayer and the shower. In other words, adults tend to be embarrassed about singing unless they have the comfort of privacy, the familiarity of ritual and/or the excuse of alcohol. When they have those permissions, they'll sing loudly—and happily.

So rather than assuming that people don't want to participate in politics, I think it's more accurate—and respectful—to recognize that politics can feel intimidating and that people simply need an environment where it feels worthwhile, safe, comfortable and normal to speak out, to share ideas and to work towards those ideas. To sing.

I'm often asked how I learned to fight for what I believe in, and I always answer the same way: "that's the wrong question." Children exhibit no signs of apathy. They know what they want, and they ask for it—often loudly. We're all activists at heart. So the question should be: what is it about our society that puts out the fire in so many people's hearts? Political apathy is something we learn. It's not a state of un-caring; it's a state of hopelessness and an erosion of faith. "Withdrawing in disgust is not the same as apathy," recited Richard in the 1990 film *Slacker*. Exactly. But the result is the same if the disgust isn't somehow resolved. If we feel that we don't have any power, we simply stop trying to exercise it. This so-called apathy goes far beyond traditional politics, appearing also in our work-places, our schools and our neighbourhoods. How many people are actively involved with a local residents' group, condo board, tenant group or parents' association? How many are actively trying to push for change in the places they work each day? The vast majority of people have simply become disengaged from the decision-making processes that shape the world around them.

The next time you notice something that you wish were different in the world, pay attention to your reaction. You may have walked past a homeless person and thought, "What can I do?" And you've likely seen headlines about climate change that make you worry about the future. When we come face to face with things that make us uncomfortable, we can try to work towards change or we can feel paralyzed by hopelessness. Taking action requires faith in our own ideas, faith in each other, faith in our leaders and faith in the system. Most people are lacking one or more of these faiths. I think many are lacking all four. This is what makes our culture so deeply biased against participation.

In the absence of these faiths, we either turn to apathy or offer our unconditional support to heroic leaders who promise to "drain the swamp." In Toronto, I remember left-leaning mayor David Miller hoisting a straw broom above his head, promising to sweep away corruption. A few years later, conservative mayor Rob Ford promised to "stop the gravy train." Again, both left and right, with a similar core message: the whole system is screwing you over, and I can fix it. And years before Trump began spouting his infamous swamp slogan, the exact same phrase was being uttered by Nancy Pelosi, a left-leaning senior Democrat. Before her, it was Ronald Reagan. We're just going in circles. None of these people can drain the swamp, because the swamp is a culture, and we're all part of it. It's bigger than any single leader, party or platform.

That said, our obsession with swamp-draining has inadvertently provided us with a useful analogy because politics *is* indeed a swamp—not in its foulness, but in its potential. Swamps—also known as wetlands—are vibrant ecosystems that filter water and provide a home to countless plants, fish and wildlife. Politics is also an ecosystem: complex, interconnected, fragile and—dare I suggest?—capable of beauty.

I've spent the last twenty years of my life exploring our democratic swamp. Like a political biologist, I've journeyed through the strange and mysterious worlds of protest movements, party politics and non-profit organizations. I've danced between conventional democratic institutions and grassroots activism, wearing a suit and tie one day and shouting through a megaphone the next. I've worked as an executive assistant at both city hall and the provincial legislature, painted do-it-yourself bike lanes on the street, organized hundreds of volunteers, started a handful of non-profits, helped draft new legislation, survived tear-gas riots in three countries, buried my car and got thrown in jail. Not in that order.

I started out protesting in the streets and then slowly learned how to navigate through the maze-like corridors of power, to effect change from inside the machine. I've learned that politics is an elaborate chess game, with dozens of forces at play: backroom strategists, lobbyists, local columnists, news producers, hidden partisan affiliations, old grudges and older loyalties. By watching the game closely, and playing both alongside and against talented practitioners, I slowly began to understand these forces and learned how to take advantage of them to move a good idea forward. But each time I think I've got a grasp on how complex the system is, I realize it's a larger labyrinth than I'd imagined. Having worked as a community organizer, campaign strategist, journalist, lobbyist, fundraiser and partisan staffer, I've seen the political ecosystem from a dozen angles. These are the two main things I've learned: first, change is possible, and regular people can have an impact; second, change is much harder than it should be because the system is indeed rigged against ordinary people. Voices are marginalized and common sense is drowned out by a political culture that feeds our worst instincts and pushes people away. So I'm left feeling both hope and rage. And I'm ready for a teardown.

Teardowns come in three flavours: demolition, disassembly and dissection.

In real estate, a teardown is a house purchased only to be ripped apart by hydraulic jaws. But for an auto mechanic, an engine teardown requires the patient and careful removal of each gasket, hose, pulley and bracket, followed by a thorough cleaning, replacement of old parts and finally an engine rebuild. And in the world of consumer electronics, a teardown is a surgical dismantling of components, simply to discover what's inside. The intent of each teardown is unique: to destroy, to repair or to learn.

Inside this book, you'll encounter a few proposals that require a political wrecking ball. But for the most part, this teardown is a meticulous surgical operation. In an article called "If You Love Your Gadgets, Tear Them Apart," *Wired* magazine explored tech tear-down culture and asked, "Why are geeks so fascinated by looking at the chips, wires, ribbons and glue—the hideous part of a gadget—when the gorgeous part is on the outside?" The answer? "It's quite simple: By peering into these gadget's 'souls,' you learn their secrets." If we're to overcome the massive failure of modern democracy, we need to look into the soul of the swamp. What are the elements of our democratic ecosystem, and how do they relate to each other? Which parts are salvageable and which are rotten to the core?

This book begins by exploring the basics: our broken voting system, the role of lobbyists, the influence of big money, the hollowness of our political parties and all the ways that our democratic spaces are designed to be alienating and hostile. But we're going to dig deeper than that, because democracy is about so much more than ballots and legislatures. We'll crack open our schools, revealing not only a broken civics curriculum but also a top-down environment that rewards both obedience and conformity, forcing kids to slowly unlearn their own leadership skills. We'll explore the harm caused by the polarization of ideas and the adversarial battlegrounds that preclude constructive dialogue. We'll deconstruct the non-profit sector and the ways that political advocacy is financially suffocated, and we'll uncover how we've drowned out community voices in our public spaces by commodifying the visual landscape. Most importantly, we'll look at all the ways we're taught to lie low, to be politically cautious, quiet and disengaged, and we'll examine why, centuries after absolute monarchy was overthrown, we still cling desperately to the fantasy of a single saviour— a great hero who will lead us and fix our problems.

I've been criticized for using words like "rigged" or "corrupt" to describe our political situation. "You're just feeding the demagogues!" I'm told. But the opposite is true: if we're afraid to state the obvious, then others will fill the vacuum and use the opportunity to push their own divisive (and sometimes hateful) agenda. We need a proper diagnosis—as grim as it may be—so we can apply the proper remedies. Admitting that our political culture is in crisis is not a declaration of defeat—it's an invitation. Those who pretend our democracy isn't broken are themselves part of the problem, because when social, cultural and political barriers conspire against our natural desires to improve the world around us, it's entirely inappropriate— and dangerous—to simply cheerlead or offer pep talks. It's like trying to motivate a room full of people to go for a jog—without telling them that their feet are chained together, torrential winds will blow against them, and someone has poured thick tar in their path. When we describe as "apathetic" those who aren't engaged politically, we're actually blaming the victim.

Have you ever had an idea for how to improve your neighbourhood? Your workplace? Your school? If you had unlimited power, what would you change about the world? Now ask yourself, "What have I done so far in my life to make those changes happen?" If the answer is "Not much," I want to help you understand why. Because I think you have a lot to contribute. We all do.

What you're holding in your hands is not an aggregation of complaints—it's a collection of solutions aimed at bringing our democratic ecosystem to life, not only in our legislatures but also in our daily lives, so that we can find our collective voice and make change happen—together.

This is a call for revolution. But not a revolution that takes place in the streets or in stadiums. I'm calling for a revolution against our own cynicism and against a spiritually carcinogenic system that has crushed our voice. Every day, decisions are made that affect our lives—our neighbourhoods, transit, hospitals, schools, parks, water and air. We can choose to be a part of the decision-making process or we can watch passively, withholding our collective knowledge and creativity.

Our greatest mistake was assuming that democracy is just about ballots. If you gave people hockey sticks but no rink and no puck, would you be surprised if they eventually put down their sticks and walked away? We need to look at the whole political ecosystem in its entirety.

The growing tides of cynicism and the rise of political leaders who are both vacuous and angry are not reasons to abandon democracy. Quite the opposite: they are the inevitable results of an abandoned democracy. In a time of looming environmental tragedy and increasing economic inequity, is it possible for us to tap into our collective creativity to build a more sustainable, healthy and inclusive society? I believe we can. Our toxic legislatures do not represent what we're capable of. They're a mockery of our true potential.

This is no time for tinkering. This is a teardown. Because the most important voice missing from our democracy, is yours.

CHAPTER 1

THE MECHANICS OF EXCLUSION

Four gallons of semi-gloss paint. Fifteen brushes. Twelve hours. That's all it took for me, my neighbours and our kids to create a five-hundred-square-foot mural on Springmount Avenue, a twisting midtown Toronto street lined with century-old homes and large trees whose branches reach out from both sides of the road, touching in the middle. Unlike traditional murals painted on walls or under bridges, the Springmount mural was painted flat on the road, stretching gloriously from curb to curb. Designed by a local artist and carefully outlined by steady-handed adults, our horizontal masterpiece was mostly painted by dozens of pint-sized

Picassos of all ages. It was colourful, gorgeous and . . . well, entirely illegal. You see, I tried to apply for a mural permit, but it turned out that our local bylaws didn't allow road murals, even though programs in other cities had successfully encouraged residents to realize the artistic potential of their pavement. My neighbours and I agreed that our roads were essentially a massive blank canvas just begging for some colour, and that the bylaws were unnecessarily restrictive, so we painted the mural anyway— without permission.

We hoped that our direct action might put pressure on the city to legalize and regulate community-driven road murals. Sure enough, our public space intervention quickly attracted media attention, and full-colour photos appeared in multiple news- papers. I was even invited to speak on radio shows about the city's restrictive policies. Our work really paid off, though, when our local city councillor agreed to put forward a motion asking city hall staff to create a proper permit process. Our painting was transforming policy!

But the city's bureaucrats recommended against the proposal. Our only hope was to convince council to vote against the staff report and overrule the recommendations of their own senior bureaucrats. I encouraged my neighbours to send letters of support to councillors, and I invited Melissa Frew, the local artist who'd designed our mural, to come to city hall and speak at an important committee meeting where councillors would be voting on our proposal. As a familiar face at city hall, I'm too easily dismissed as an "activist," so I felt that Melissa's voice would show we had support in the community. She'd never been to a meeting at city hall and said she was nervous, but she hesitantly agreed to attend. This was participatory democracy in action!

At the meeting the following week, Melissa didn't show up. I sent her a text to find out where she was, and she wrote back immediately to explain that she had arrived at city hall but had trouble finding the room the meeting was in. And when she did find the right door, it was closed. Councillors, city hall staff, lobbyists, political insiders and activists (like me) know that the committee room doors are *always* closed, and that everyone is welcome to open them and walk in. But to someone attending a committee meeting for her first time, a closed door sends a strong message: keep out. Remember what I said about singing? People often need to feel a sense of permission; without it, they revert to caution and disengagement. When Melissa encountered the closed door, she wasn't sure if she was allowed in. She did crack the door open slightly to listen, but when she couldn't determine if she'd missed the item or not, she decided to go home. "I didn't feel that I could walk in," she later told me. "I thought I would be interrupting."

Here's a challenge: go to any indoor shopping mall and find a store with its doors closed. You can search for the rest of your life, but you'll never find one. Retail managers know that the smallest details can encourage shoppers to come in or walk past. We often hear conservatives say that we should run government like a business, while progressive voices strongly push back, arguing that a democratic society cannot be defined merely as a set of financial transactions. Both sides are right. On the one hand, governments are not corporations driven solely by their bottom line, and citizens are so much more than simply taxpayers. On the other hand, governments can learn a great deal from the private sector. Indeed, every day I notice examples of businesses doing a much better job than government when it comes to informing, engaging, attracting and inspiring people. So despite my somewhat centre-left political views, much of this chapter is devoted to how we should in fact run government more like a business. Here's why: When Melissa responded to my text message, I encouraged her to come back to city hall. She returned, opened the committee room door and ended up speaking eloquently to the councillors. A few minutes later, we won the vote and our community project was approved. For the first time in Toronto's history, citizen-driven neighbourhood road murals were legal. Once she'd found her way through the door, Melissa was able to interact with the decision-making process and witness her own impact on public policy.

Our democratic institutions can feel inviting, alienating or even invisible, depending on how they're designed. When we talk about democratic reform, we focus on the biggest and most obvious design flaws, such as our voting system or the influence of "big money" (both of which I'll address later in this book). But during my twenty years as a community organizer, I've seen how small, overlooked flaws can collectively serve as a significant obstacle to participation. Just as a city's billion-dollar sewer system can get blocked by wet wipes and dental floss, a democracy can be clogged when the smallest details coalesce into layers of obstruction. If something as simple as a single closed door can deter a grown adult from participating, try to imagine the cumulative impact of these layers and how they reinforce the idea of politics as an insiders' game. These are the often-overlooked mechanics of exclusion, and this is what makes our system rigged against ordinary people. A healthy democracy must be accessible, comfortable, understandable and convenient. Every aspect of the system needs to be dissected and assessed based on how it impacts these four necessities. If we want to create a culture that invites people in rather than pushing them away, the first step is to open the doors—both physical and metaphorical. Once these doors are open, I believe we can create a participatory democracy unlike anything we've ever seen before.

BELOW GRADE

The way that governments design public notices to communicate with citizens offers us a perfect example of what I'm talking about. When I presented a TEDx Talk back in 2010, I showed the audience what a public notice looks like in Toronto, and then I showed how ridiculous a Nike ad would look if the company used the same approach.

The ensuing laughter was expected. We all know that companies like Nike produce fun, sexy, effective advertisements, while governments have cornered the market on useless communication.

 **TORONTO**

Ulli S. Watkiss
City Clerk
www.toronto.ca

City Clerk's Office

NOTICE OF APPLICATION(S)
(Under the Planning Act)

The City has received the following application(s) under the Planning Act:

NORTH YORK COMMUNITY COUNCIL AREA:
City Clerk, attention: Francine Adamo, Administrator
North York Civic Centre, Main Floor, 5100 Yonge Street, Toronto, ON M2N 5V7
Fax: 416-395-7337, E-mail: nycc@toronto.ca

Application No.: 10 184490 NNY 10 OZ
Application to Amend the Official Plan to permit the construction of a 7 storey building
containing office uses, retail uses and 22 residental dwelling units.
4362-4370 Bathurst Street
Southwest corner of Bathurst Street and Sheppard Avenue West
Ward 10 - York Centre
This land is also sibject to an application under the Plannign Act for an ammendment to a
zoming by-law Application No.: 10 175209 NNY 10 OZ.
Christian Venresca, Planner at 416-395-7129 or E-mail: cventre@toronto.ca

Application No.: 10 227038 NNY 24 OZ
Application to Amend the Official Plan and Zoning By-law and to amend the Draft Plan
of Subdivision to redessignate Park and Mixed Use blocks, to amend the zoning by-law
performance standards including height and density and to revisethe street and block
pattern
1001-1019 Sheppard Ave East
South of Sheppard Avenue East and west of Bessarian Road
Ward 24 -- Willowdale
Lynn Poole, Planner at (416) 395-7136 or E-mail: lpoole@toronto.ca

---

Nike inc.

Oct 25 2011

Notice of Retail Purchase Opportunity

Our regional distribution centre has received notice
that product #372G (running shoe) will be available
for retail purchase at certain locations, as of October
2nd. Product 372G has a mesh and synthetic nylon
material shell with a carbon rubber outer sole. This
sole has a circular "waffle" tread for traction. The inner
sole is injected with Phylon material. This product is
available in men's, women's and children's shoes.

Nike has effective ads because the company wants you to buy its products. But the message we get from bland public notices is that governments are completely uninterested in having regular people involved in community planning. In other words, these government notices are rigged. Rigged to keep you uninformed and uninvolved.

One year after the TEDx presentation, I wrote a blog post inviting designers to create an ideal public notice, the polar opposite of the Toronto example. I asked them to ensure that each design contained four elements:

1. It should be gorgeous. We get bombarded with messages all day, on TV, on billboards, in magazines and on our phones. The design had to break through the mental clutter and catch people's attention.
2. It should highlight the most important information. Someone should be able to glance at it and get the basic idea of what it's about in only a few seconds.
3. It should clearly highlight opportunities for engagement. Is there a town hall meeting? An online survey? A design workshop?
4. It should include a call to action. "Your voice matters." "This is your chance to be heard." "We want your opinion." Remember: we need permission to sing.

Shortly after my posting, I received a dozen spectacular submissions from all across the country. Their beauty and clarity instantly revealed the gross negligence of our cities' administrators and elected officials. I posted the designs on my blog, and a year later, I received an unexpected email from Jill Brooksbank, the communications coordinator of the small town of Pemberton,

British Columbia. After watching my TEDx Talk and seeing the beautiful designs on my blog, Brooksbank completely redesigned the official template for Pemberton's public notices based on the guidelines I'd provided. The *National Post* published a story about the town's revised design, with the headline "How One B.C. Municipality Is Trying to Get People to Actually Read Public Notices." This was an exciting breakthrough for my crusade, but at the same time, I couldn't help thinking how sad it was that a well-designed public notice was worthy of a headline in a national newspaper. You'd never see a headline stating that a garbage truck has picked up garbage, or that librarians have put books back on the shelves. But that's where we're at. When governments try to engage the public, it's news.

I wanted Jill's efforts in Pemberton to catch on, so I decided to give them an award. The goal was to use shame, embarrassment and jealousy to encourage other cities to follow Pemberton's lead. I admit, the award was a bit of a scam. I designed a certificate on my laptop, printed it at home, flew to BC, bought a cheap picture frame in Vancouver and drove two hours to Pemberton to deliver the inaugural Dazzling Notice Award (DNA). Even though the award was just a random act of appreciation from a lone crusader, Jill and her colleagues—Mayor Jordan Sturdy (right) and Daniel Sailland (left), the town's chief administrative officer—were thrilled.

Sure enough, my devious plan worked. Other cities started contacting me: "Dear Mr. Meslin, our municipality would like to inquire about the application process for the Dazzling Notice Awards." Within two years, I'd given awards to Ottawa, Hamilton and Vancouver. Then Oakville, Brampton, Niagara Region and others. I was ecstatic, but to be honest, I was also terrified of

being exposed as a distributor of fake homemade awards. So I've teamed up with the International Association of Public Participation (IAP2) who now manage the awards using formal criteria for evaluation and a panel of judges. (The first two awards were given to Squamish, BC, and Waterloo, Ontario in 2018).

Of course, good graphic design is just the beginning. The effective use of colours, images, fonts and layout is great, but if the words themselves don't make any sense, you've still got a useless leaflet, web page or sign. Take this development notice, for example, which I saw on a large board in front of a downtown building:

Development Proposal
587-599 Yonge St.
2-4 Dundonald St.
7-9 Gloucester St.

An application has been filed to amend the City of Toronto Zoning By-law 438-86 to permit a mixed-use development with one 49-storey tower (163.16 metres including mechanical penthouse) including a 4 storey podium (19.9 metres). The development would contain 513 residential condominium units and retail uses at-grade and on the second-storey. The residential lobby is proposed to be located at the southeast corner of the building and accessed from Dundonald Street. Four levels of below grade parking containing 202 vehicular parking spaces are proposed. There are 529 bicycle parking spaces proposed. Exterior amenity space is to be provided on the roof of the podium, on the third and fifth floors, and interior amenity space is to be provided on the second, third and fifth floor. The existing row houses at 7 and 9 Gloucester Street are to be retained except for the rear extensions which are proposed to be demolished.

STATUTORY PUBLIC MEETING:
Information will be posted once meeting is scheduled.

TORONTO FILE# 12 235622 STE 27 OZ
For Information:
City Planner: Sarah Henstock
416-392-7196   shensto@toronto.ca

No one knows what Zoning Bylaw 438-86 is, so why would you use it in your opening sentence? It's a great way to make sure that no one continues to the second sentence. You also won't find many ordinary citizens who know that the word "podium" in this context refers not to a lectern with a microphone but is an obscure architectural term for the base of a tall building—the wider floors underneath a narrow tower above. Similarly, the term "below grade" is used by engineers to describe things that are under the ground—a situation normal people universally describe as "underground." There's a reason that London's subway system is called the Underground and not the Below Grade. It's the same reason that there's no rock band called the Velvet Below Grade. "Mechanical penthouse" refers to a storey of a skyscraper that contains the heating and ventilation systems, air-conditioning, generators and water pumps. No one cares about these floors, or even knows about them, so these words are just clutter on the page. And I imagine that an "exterior amenity space" is some kind of patio or deck, but to be honest, I'm not sure. I am sure of this: never in my life has someone said, "Dave, let's meet up later at the exterior amenity space." Not once in forty-four years. Lastly, one surefire way to decrease attendance at a statutory public meeting is to call it a "statutory public meeting." It not only sounds terribly dull but also implies that the city is being forced to hold it against its will—which may actually be true, owing to provincial guidelines. What's wrong with calling it a town hall? Or just a public meeting? Or a neighbourhood meeting?

Even worse, I've seen public notices where the language is entirely misleading. For example, advertising companies in Toronto have been trying to install massive digital billboards near residential homes. However, these megaboards, which flash a new image every ten seconds, aren't allowed near residential areas so the companies have to apply for a special exemption. City officials then send out a public notice to affected households, to solicit residents' input and approval. But these notices—which are allegedly intended to inform neighbours about a bright billboard that will flash thousands of times each day—don't mention the words "billboard" or "flashing." In fact, the public engagement notices refer to the billboards as "static electronic signs." I'm not joking. They use a word that's the *exact opposite* of what they're attempting to describe. None of the residents respond to these notices, of course, since a "static" sign sounds quite harmless. But the next thing they know, there's a digital billboard the size of a drive-in movie screen outside their bedroom windows. And we call this public consultation.

Here's the bottom line: people have busy lives. It's a lot to ask them to take time out of their days to participate in local decision-making. So every time we make the invitation a little more complicated or confusing, we're giving citizens one more reason to tune it out. Words themselves can be rigged. According to a report called "Municipal Gobbledegook," written by the Toronto Bureau of Municipal Research: "Public notices, rather than clearly informing people of decisions that are pending, may only confuse or perhaps frustrate or even antagonize them. It is too easy to view the notices as mere legal formalities. But they are much more. These notices not only convey specific information to particular individuals, but also are an important mechanism through which citizen participation may be encouraged and informed or discouraged and possibly nipped in the bud."

Wise words. Sadly, that report was written in 1972—before I was born. People have been hopelessly advocating for plain-language policies for decades. But using understandable words is just one small part of effective communication. Another element, equally important, is how numbers are presented. Government policy is all about data: how much of our money they've collected, how they plan on spending it, and how they will measure its impacts. But when we read—even in plain language—about millions or billions of dollars being spent on transportation, education or healthcare, the numbers begin to seem abstract and it can be difficult to grasp the trends and relationships between enormous pieces of data. The solution to this is called "data visualization," which is just a fancy term for making numbers pretty.

An example of data visualization that you encounter every day but have probably never thought much about is the weather. There are 1,480 weather stations across Canada and more than 8,000 in the United States. They collect information about temperature, precipitation, humidity, pressure and wind. The raw data looks like this:

METAR KNXX 121155Z 03018G29KT 1/4SM +TSSN FG VV002 M05/M07 A2957 RMK PK WND 01029/1143 SLP026
SNINCR 2/10 RCRNR T2 SET 6///// 7//// 4/010 T10561067 11022 21056 55001 PWINO PNO FZRANO

Computers take those numbers, calculate the forecast and then output revised data that looks like this:

"Temperature_max" : [7.20, 8.57, 10.11, 9.32, 9.80, 8.60, 9.05]
"Temperature_min": [2.58, 0.39, 3.14, 3.38, 3.36, 1.73, 2.11]
"Precipitation_probability": [29, 11, 11, 11, 11, 16, 24]

But that's not what you see when you look at a weather forecast. Instead, you get colourful charts, graphs, icons and maps. While a trained meteorologist might be able to look at the raw numbers and know what they mean, it's the colourful charts and maps that make that data understandable to ordinary people like you and me. Any government serious about citizen engagement needs to ensure that there are creative visualizers working alongside the accountants, data analysts and finance specialists. If your data isn't beautiful, you're not communicating.

When it comes to hearing from our governments, we desperately need a massive dose of creativity. Good design, plain language and data visualization are fundamental to public participation. Nothing short of a complete overhaul of every governmental communications department will suffice. When that happens, we can find our nearest above-grade exterior amenity space and raise a glass.

OPENING THE DOORS

But what about the physical spaces of democracy? Our city halls and legislatures were intended as palaces of participation: public spaces that would allow regular people to witness, and participate directly in, the democratic process. Designed as temples of transparency, these buildings are supposed to serve as the guarantee of accountable and responsive government, and your personal gateway to engagement. But like government materials that are designed to exclude, these spaces too can be rigged. Any physical space or public event can be designed in a way that makes it feel friendly or hostile, welcoming or alienating.

Again, the contrast with the private sector is astounding. Businesses invest enormous amounts of time, thought and money into making their spaces both noticeable and comfortable. Not only do they want to you find them and walk through their doors, but they want you to come back. Governments seem to operate with the opposite philosophy—their buildings appear designed to make you feel confused, uncomfortable or lost. In the story I shared earlier, Melissa Frew's feeling of being worried about opening the door of a committee room is what people feel all the time in these buildings. My favourite example is Halifax city hall. Nearby, colourful signs announce the presence of a bank, a hotel and a restaurant. But curiously, it seems that no one ever thought of putting up a sign for city hall. If you walk close enough, you'll notice a couple of inconspicuous miniature plaques, some including the words "city hall" in a font so small you could completely obscure the text with a Pez dispenser. A citizen could walk past the historic building hundreds of times and easily imagine it to be a courthouse or a museum. On a recent visit, as a fun experiment, I asked a few people for directions to city hall—while I was standing directly beside it. Local residents would stop under the anonymous towering stone of their own government building, thoughtfully glance up and down the street, and apologetically confess that they didn't know where city hall was. Even if they did manage to somehow identify the building, their next challenge was to figure out how to get inside. Every single doorway facing the street is locked. Most of these doors are solid steel, with no windows or doorbells. Some have security cameras pointing at you as you bewilderingly look back. One door on the east side of the property has a sticker that says, "Keep away. Do not touch anything. You can be badly hurt or killed." If you eventually make your way to the west side of the building, which faces a lightly travelled one-way side street, you'll pass another locked door and then an opening in a concrete railing, marked with two helpful signs: "Authorized parking only" and "No skateboarding." Through that opening, you'll find a secret public square and the single open door. This "front door" is hidden on the back of the building, leaving only stone walls facing the street. Upon entering, you'll find yourself at a security checkpoint, face to face with a friendly guard asking why you are there—and wondering how you possibly found your way in.

With no signage and an obscured entrance, Halifax city hall has the look and feel of a members-only club. Like the Citadel, the historic military fort just a few blocks away, the building seems intentionally designed to keep people out.

Closed committee room doors, poor signage and obscured entrances are obvious obstacles. But they're also the easy targets. Hundreds of smaller details contribute to a cold and unwelcoming environment that discourages regular citizens from participating, giving an enormous advantage to paid corporate lobbyists and representatives of big business, who will always find a way to have their voices heard. It's literally their job. Time after time, I've seen ordinary people dip their toes into the waters of political participation and then pull back because it feels cold and murky. It's almost as if someone came up with a list of all the things that would make it more comfortable and convenient for citizens to engage politically, and then implemented the opposite.

For example, our governments hold their most important public meetings during regular work hours, presenting an enormous obstacle to those who want to speak at a meeting or witness a crucial vote but can't take time off work or school. Timing is everything. That's why *Dancing with the Stars* doesn't air at noon and restaurants don't send their staff home at five. But even if you are able to attend a daytime meeting of your local government, you'll quickly encounter one of the most annoying aspects of the political system: there's no schedule. If you want to speak about a specific item, you just have to wait around until the item comes up. It might be discussed in the morning, the afternoon or maybe even the next day. Most people will simply leave in frustration— or not show up in the first place. As a political organizer, I can tell you that when I try to mobilize citizens for an important meeting,

I have much more success if I can tell them to be there at 10 a.m. or 6 p.m., rather than asking them to hang around for hours. To be fair, it would be difficult to have a fixed schedule for every item because no one knows in advance how long each debate will take. But councils could easily schedule the most important items into two or three predetermined slots. Better yet, we could have a process where citizens are able to request a scheduled item by collecting a set number of signatures. This is a no-brainer. No one would ever attend movies, plays or sports events if they didn't know what time these things began. People are busy and need to schedule their lives. Daytime meetings and the lack of a clear schedule effectively silence community voices while amplifying the voices of private interests.

But timing is just the beginning. Equally important is the atmosphere citizens encounter when they try to participate for the first time. The smallest details can completely transform a space. Serving food, for example, is a universal gesture of warmth and hospitality. When I started out as a community organizer, two decades ago, I promoted all my public meetings with the phrase "juice and cookies will be served." That one simple sentence made it clear that I genuinely valued people's participation, time and effort. As they say, food is the way to a person's heart. The private sector has also figured this one out. Some of the most successful companies in the world offer free meals to their employees— Google famously has dozens of café restaurants at its California headquarters, each serving free breakfast, lunch and dinner. (Google co-founder Sergey Brin once told his office designers, "No one should be more than 200 feet away from food.") Some businesses even offer free snacks to their customers. I've seen banks serving coffee and cookies, a nail salon serving smoothies, car dealerships giving away biscotti and tea, a garage offering slushies, hair salons serving beer and wine. Most popular of all is popcorn—available at stores selling everything from tires to hardware to jewellery.

But at city hall in Toronto, not only are no snacks served but people aren't even allowed to eat. Every Tim Hortons has a sign that says, "It's nice to see you!" but the only sign that welcomes guests as they enter Toronto's council chamber reads, "Council regulations: No food. No drink. No signs. No banners." In other words, thanks for stopping by, but please refrain from all activities related to human expression or survival. Similar signs can be found in Toronto's regional municipal buildings. The North York Civic Centre, for example, offers the following friendly all-caps sign: "NO FOOD OR DRINK ALLOWED IN COUNCIL CHAMBER." Can't you feel the love? But let's be clear: *regular citizens* (you and I) aren't allowed to have food in these chambers, but if you're a councillor, you can set up a salad bar on your desk or make fondue. City staff claim that allowing food would create a mess. And yet somehow, movie theatres have figured out how to purchase and use vacuum cleaners, while our city halls and legislatures are still researching the topic.

Providing even the most basic frills, like free Wi-Fi, seems to be a struggle. Somehow, every café and fast food joint in North America has discovered that providing connectivity is a great way to create a comfortable and inviting space, yet thousands of government buildings across North America still have no public internet access. Even a place like Toronto city hall, with its annual budget of $10 billion, didn't begin experimenting with public Wi-Fi until just recently. The first attempt required a new alphanumeric password each day. This was printed on paper and taped to a metal stand. Each time you closed your laptop, you'd be bumped off the network and would have to make your way back to the stand to type in the new password again. Meanwhile, Starbucks had been offering free and convenient Wi-Fi for more than a decade.

Connectivity also requires electricity, a fact widely known outside of government buildings. Everywhere I go, I have no trouble finding an outlet to charge my laptop or phone. Some businesses even have charging stations for phones, with cables provided (the gold standard is a small cubby with cables and a locking door—your own personal phone-charging vault). But I can't tell you how many times I've had to leave a Toronto city council meeting because my laptop or phone needed a charge—especially on days when I've had to wait hours upon hours for an unscheduled item to come up. Somehow, city hall techs have managed to install outlets on all the politicians' seats, but none in the public seating. Again, a double standard.

Oh, and while you're sitting there—thirsty, hungry and offline—make sure to refrain from expressing yourself by applauding a speech, presentation or vote. Clapping is banned too. I'm not talking about rowdy or disruptive behaviour—just polite applause. Yet again, a ridiculous double standard, as silent citizens watch their elected officials clap, laugh and heckle. Efforts to maintain a strictly passive public have reached absurd heights, with councils across North America passing formal "no clapping" regulations that have resulted in applauding citizens being escorted out by officers or even handcuffed and arrested.

Over-policing, in general, has become common in political spaces. Security cameras, armed guards, locked doors, bag checks and metal detectors are the new normal in government buildings.

Earlier this year, I was invited to Queen's Park to witness the introduction of legislation I'd worked on, but it felt like I was visiting a maximum-security prison rather than the people's legislature. After I'd signed in at the front desk and got a personalized visitor's pass, my knapsack and laptop were confiscated. I then went through a metal detector and was told to hand over my cellphone. (Forget about Wi-Fi or charging stations. I no longer had any device to plug in!) When I was asked if I had anything else in my pockets, I held up a standard yellow HB pencil. They took it. I kid you not.

While increased security is clearly warranted in light of recent terror attacks, each tactic has to be measured against the culture of fear it creates and the negative impact on legitimate public participation. We all want to feel safe, but we also feel uncomfortable when we're unfairly scrutinized, suspected or inconvenienced. Any security measure must be based on evidence, rather than fear and sensationalism. And as horrifying and memorable as political attacks have been, the evidence paints a clear picture: American politicians are three times as likely to be killed by lightning as they are to be killed by another human being, and in Canada, the likelihood is much, much lower. There are extremely rare cases of direct attacks on government buildings, such as the 1984 shooting at the Quebec legislature or the 2014 shootings on Parliament Hill, and no one would suggest that these buildings should not be protected by armed guards who can respond with force and defend those who are being targeted. But the focus should be on security measures that are invisible rather than intrusive.

The most excessive examples of over-policing are at our city halls. I say excessive because as rare as terror attacks are at the national level, they are unheard of in municipal buildings. Over the last 150 years in North America, only a handful of local politicians have been the targets of violence, and almost every attack happened either inside the victim's own home or at the hands of a fellow politician—not a member of the public. Yet city halls across Canada have been rapidly increasing security, as if they are under siege by an armed militia.

When I first got involved with municipal politics in Toronto, for example, our city hall felt open and inviting. Slowly, new security features were added that made it harder for ordinary citizens to move around the building. Councillors' offices were placed behind a newly-built set of locked doors, accessible only by those with an official pass and a staff escort. Then most of the doors to the building were locked, with one single open door placed under the watchful eye of a uniformed guard—a situation *Toronto Star* reporter Jennifer Pagliaro described as a "lockdown-style operation of all entrances and exits." Now they've recently added bag screening as well, with security guards shining flashlights into people's personal belongings, and Council is considering even further measures including metal detectors and glass barriers to physically separate politicians from members of the public during meetings.

None of these so-called "security" measures are in response to any credible threat, nor is there any evidence that they would prevent an attack. They're simply a response to fear. When Calgary City Hall implemented similar measures, the manager of security flatly admitted, "There's no specific event that's actually brought this on." According to the *Calgary Sun*, the most violent attack that their city hall had ever witnessed was a woman who threw a book in the chamber.

Barricades, visitor passes, property confiscation and armed guards all create an atmosphere of militarization, unfriendliness and inconvenience, threatening the openness and comfort required for a healthy and participatory democracy. No other sectors would tolerate the levels of inconvenience that we've created in our government buildings, because they actually use evidence-based risk assessment to measure benefits against unintended negative consequences. When a woman stabbed a complete stranger to death in a Toronto Shoppers Drug Mart in 2015, did the retail chain respond by adding metal detectors, security guards and bag-checks at all its locations? Of course not, because such a response is statistically unwarranted and would hurt business. Personally, I'd switch to Rexall.

Which brings me back to my main point: Why are political spaces designed and treated so differently than commercial spaces, in terms of convenience, accessibility and comfort? Civic engagement is constantly thwarted by details that create a hostile and confusing environment that discourages participation. Meanwhile, lobbyists saturate the system, easily drowning out the handful of citizens who defy the odds to take part. Your voice, and the voice of your family and neighbours, is lost. To level the playing field and attract regular citizens into the process, the system needs to make every step as easy and as comfortable as possible so people like you can fit a little democratic participation into their busy lives. But rather than simply compiling a checklist of the hundreds of small details that need to be fixed, let's dig a little deeper and explore why companies invest millions to attract and retain customers, while our governments create experiences that feel like a cross between a high school detention and a funeral.

DEPARTMENT OF USER EXPERIENCE

Almost every topic I've discussed in this chapter so far can be summed up with two words: user experience. In the world of technology, user experience (or UX, for short) is about maximizing the simplicity and comfort of a device or application—especially for first-time users. But UX doesn't apply only to laptops or smartphones. Anything can be designed with UX in mind: a store, a car or even a pen. All the commercial products and places we interact with daily tend to have incredible UX design. Companies invest effort, attention and money into making you feel as comfortable as possible. Governments do not. In fact, they seem committed to creating uncomfortable environments. The reason for this contrast can be found by comparing the incentives and motivations that drive both sectors.

Corporate managers operating in a competitive environment have a clear incentive to invest in UX: happier customers lead to higher revenues. For a store, restaurant, movie theatre or sports arena, good UX design brings nothing but benefits to the owner. But in government, the opposite is true. Not only do governments operate within a monopoly, but they actually have an inverse relationship to public participation. After all, if ordinary people begin to participate in politics, they might get involved with an advocacy campaign challenging government policy, volunteer for a political opponent or even decide to run for office themselves. For government, good UX design can threaten those in power. In other words, politicians are literally in a conflict of interest when it comes to civic engagement.

Now, I'm not suggesting that politicians ignore UX intentionally. There's no need for a conspiracy theory here. UX gets ignored in political environments out of passive neglect, because there's no incentive to prioritize it. For that reason, I propose that every government body have an independent, arm's-length department of user experience with a substantial and stable budget, untouchable by elected officials. This is not to be confused with an auditor, who looks at the effectiveness of service delivery. This department would be responsible specifically for the UX design of political participation.

If governments already had these UX departments, I wouldn't have had to write this chapter. The problem is that no one is being paid to ask, "Will anyone understand this notice?" Or, "Is this room comfortable?" Or, "Is this meeting accessible?" If those questions were being asked, staff would have realized years ago that government materials need to be redesigned, that meetings need clear schedules, that excessive security is a deterrent to participation, that serving food is a simple way to boost engagement and that allowing people to bring pencils into Parliament may make their experience a little more constructive and participatory. On average, companies spend 10 to 20 percent of their budget on marketing and UX design. If governments took just a tiny fraction of that—even 0.1 percent of their operating budgets—and invested it in permanent steady funding for an independent department of user experience, our relationship to politics would change overnight. If I were hired to work in a properly funded department of UX, here are some simple reforms I would try to implement right away:

- **GREETERS:** The moment you enter a building, you can develop an instant sense of belonging and comfort or confusion and alienation. That's why Walmart, Apple and Best Buy have full-time greeters standing at each doorway, offering both a smile and a "How can I help you?" It would be nice, at our city halls, to be greeted by a smile instead of a security badge.
- **CHILDCARE:** Most participants at public meetings are younger than thirty or older than fifty because those in between are busy raising kids. Once again, we can look to the private sector for inspiration here. Numerous companies offer free in-store childcare, the most famous example being IKEA's Småland, which has been serving as a temporary babysitter for millions of kids since 1958. Similar programs exist all across North America, and even small businesses offer free childcare. (My favourite example is a San Francisco manicure studio that had a program called "Mani and Nanny.") But with no childcare facilities at public meetings, only those who can afford private care or have a live-in nanny are in a position to engage with their government. The size of your wallet should never determine your capacity to participate as a citizen.
- **DIRECT MAIL:** At election time, you'll hear a lot about the "front-runners" or about leaders of the major parties. But there are dozens of other candidates and parties that you won't hear about until you see them on the ballot. My UX department

would mail election menus to every household, showing all
the candidates, parties and platforms. We'd also distribute
detailed and colourful catalogues that explain how to participate in decision-making between elections so voters can have
an impact on issues that affect them. We'd deliver these catalogues to homes, community centres, libraries, schools and
government buildings. I've asked government staff why they
don't already do this, and I'm always told that the internet
has replaced the need for printed materials. But a website is
effective only if someone actually sees it. Even then, it takes
just one click to close a browser tab, while a printed leaflet
is more likely to lie around the house and get noticed. That's
why the executives at IKEA (again) spend well over half of
their annual marketing budget on a printed catalogue. With
more than two hundred million copies printed worldwide,
it's actually the most printed book in the world (even more
than the Bible). Canadian Tire ditched print marketing a
decade ago, but then returned to publishing twelve million
copies of a two-hundred-page catalogue, explaining that the
print catalogue served as a "gateway" to the online catalogue.
The exact same thing happened to J.C. Penney, which also
cancelled its print catalogue, only to bring it back five years
later because, as CEO Mike Ullman told the *Wall Street
Journal*, "we lost a lot of customers." Bingo.

But aside from running its own programs, a department of user
experience could also make recommendations to other departments
or directly to legislators. For example, UX experts might suggest
loosening dress codes for political meetings. While the private sector
is beginning to ease office fashion regulations, led by comfort pioneers such as billionaire Richard Branson ("I've always hated ties,"

he once said, because they're "uncomfortable and serve no useful purpose") or investor and NBA team owner Mark Cuban ("I don't wear a suit and can't figure out why anyone does"), politicians across North America have been prevented from speaking in their own legislatures or chambers for not wearing a tie. Some have even been escorted from their seats by security for dress code violations. Our own House of "Commons" forces all male members to wear ties, lest they look too . . . common? The sad irony is that business attire is supposedly worn as a gesture of respect and seriousness, and yet our elected reps throw shameless partisan insults across the room while dressed in suits and heels, resembling a group tribute to Boss Baby.

A department of user experience could also oversee the implementation of existing policies. For example, most governments have already committed themselves to a plain-language policy (a universal ban on bureaucratic jargon so average citizens can easily read government documents without requiring a degree in economics, business management, public policy or Latin). But it doesn't seem to be in anyone's job description to oversee the implementation of the policy. Good intentions can evaporate quickly without oversight. Lastly, the department of UX could carry out thorough audits of existing programs, measuring their openness, convenience and accessibility. An audit of elections, for example, would quickly point out systemic inconveniences that likely discourage participation, such as:

- WEEKDAY VOTING. Major public events are never, ever held on weekdays . . . except for elections. Imagine the Santa Claus Parade or Grey Cup being held on a weekday afternoon while kids are at school and their parents are at work. That would be crazy. Yet in Canada we hold all our federal and provincial elections on Mondays, Tuesdays or Thursdays. Globally, weekday voting is actually quite rare, with citizens of more than fifty countries (including most of Europe and South America) casting their ballots on Sundays, and those of a dozen others (including Australia, New Zealand and Taiwan) voting on Saturdays. "But isn't your employer obligated to give you time off to vote?" you might be thinking. This is a misunderstood rule. Your employer is only obligated to ensure that you have three consecutive hours to cast your ballot within the hours of voting. So if you work from 9 a.m. to 5 p.m. and the polling stations are open from 9 a.m. to 8 p.m., your boss is not required to give you anything. You're just supposed to leave your kids at school and skip dinner while you vote. And it's absurd to think that people in precarious minimum wage jobs are going to walk out the door for a few hours in the middle of their workday. Think weekends are for relaxing and not voting? Then how about keeping our elections on a weekday, but declaring it an official paid holiday? *Toronto Star* columnist Emma Teitel proposed this very idea in a 2016 column and summed up the issue perfectly with one question: "What's the use of observing Canada Day, a national holiday marking the moment our democracy came into being, if we don't also grant our citizens ample time to participate in its continued existence?"

- **DIGITAL VOTERS LISTS.** I've voted in nineteen elections in my life, and each time I've had to line up at an assigned polling station, wait patiently for my name to be found on a paper list and then watch it get carefully crossed out with a ruler and pen. Imagine if every time you bought a pair of jeans, you had to wait for the sales clerk to update her inventory list with a pen. Or if Costco allowed you to shop at only one location because each store had a different printed member list rather than an integrated shared database. Our polling stations should be subsidized by the Canada Council for the Arts or perhaps the Department of Canadian Heritage, since they are essentially live theatrical re-enactments of how information was managed in the early 1800s.

- **ONLINE VOTING.** For those of us who grew up in a pre-internet world, it may not seem strange to line up at a voting booth on election day. We also used to line up at banks to withdraw twenty dollars and in video stores to rent plastic boxes full of magnetic tape. But today's young people have no idea what a video store was, and to them, polling stations must seem like a strange ancient ritual on par with making mixtapes or sacrificing animals. Concerns about hacking and electoral fraud can be dealt with through various forms of public data verification, and coerced voting can be remedied by simply allowing people to recast their votes. Estonia has been offering online voting in its general elections since 2005. Meanwhile, voters in Canada are asked to stand in the cold, waiting to put a piece of folded paper into a cardboard box. No wonder half of them stay home.

I want to be clear that there are a handful of politicians who are indeed trying to make progress on democratic user experience. People like Bruce Archer, a city councillor from Mesquite, Texas, who recently convinced his colleagues to switch all their meetings to the evening. "It's changed everything!" he told me. "When I was first elected, meetings were at 3 p.m. Since we've gone to night meetings, we're having good crowds at every meeting, and you can feel a lot of enthusiasm and energy." Or Edmonton councillor Scott McKeen, who pushed back against a proposal for metal detectors in the council chambers and a physical barrier between councillors and the public. "We live in a world where fear is being heightened and marketed," he told reporters. "When we react to that, I think we make it worse and the possibility of a negative outcome actually increases." Or Councillor Maureen Cassidy, of London, Ontario, who successfully proposed that food be allowed in the chamber—her first motion as a rookie councillor. "I remember sitting for hours in the gallery as a member of the public with my stomach growling," she explained. "The rules seemed a little bit as if we were treating grown adults like children. To encourage greater participation in civic life, we should make it as easy and comfortable as possible."

Some bureaucrats are also pushing for reform. I've met incredibly passionate civil servants like Jason Darrah, Edmonton's former director of public communications, who believed that rather than trying to attract people to traditional consultations at city hall, the city should bring discussions directly to citizens. For Edmonton's long-term transit strategy, Darrah's department hosted spontaneous meetings on public transit buses, giving free rides to passengers who would participate in a pop-up focus group. To get input on snow and ice removal, city staff went to senior centres and offered free meals to those willing to share their ideas. They've connected with Indigenous seniors groups by attending their tea and bannock gatherings, and they have a van called the City Hall Express that travels to community events, festivals and powwows. But my favourite innovation is the pizza party, where Darrah provides workbooks, instructions, an optional facilitator and, most importantly, free pizza to citizens who want to host informal focus groups in their own homes. "People are darn busy," he told me. "That means that we have to come up with different ways to connect, to make it easier and convenient. We're trying to retool the way we listen and learn from citizens. It's not us controlling the environment. It's respecting people's time."

Another civil service hero is Barb Clifford, Calgary's former returning officer. After seeing a public transit bus in Boston that had been repurposed to provide meals to the homeless, Clifford invented a Vote Bus based on the same idea. Her mobile voting station—a retrofitted bus borrowed from Calgary Transit—drives around the city and parks in front of LRT stations, looking for voters. Following Calgary's experiment, Sudbury also rolled out an Election Bus, parking it in high-traffic destinations such as colleges and universities or outside of Sudbury Wolves hockey games. This is incredible UX design for voters.

But for every example of a government opening its doors, I can find you ten of doors remaining closed or, just as frequently, being pulled closed even tighter. Not only are innovative UX ideas incredibly rare in government, but they don't spread quickly when they do happen. Take online voting. A few brave municipalities have introduced internet voting as a supplement to traditional voting booths, and the results are fantastic. The most conservative estimates suggest that internet voting triggers an automatic 3 percent bump in voter participation, with some experiments showing much, much higher results. You'd think that after a few cities tried it, the rest would simply join in. But no. You and I continue to use online banking without any problems, we tap our digital credit cards daily, we store personal information in the cloud—but we vote with pieces of paper and cardboard boxes.

Even when governments launch UX projects that seem incredibly innovative, they're often just playing catch-up to the private sector. Calgary's Vote Bus, for example, seems like a really creative and edgy idea. But if you think about it, the concept of putting impulse items right in front of consumers is not new at all. Heck, ice cream vendors figured out a century ago that mobile retail efforts led to impulse purchases. Toronto has 136 ice cream trucks—twice the number of fixed-address ice cream stores! And of course we have mobile food trucks, fashion trucks, knife sharpeners and so on. The secret of their success is that they come to you, rather than forcing you to go to them. It's an old trick—not a new one.

But the most important part of my proposal for a political department of UX is the budget. Good UX design isn't cheap. When civil servants and bureaucrats try to improve things, not only are they outliers but their efforts are sabotaged by politicians who refuse to invest in UX. So we end up with half-assed attempts that we'd never see in the private sector. A simple example is live-streaming and video archiving of government meetings, a reform that is slowly rolling out across the country. The intention is good, but the results so far are sloppy at best. Most of the live feeds are difficult to find, buried deep inside poorly designed websites. Very few have text overlays explaining what item is being discussed and who's speaking. (Imagine tuning into a baseball game and not seeing the score, what inning it was, or who is up to bat!) Some archived videos haven't even been trimmed of "dead time"—like lunch breaks. I found one video of an Edmonton council meeting that begins with ten minutes of people simply walking around the room. And before that, there was—no exaggeration—one full hour of a black screen. Total darkness. For an hour.

A teardown reveals the mechanics of exclusion, details often missed because of their scale and seeming insignificance. Every single failure I've mentioned so far is the inevitable result of an institutional absence of effort and resources related to public participation. So if we want to have any hope of seeing governments opening their doors, we'll need dedicated staff members who focus solely on UX and ensure that they have a corporate-size budget to get the job done. If we can achieve that goal, thousands of small changes would begin to unfold and our political culture would be turned inside out. It's time for us to raise our expectations and work towards political systems that are comfortable, convenient, accessible and understandable. Only then can we breathe life back into democracy by drowning out elite players in a tidal wave of ordinary people.

CHAPTER 2

LEVELLING THE FIELD

It's one thing to get people in the door and make their experience as comfortable as possible. But even with the best UX design in the world, our political systems will still be complex and difficult for the average person to navigate. Before any legislation, bylaw or policy is approved, it weaves its way through reports, consultations, committee hearings, revisions, public debates and votes. Decisions are influenced by dozens of forces within the political ecosystem, such as bureaucrats, politicians, citizen groups, business interests and the media. Each of these groups has its own subsets and internal ecosystems, and all are competing to shape policy by strategically exerting pressure at the right time and the right place. Those who know how the process works have an enormous advantage over those who are walking aimlessly through the legislative labyrinth. Wouldn't it be great to have a personal guide who could take you by the hand and explain how you can maximize your influence at every stage of the process? Those navigators exist, and they're called lobbyists.

Professional lobbyists provide a variety of services to their clients. They have access to decision-makers through personal relationships and can assist with the framing and branding of a client's message. But one of the most valuable skills they offer is an ability to decipher the complexities of the political process. These services are invaluable to any corporation, and lobbyists get paid well to deliver the goods. Many multi-billion-dollar industries have obstructed good policy through effective lobbying, including tobacco companies, oil producers and fast food chains, but lobbying isn't limited to these massive corporations. Every local advocacy campaign I've ever worked on as a community volunteer—from toxic garbage dumps to bike lanes to protecting public spaces—has had to deal with sabotage by high-paid lobbyists who had more time, more resources and more connections.

Corporate lobbying is one of the greatest forces contributing to the imbalance of power in society and the disproportionate amplification of wealthy voices at the expense of your own. It wasn't always like this. The history of lobbying is fascinating and reveals a massive shift in public tolerance. One hundred and forty years ago, the US Supreme Court described lobbying like this: "If any of the great corporations of the country were to hire adventurers who make market of themselves . . . to procure the passage of a general law with a view to the promotion of their private interests, the moral sense of every right-minded man would instinctively denounce the employer and employed as steeped in corruption. If the instances were numerous, open, and tolerated, they would be regarded as measuring the decay of the public morals and the degeneracy of our times." Shortly afterwards, the Georgia constitution was amended to declare lobbying a crime. Even a few decades ago, professional lobbying barely existed in North America.

Yet corporate advocacy has grown exponentially in my lifetime, and it has become one of the defining characteristics of our city halls and legislatures today. The very recent proliferation of digital billboards along our highways offers us a clear example of how powerful lobbyists have become. The leading cause of fatalities on our roads—more than speeding or drunk driving—is driver distraction. Yet the outdoor advertising industry is literally trying to increase and monetize highway distraction with flashing roadside billboards that take advantage of a captive audience. It's TV with no remote control—an advertiser's dream. These billboards offer no public benefit and serve only as an annoying visual blemish on our landscape. But their overhead costs are low and their profit margins enormous, and a huge chunk of that revenue is spent on lobbyists. And it works. As legislators introduce new policies to crack down on distracted drivers, these billboard companies— enabled by those same legislators—invest millions to develop ways to distract those same drivers. That's the power of lobbying.

So what can we do? Countless jurisdictions have attempted to put limits on corporate lobbying, but since there are so many tactics available to influence decision-makers, these mechanisms have often proven ineffective. You close one loophole, they'll squirm through another. But the situation is not as hopeless as it sounds. American academic and activist Zephyr Teachout has proposed a brilliant solution that is radically counterintuitive: we need *more* lobbying. Rather than trying to reduce the voice of wealthy corporations, why not simply level the playing field and increase the voice of everyone else? Lobbyists for all!

How would this work? Well, the government could provide direct funding to community groups that want to hire a lobbyist. If a small advocacy group could prove that it had a certain amount of support from the community (perhaps by collecting signatures), it would get an automatic government subsidy to hire a lobbyist. Or corporations themselves could be forced to pay for their opposition's lobbying costs—a proposal put forward by political scientist Lee Drutman. Or as Teachout has proposed, governments could create an Office of Public Lobbyists and staff it with full-time advocates who assist community groups. Just as courts appoint lawyers to low-income defendants, public lobbyists would be assigned to citizen groups that have few resources.

The premise behind this approach is not only that corporate lobbying can't be stopped, but that lobbying is actually a good thing—as long as there's a level playing field. Drutman points out that politicians can only make the best decisions if they've been exposed to all points of view and the most information possible. "Any attempt to cut [politicians] off from the pressures of society is a betrayal of both the idea of representative democracy and the potential for collective intelligence," he writes in his book *The Business of America Is Lobbying*. "The Washington lobbying community is full of many bright policy minds, and the expertise and knowledge that the business community can provide make for a more informed policymaking process." The problem is that the current imbalance of lobbying "turns our government from a fundamentally public-facing entity to a private facing-entity," Teachout asserts. "If we do not radically change the role of the lobbying industry in decision-making, laws will increasingly tend toward complex mechanisms that redistribute power away from the people and toward the clients of the most effective lobbyists."

As I think back to each time that I've personally experienced lobbyists successfully interfering with the public good, I realize that the actual problem wasn't their efforts, but rather the lack of a counterbalance. I find myself thoroughly convinced by both Teachout and Drutman: as backwards as it may seem, the solution to lobbying is more lobbying. A large dose of professional assistance to help community voices influence the political process would go a long way to creating a more balanced dialogue in our legislatures. Without it, voices like yours will be left unheard and decisions will be made in the interests of those who have the financial capacity to navigate the political maze.

The other piece of the puzzle, however, is education. After all, one reason we so desperately need navigators to help us understand the complexities of the decision-making process is that our schools do such a terrible job of teaching us about democracy in the first place. Tour guides are beneficial only in an environment where you would otherwise feel lost or confused. If kids grew up developing a deeper understanding of how governments operate, then the ability for corporate lobbyists to distort that process would be severely eroded. Most school boards do have some kind of limited civics program, but the courses are generally treated as a fringe part of the curriculum. It would be easy to blame students for this failure. Kids just don't care about politics, right? Well, not necessarily. It all depends on how you approach the topic.

Several years ago, I was invited to speak to a few hundred high school students in Markham, Ontario, and I started by telling them about all the political themes that get me excited: bicycle infrastructure, public space reclamation and voting reform. I'll be honest— they didn't care. The students looked bored and disconnected, so I shifted gears and asked them a simple question, hoping it might trigger their attention: "What do *you* care about?" No one answered, so in an effort to make the question more concrete, I asked them to imagine what they would change if they were the prime minister for a day. Again, no answer. What if they were the premier of Ontario? Silence. The mayor of Markham? Awkward stares. Finally, I made it as tangible and local as possible: "What if you were the principal of this school? What would you change?" After a few moments of further silence, one solitary hand rose nervously above the hundreds of sleepy heads. The teenage boy said simply: "Hats. We're not allowed to wear hats." Some of the teachers looked at me nervously. I smiled with excitement. "You're not allowed to wear hats?" I said. "Let's talk about that." Suddenly, eyelids that had seemed heavy just moments earlier were opening wider because I was discussing something the students could relate to. We talked about how rules are made—and how you can change them. I gave them tips and ideas about how to run an effective advocacy campaign. I suggested they start a petition and a Facebook page, hold a media event and recruit endorsements from open-minded parents. I encouraged them to do some research and find data to support their cause. Surely someone has written a PhD thesis on the impact of dress codes on academic performance, schoolyard violence and dropout rates. I also recommended that they propose a pilot project, maybe called "Hat Fridays," to make the change more palatable for the administration. The first step, I told them, was to meet with the principal and have a discussion about it. By the end of my impromptu Activism 101 workshop, these kids looked attentive, interested and engaged. They'd been transformed by the realization that democracy is not an abstract topic about ballots, procedures, bylaws and legislation. It's about our lives, it's about power and freedom, it's about choice, expression, struggle and change.

Now, you may be thinking, "Aren't you just teaching them about selfishness? Shouldn't they be worried about poverty and environmental catastrophe, rather than hats?" My answer is this: gateway drug. Get them started on something easy, accessible and relevant to their daily lives. Help them see the connection between taking action and changing the world around them. Once they understand that they're capable of sparking change, even in a small and materialistic way, the message will sink in. After all, kids don't like poverty or pollution any more than we do. The task for us isn't to make them care about social problems but rather to bring the idea of civics alive, make it relevant and help students realize that they aren't powerless—that they can have an impact.

I would start by changing the name. Going back to the idea of plain language, I propose getting rid of the term "civics" from our curriculum and replacing it with something kids will actually relate to, like "Shaping the World," "Your Voice," "Sharing Power" or simply "Power." After all, that's what civics is all about: who has power, how it's shared and how it's exercised. Kids will be much more excited to learn about power than they are to learn about civics. The next step would be to massively increase the amount of space in the curriculum devoted to democratic skills. Most provinces don't have a mandatory civics course at all, and for those that do, it's a mere crumb. Ontario, for example, offers only a single half credit civics course. Imagine math being taught in only one year, as a half credit. And yet, how is math more important than learning about power? Having been exposed to the inner workings of government and community organizing for two decades, I can tell you that we could teach a full course about democracy in each year of school, and we'd still just be scratching the surface. One high school credit should be dedicated to the mechanics of local government and another to our parliaments (both provincial and federal).

These courses would explore voting systems, budgets, revenue sources, accountability, balance of power, proposals for reform, opportunities for public participation and so on. A third course could look at charities, non-profits, grassroots community groups and foundational elements of community organizing, advocacy and protest. These are the building blocks of a democratic society. It's absurd that we don't teach how these structures work, demystify the process and explain that anyone—even kids—can participate and take a leading role. A further course could explore media literacy in the context of political messaging. We keep hearing about the crisis of fake news and paid political interference online, which has led to new proposals to censor, screen and moderate news feeds to ensure that all news is "real." But it's a slippery slope to have any central body (whether it's the government or Facebook) moderating the truthfulness of our news. A more practical solution is to ensure that citizens have the skills to interpret news from diverse sources and the mental filters to compensate for bias and partisanship.

Instead of these valuable courses, we get civics classes that are rushed and oversimplified, and often focus on memorizing facts and dates rather than imparting practical knowledge that is actually relevant to students. Even more problematic is the tendency to replace a proper civics education with charity fundraisers. Don't get me wrong—there's nothing wrong with teaching kids about charity and the importance of giving to those who have less. But that's not the same thing as learning to engage with the system in a meaningful way and to exercise collective power to effect permanent change. Kids need to understand the connection between policy and outcomes because neither poverty nor pollution happens in a vacuum. These things are directly impacted by our political decision-making process.

Lastly, a big problem with our current approach to civics is the teachers themselves. While there are a handful of civics teachers who feel passionate about the topic, the vast majority appear uninterested in teaching it in the first place. It's not their fault, really. Civics is one of the only courses that doesn't have its own certification. In other words, unlike maths or sciences, there is no way for a teacher to be formally trained to teach civics. The end result, predictably, is that very few educators have the knowledge, skills or desire to teach it. Stephen Young, the founder of Ontario's Civics Education Network (CEN), admitted in a recent interview that civics classes have "a bad reputation among students and teachers across Ontario." He explained that "the schools themselves perpetuate this, often putting new, inexperienced or uninterested teachers into the course. These teachers then teach to the text . . . not making any effort to inspire and motivate their students." A report from CEN goes even further, saying, "It appears to be common practice for a principal to 'slot in' any teacher who has free space in their schedule. Worse, assignment to a civics class is oftentimes seen as a punishment." So if the principal doesn't like a certain teacher, she gets *sent* to civics? It's the Siberia of our curriculum? Folks, we have a major problem here. The CEN report ends with this worrisome conclusion: "Recent research concludes that [Canadian civics classes] focus almost exclusively on political and military events, avoid controversy, and construct citizenship in more elitist and passive terms than in other democracies. Indeed, many academics have criticized Canada's existing civic education as brainwashing at worst, and unreflective of the changing nature of societies at best."

When teachers and academics themselves are describing a curriculum as "unreflective," "brainwashing" and "punishment," it's definitely time for a teardown. It's hardly surprising that our current approach is failing. Imagine trying to get kids excited about playing baseball by placing them in a class called "Sphere Contact and Diamond Circumnavigation," in which they sit at their desks endlessly memorizing obscure game scores from the 1960s. Now imagine that class is taught by someone who not only doesn't like baseball but has never swung a bat in his life. How do you think that would turn out? These courses need a top-to-bottom make-over if we want to provide our kids with the tools required to learn how to participate in our democracy, how to be engaged citizens, how to find their own voice and how to help change the world around them.

Alberta's City Hall Schools offer an incredible template of what's possible. While most Canadian city halls put on some kind of superficial half-day tour for school classes, both Calgary and Edmonton have a full-size permanent classroom where students spend an entire week learning about democracy through a custom-ized hands-on participatory curriculum. I visited both schools and loved what I saw. Rather than being isolated in a basement or a far-off corner, the schools are built into the main floor of their respective city halls. In Calgary, the classroom is directly across from the council chambers. Floor-to-ceiling windows facing the lobby remind the kids that they belong there, and that they're part of the building's purpose and function. These students spend five days meeting city staff and politicians, working on group projects and participating in mock meetings in the council chamber. Kids of all ages take part, with the content tailored to their needs. In Edmonton, kids in a grade one class were asked to design a new bridge for rapid transit. Afterwards, a senior planner came to the classroom and stamped each drawing with an official seal. Very cute, but also educational: a window into the vast world of deci-sions that shape our surroundings.

Older kids delve deeper, of course, and form a new understanding of what government does and how it affects them. When I spoke to a group of grade five students, I heard a common theme: that single week had opened their eyes. "I always thought that city hall just kinda stood there, and that it was just a building and that it didn't have any use," a young student named Dianna explained. Her friend Chloe, echoing her, confessed, "I thought that city hall was just this big clock, and I didn't know it actually had things in it. I didn't even know that Calgary had a government." Many students expressed surprise at how interesting their time in city hall was, and how much they actually enjoyed it. Interestingly, I noticed this same sense of surprise coming from some of their parents as well—and even from the teacher! Linda Hut said she'd always loved taking her students on field trips to the zoo or the museum, but when she heard about City Hall School, she admits that her first reaction was skepticism. "City hall? Really? For a whole week?" But she tried it, and she liked it so much that she now runs the entire program. I asked her what the attraction was for her.

"The students get a sense for how complex city government is," she explained, "with different sides to each issue—how everybody has a voice and how people can make a difference by standing up, by sharing their view and also the chance to meet people that are connected with their city. It's the connection with people that plants a seed for future activists, for future leaders, for future city workers, future councillors and just future engaged citizens."

During my visit to Calgary, students were asked to figure out how many votes were needed to win a motion at city council. There are fourteen members of council, plus the mayor. "Eight votes," the kids all quickly said. Then one student asked, "But the mayor has the final say . . . right?" Jody Danchuk, the teacher, asked the kids what they thought the answer was. When there was no consensus, she simply said, "Well, we're going to be meeting the mayor later in the week. You can ask him the question yourself!" What an amazing and empowering experience—to spend time at city hall, develop questions about how power is shared in our democracy and then have a chance to ask those questions of those who currently hold power. If kids aren't given a roadmap to democracy, they're unlikely to participate politically when they're older. City Hall School is the best example I've seen of what that roadmap can look like.

But enough about kids. Teaching young students about government and power is important, but what about the rest of us? Education doesn't end when we leave school, right? We've got adult classes for cooking, pottery, kick-boxing—you name it. Why don't we have free courses teaching adults how democracy works and how they can get involved, take the reins and make a real difference? This is another area where government could learn from business. Think of Home Depot, which offers free workshops every Saturday morning on how to install moulding or how to tile floors. These classes not only get people in the door but also create active customers.

The skills they learn encourage them to initiate renovation projects at home. After all, you're not likely to buy lumber, tile or tools if you have no idea how to use them. Democracy is no different: when people lack knowledge, skills and a sense of familiarity, they simply tune out, which gives more power to a small group of influencers.

A few city halls do offer adult democracy courses, but none come close to allocating the kinds of resources that Home Depot does to its customers' skills development. Edmonton offers a series of courses through its Planning Academy, but only once a year and for only forty students at a time. In Ottawa, a small non-profit called Synapcity hosts a free civics boot camp, also for forty people, with no government funding at all. But the best example I've ever seen is Toronto city hall's Civics 101, a free educational program offering six in-depth evening sessions. The project was launched in the spring of 2009 with a fantastic advertising campaign featuring three short sentences: "Curious about your government? It's your city. What do you know about it?" The promotional materials were translated into seventeen languages, and participants were offered assistance with childcare and transportation. Incredible UX design, and it paid off. Over 900 applications were submitted—many more than anticipated. The program could accommodate only 175 students, unfortunately, leaving more than 700 eager applicants out of luck. But the sessions were a huge success. Ninety-four percent of participants said they had learned how city government works, and 84 percent were inspired to get more involved. Testimonials in the final report showed that the participants were not only happy with the program but hungry for more. "This whole program exceeded all my expectations. I encourage you to repeat this every year! So many people would become engaged and informed," gushed one student. "I would love to attend a Civics 201," said another. "This is only the beginning."

Pretty cool, right? But here's the punchline: despite all the effort invested in creating the program, the avalanche of applications and the fact that participants loved it and wanted more, the entire program was shut down after only one session. I can't think of any better example of how apathy and disengagement are encouraged and perpetuated by those in power. I'm not blaming the city staffers who ran the program—it was the councillors who decide what gets funded and what gets cut each year. Every city, town, province and territory should be offering free programs like Toronto Civics 101. The failure to do so is an admission that citizen engagement is not valued—that *your* voice is considered irrelevant.

TRICKS OF THE TRADE

People attempting to engage in our political system for the first time, even if they've been briefed on the basics, will likely feel mystified or disoriented as decision-makers dip into a bag of tricks used to create illusions, confuse onlookers or even make things disappear. These acts of wizardry serve as yet another layer of obstruction, giving lobbyists and insiders even more of an advantage. Vanishing acts used to obscure otherwise transparent debate and dialogue are especially common. Some have clear names such as "closure" (a legislative ruse used to close down an ongoing debate), but others are masked behind a web of jargon intended to further confound the citizenry. Vague terms such as "routine motion" or "the previous question" are assigned to tools used to minimize transparent discourse in the legislature, while others have Orwellian titles such as "time allocation" (a procedure that allocates *less* time for debate than normally allowed). Then we have the controversial omnibus bill. No, that's not the name of a public transit system or a Transformers character—it's a mega-sized piece of legislation that combines unrelated issues into a single vote. Like a shell game, a government can use an omnibus bill to pass an unpopular item by hiding it inside another piece of legislation and hoping that no one will notice. I witnessed this first hand in 2006, when the Ontario Liberal government proposed expanding municipal council terms from three years to four. City councillors and mayors loved the idea, of course, but municipal advocates were shocked that such a major reduction in democratic accountability could happen without consultation or a public referendum. A century earlier, eight separate referendums were held before the municipal term was changed from a single year to two. (On average, the No vote was 60 percent.) But this time, the government decided not to seek input or even have a transparent vote in the legislature, and instead buried the item deep inside an omnibus budget bill. The media ignored the issue and the public didn't know about it. I pulled together a multi-partisan citizens' campaign opposed to the change, but it felt like we were campaigning against a ghost. The proposal was adopted in a vacuum.

A similar voodoo tactic used by city councils and school boards is called a consent agenda. This was supposed to be a time-saving tool used to combine dozens of small administrative items into one simple vote. But a council or school board can use it to make important decisions behind closed doors and then simply rubber-stamp these decisions in public. A staff person at the Toronto school board recently told me that many parents and families used to attend the meetings, but "barely anyone comes anymore" because of the frequent abuse of consent agendas.

Why stop at making a proposal or a debate disappear? Why not make the government itself disappear? This can be done provincially or federally by proroguing the legislature—a fancy word for shutting down the entire government, bringing all proposed legislation and debate to an abrupt end. Prorogation has been used by prime ministers and premiers for many decades as a way to avoid embarrassing votes. This term also has an Orwellian name, since it can be traced to Latin and French roots meaning "to ask publicly" or "to prolong, extend"—the exact opposite of what it does.

Another way to make an entire meeting disappear is to go in camera—probably the most misleading term in the entire political dictionary. You might imagine that when a meeting goes in camera, lights and cameras are turned on and public scrutiny is heightened. But an in camera meeting is essentially a secret session that no one is allowed to watch—there are no minutes taken, and there are definitely no cameras! The politicians become invisible. Ta-da! The term actually has nothing to do with cameras, but rather comes from the Latin for "in a chamber"; it refers to part of a trial when the judge and lawyers retreat into the judge's private office (the chamber) to discuss something, away from the public and the media. In government, in camera sessions are supposed to be used only for confidential personnel issues, legal concerns or contract negotiations. But they are frequently used purely to avoid public scrutiny and—coincidently—cameras. Former Ontario ombudsman André Marin wrote in 2013 that at least 20 percent of the in camera meetings he investigated were illegal. "Unfortunately, some councils appear to be addicted to secrecy," he said at the time. "There is, in my view, a putrefactive decay in democracy at the municipal government level due to the insistence on officials to continue conducting city business secretly and illegally. Hanky-panky continues to take place in the backrooms, and councils are continuing to cling to cloak-and-dagger old-school boardroom politics."

Speaking of cameras, even when governments aren't hiding behind closed doors they still manage to create optical illusions by controlling who is allowed to document the meeting. In the House of Commons, for example, only one single TV camera is used, and it's controlled by the legislature staff. This official camera feed is shared with all the media outlets, but it's carefully focused on one politician at a time, allowing the rest of them to act like clowns, heckle and make rude gestures without being seen by the public. In fact, this single controlled camera allows members of Parliament to leave the room altogether, unnoticed. When I was working as a legislative assistant in Ontario's parliament building, I once watched a politician deliver an enthusiastic speech to an almost empty legislature. A handful of other politicians had been strategically placed around him to fill the camera shot and make it look like the room was full, but he was talking to hundreds of empty chairs. I was stunned to find out that this happens all the time, both provincially and federally.

"More than 38 years after television cameras were allowed in the Commons, Canadians still don't really see what happens there" wrote the *Toronto Star*'s national affairs columnist, Tim Harper, who has spent two decades in Ottawa watching Parliament up-close.

He suggested that if mainstream media outlets were allowed to use cameras in the House of Commons, politicians' behaviour would quickly improve. "If Canadians see who is doing the shouting, a public shaming on camera might stop some of these inanities that litter our political discourse." Another option, of course, is simply to let ordinary people like us bring our own cameras. Currently, we're not allowed to take any photos of our own government, since all electronic devices are confiscated at the door. Somehow, in our modern world of non-stop documentation and ubiquitous closed-circuit cameras, we tolerate archaic laws that allow politicians to hide from public view.

It gets worse. I mentioned earlier that you aren't allowed to bring pencils into Ontario's provincial legislature, but it turns out that the pencil ban isn't a security precaution at all. Pencils are banned because there is actually a formal ban on writing found in the official rules of Queen's Park. The same is true in our national House of Commons, where visitors are offered the following stern warning: "Some items are not permitted (including cameras, recording devices, binoculars, umbrellas, overcoats, bags and parcels) . . . Visitors are not allowed to read, write or speak during the debates."

Excuse me? Citizens aren't allowed to read or write in our own government buildings? I got in touch with the Clerk's Office at Queen's Park to ask why such a rule exists. I received a letter explaining that no pencils or other writing materials are allowed because of a ban that "apparently originated with the concept that the debates of the House should be kept secret from the Monarch." Well, I'm glad to hear that the legislature hasn't updated its policies since the 1800s. "The prohibition has continued over into modern times on the basis of long-held tradition," the letter went on to say, "but also because having people who are supposedly present to observe proceedings, also rustling paper and writing things down, could be disruptive or distracting to the House and to the MPP speaking and so we continue to disallow it. We also require people in the galleries to relinquish their smartphones as well, on the same basis. Taking 'virtual' notes and pounding away at keyboards would also likely be a distraction."

The letter writer concluded with "I hope this answers your questions." No, it doesn't. Not at all. In fact, the answers are unfathomably condescending and nonsensical. Members of the House of Commons and our provincial legislatures spend much of their day yelling insults at each other, laughing out loud and clapping like trained seals every time someone from their party speaks a word—but somehow a member of the public will create a "distraction" by using a pencil or gently touching the screen of her phone? The most basic step towards transparency in any democracy is allowing people to watch and document the decision-making process. Yet inside the one room that should have the highest level of transparency in the entire country, all forms of public communication and documentation have been banned—an astonishing example of how elected leaders strive to remain unaccountable to the very people who elect them, and how we as citizens have set our own political expectations so low that we fail to realize when we're being treated as children by our own government.

The good news is that reform is possible. History shows us that democratic obstructions are vulnerable to public awareness and calls for change. History also teaches us that change happens incredibly slowly and requires constant vigilance and pressure. Let's look at the history of omnibus reform, for example. Political commentators and activists have been calling for change for decades. Even political parties have been demanding—and promising—change for my whole life. Back in 1982, when I was in the second grade, the federal Conservatives felt that Pierre Trudeau's Energy Security Act dealt with too many topics and asked the Speaker of the House to break it into smaller pieces. The Speaker refused and when the parliamentary bells rang out to call the vote, the Conservatives used an obscure rule to trigger a procedural delay. Instead of ringing for thirty minutes as usual, the voting bells rang—non-stop—for two weeks. (Earplugs were handed out to the security guards on duty.)

In the end, the Conservatives won the battle and the government agreed to divide the bill into eight separate pieces of legislation. But twelve years later, omnibus bills were still being used by the Liberals, so a young Conservative MP spoke out in the House of Commons. "In the interest of democracy I ask: How can members represent their constituents on these various areas when they are forced to vote in a block on such legislation and on such concerns?" the MP inquired. "We can agree with some of the measures but oppose others. How do we express our views and the views of our constituents when the matters are so diverse? Dividing the bill into several components would allow members to represent views of their constituents on each of the different components in the bill."

The MP was thirty-five years old, serving in only his second year as an MP. His name was Stephen Harper. Two decades later, Harper was prime minister and began introducing omnibus bills that were longer than anything we'd ever seen before. His government's annual budget bills altered dozens of pieces of existing legislation, affecting topics as varied as bridge tolls, information sharing with the United States, the Temporary Foreign Worker Program, overseas mail delivery and environmental assessment legislation. Harper's 2014 budget was called a "monster" by the NDP, and Green Party leader Elizabeth May said it represented a "disappearing democracy." The media was equally critical. CTV called it "bloated," and a *Globe and Mail* editorial said that "Harper's Ottawa is omnibusted," and that the bill was "an abuse of process" that shows "contempt for Parliament by subverting its role." According to Queen's University political science professor Ned Franks, budget implementation bills used to average only twelve pages, but from 2001 to 2008 that number jumped dramatically, to 139 pages. In 2009, Harper's budget bill came in two parts, adding up to a staggering 580 pages. His 2010 budget implementation bill surpassed 800 pages.

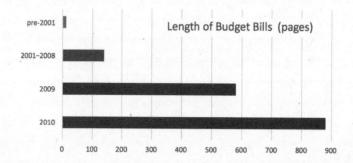

To their credit, Justin Trudeau's Liberals (after introducing their own enormous omnibus budget bill) did table legislation that allows the Speaker of the House to break up bills into smaller pieces. It's a step forward, but hardly a revolutionary or innovative move, considering that governments across North America have rules against omnibus bills. Many US states long ago banned bills that deal with more than one subject at a time. For example, California's constitution requires that "a statute shall embrace but one subject, which shall be expressed by its title." This rule was adopted more than 150 years ago, after the state court described omnibus bills as "a crying evil" causing the "confusion and distraction of the legislative mind by the jumbling together of incongruous subjects." There is nothing new about the calls for reform, or the availability of clear solutions. Yet Canadians had to wait thirty-five years after the Conservative protest against Pierre Trudeau's omnibus bill before change was delivered by his son—who was only eleven years old when those bells rang for two weeks.

But the painfully slow pace of reform isn't the only problem. Each reform comes with loopholes that the next government can easily abuse, creating a whole new set of tricks. Canada's new omnibus rules have already been criticized by the advocacy group Democracy Watch for including exemptions for budget implementation bills. In other words, securing the reform is only the first step. Constant vigilance and political organizing are required to ensure that each reform actually achieves its goals. Take open data, for example. Designed to increase transparency and participation in government, open data programs create portals that members of the public can use to download information. The results can be extraordinary, with a growing number of examples of citizen-led community projects that rely on open data. But according to leaders within the tech community, many open data programs aren't living up to their name. In particular, there are complaints that governments are releasing the lowest-hanging fruit—unhelpful data sets like registered dog names—rather than useful information such as land development applications or even postal code maps. (The Global Open Data Index ranks Canada eighty-first in terms of access to postal code information, behind countries including Colombia, Rwanda and Kazakhstan.) In effect, the government is creating the illusion of openness and reform without actually opening up.

The same thing can be said for freedom of information (FOI) programs that allow citizens to ask for specific government information that isn't otherwise publicly available. FOI programs are supposed to serve as a last resort for public access to information. Like open data, FOIs sound great—but the reality is less exciting. The release of information under these programs is often stalled by bureaucratic paperwork or obstructed by political interference. Even if you get your FOI request approved, the released document might be covered with black stripes called redactions. These allegedly exist to protect confidential

information, but the more likely goal is ███ █ ███ ██ ████ ██
████ ███ ████ or ██ ████ ████ ████ ██████ ██ ███ ██. My favourite
example involves an FOI request filed by realtor Russell Quirk asking
for details about a multi-million-dollar development deal in his
London (UK) suburb of Brentwood. He received 425 pages of information from the local government, but every single word was completely blacked out. Another political vanishing act.

Just like omnibus bills, we've seen decades of broken promises for
FOI reform. As leader of the Opposition, Stephen Harper once said,
"Information is the lifeblood of a democracy. Without adequate
access to key information about government policies and programs,
citizens and parliamentarians cannot make informed decisions, and
incompetent or corrupt governance can be hidden under a cloak of
secrecy." But just a few years later, when he was prime minister,
Harper was engaging in the very practices he once lamented.
Information law scholar Stanley Tromp, in a report titled "Fallen
Behind: Canada's Access to Information Act in the World Context,"

exposed how dozens of failures in Canada's access to information system resulted in loopholes, exemptions, slow response times and no access for permanent residents. In 2010, a British report ranked Canada last out of five parliamentary democracies, behind Australia, New Zealand, Ireland and the United Kingdom. Canada's former information commissioner, Suzanne Legault, has also been critical of the government's snail's-pace reforms, describing unnecessary exemptions, political obstruction and unreasonable delays. In 2015, her office took the federal government to court (and won) when a citizen's FOI request was "delayed"—for three years. In a separate case, involving the Harper government's attempt to destroy information related to the federal gun registry, Legault wrote, "You cannot escape the analogy that the federal government . . . was attempting to erase this history into a Memory Hole of the Records Department of the Ministry of Truth." You know things are bad when your country's official information commissioner publicly compares the government to George Orwell's *1984*. But don't blame Harper for this particular lack of transparency. Legault has pointed out that most of the eighty-five recommendations she's put forward to modernize the Access to Information Act have been proposed at some point over the past thirty years by other commissioners and in ten separate formal reviews of the act. Over those three decades, the recommendations have been ignored by ten parliaments, led by both Liberals and Conservatives, with the NDP often holding the balance of power.

Disappearing legislation, disappearing politicians and disappearing debate. Politicians use their toolkit of tricks, loopholes and illusions to limit discussion, reduce transparency and sometimes literally hide from us. Stronger rules are required, but the most important remedy is increased public awareness—yet another reason why we desperately need a makeover for our hollow "civics" classes. If people don't know how these manoeuvres work, or even what they're called, then politicians will continue to use them freely. In the meantime, let's at least clear up the terminology to reduce the chances of procedural abuse or evasion. Zee Hamid, a city councillor in Milton, Ontario, just west of Toronto, recently proposed that the term "in camera" be changed to "confidential session." "I realized that outside of the legal and political circle, most people did not understand what 'in camera' was," he told me. "The goal of changing it was to make it transparent that the council was going into a confidential session so residents could watch over us and decide whether the issue justified a confidential discussion or not." Small changes like this could go a long way.

Our governments aren't accountable unless we can see what they're up to. While opposition politicians frequently call for more transparency, they're quick to change their minds once in power and protect the broken systems that are already in place. I can't stress enough how all these acts of political sorcery contribute to our collective disengagement. I've seen it first hand, over and over. And yet it doesn't affect me as much anymore, because I've learned how to spot the tricks. In a way, I too have become an insider. But for any political newcomer, these procedural sleights of hand are a huge turnoff and will likely discourage further participation. We all want a little magic in our lives, but when it comes to democracy, there's no room for illusions and vanishing acts.

BITE-SIZED DEMOCRACY

You've probably heard the adjectives "lower" and "higher" used to describe our three levels of government, with municipal government being the lowest and federal government the highest. These descriptors imply not only a geographic status but also a level of importance, with our provincial and federal legislatures taking on complex issues of great importance while our city councils simply ensure that the garbage is picked up on time. This perceived hierarchy is reflected in our voter turnout, with municipal elections consistently attracting much less participation. But during my twenty years of community organizing, I've learned that we've got it all backwards: municipal government is where it's at.

Most of the public services we interact with on a daily basis are legislated, funded and implemented by municipal governments. Police, fire, schools, libraries, housing, childcare, drinking water and public transit are all managed by our city councils and local boards, as are complicated and controversial issues such as gambling, long-term care and drug addiction. Not only that, but this "lowest" level of government is intended to be most the participatory. We accept that national and provincial governments will inevitably feel somewhat inaccessible to ordinary people, but we have higher expectations for local government. You and I are unlikely to play a direct role in shaping a new foreign policy, for example, but it shouldn't require a stretch of the imagination to see ourselves actively participating in decisions that affect our cities or neighbourhoods. That's the promise of what we call local government: it's our gateway to the political world—the one level of government that is supposed to be nearby and approachable.

But what happens to this promise when our cities' populations reach into the millions? Toronto started out as a small town, but now it has a "local" government representing a population larger than that of Newfoundland and Labrador, Nova Scotia and Manitoba—combined! Fifteen American states and ninety-one countries have smaller populations than my hometown. And it's not just our megacities that have outgrown their municipal model. Even Hamilton, Surrey (BC) and Quebec City, each much smaller than Toronto, have populations three times the size of PEI's and larger than Malta's and

Iceland's. As these cities have grown, their public institutions have also expanded: more schools, more fire halls, more hospitals, more everything. But, while every other institution adapts proportionately to population growth, government operates inversely. We've actually *shrunk* the size of local government, drastically increasing the ratio of residents to representatives. Toronto, for example, used to comprise thirteen independent towns, each with its own city or town hall. There were eighty-seven councillors across those towns, each representing about twenty-three thousand local residents. In 1967, half of those towns were annexed by the others, leaving sixty-four councillors, each with thirty-seven thousand residents. Half a century later, with the population having grown from two million to almost three million, the remaining six cities have been amalgamated (a clever synonym for "dismantled") into the present-day City of Toronto, with only forty-four councillors, each responsible for sixty thousand residents. Just when it seemed council couldn't get any smaller, right in the middle of the 2018 election, Premier Doug Ford slashed council down to twenty-three. Over half a century, twelve independent councils were completely dissolved over a period of fifty years (a reduction of 92 percent) and the number of councillors cut by three quarters—all while the population grew by 50 percent!

Think of it like a school. Just as smaller classrooms allow teachers to give more attention to each student, smaller wards or ridings increase a politician's responsiveness. Let's say a school's enrolment grew by 50 percent and the administration responded by laying off most of the teachers and closing 92 percent of the classrooms. That's exactly what's happening to our cities! It's a catastrophic dilution of democratic representation, making our "local" government feel more distant and disconnected from ordinary people.

This endless shrinking of local democracy not only changes the ratio of political representation, but also physically moves your city hall farther away. Residents who used to live within walking distance of city halls in North York, Scarborough or Etobicoke, for example, now live over twenty kilometres from Toronto City Hall—ninety minutes by public transit. Not very "local" at all. In other parts of Ontario, especially rural areas, amalgamations have been even more devastating to local democracy. Northeast of Toronto, nineteen independent townships were merged into one mega-municipality called the City of Kawartha Lakes, which, despite having a population of only seventy-three thousand, covers more than three thousand square kilometres, making it the sixth-largest city in Canada by area. This municipality is a hundred kilometres long from top to bottom and twenty-six times bigger than Vancouver, leaving some residents with a forty-five-minute highway drive to their city hall.

This dilution of democracy presents us with yet one more way in which system is rigged against ordinary people. Even if we had better UX design, public lobbyists and four high school courses about power, we'd still be stuck with a system that's designed to be colossal and distant.

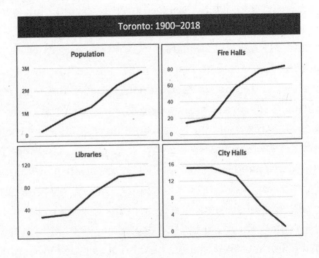

You might be asking, "Doesn't it make sense to streamline debates and discussions across a region?" Sure, if city councillors were responsible for making decisions and nothing else. But councillors are more than just company directors. They also serve as both conduits and ambassadors for government. They're the human face of representative democracy. And the physical buildings that house our council chambers serve as access points for democratic participation. For these roles, proximity, scale and access are vital ingredients. People understand this equation intuitively. In fact, each one of the amalgamations I've mentioned was opposed by the people who live there. In Metro Toronto, residents in all five dissolved cities voted overwhelmingly against the elimination of their local governing body. The highest No vote was 80 percent in East York, and even the lowest No vote, in Etobicoke, was 70 percent. Three years after the Kawartha Lakes amalgamation, residents voted to de-amalgamate. All these voters wanted to keep their local council, their local mayor and their local city hall. Sadly, all these referendums were ignored.

The combination of population growth and amalgamations makes your voice infinitely smaller. De-amalgamation has been proposed as a solution, but that doesn't really solve the larger problem: our cities are growing endlessly in size and density. Also, there are some valid arguments in favour of the kind of regional decision-making that amalgamated councils can offer. So the question is, How do we allow municipal amalgamations and regional planning to take place, while preserving the benefits of local democracy? The answer is actually quite simple. When any municipality grows to a certain size, a fourth level of neighbourhood government, responsible for local decision-making, should be created. These micro councils could be split into smaller and smaller units to maintain bite-sized ratios. This fourth tier of democracy would be designed to be closer to the people and more participatory than our existing city halls. Toronto attempted this with the creation of four community councils. But the members are the same people who already sit on city council, and each mini council represents close to a million people, which isn't really a "community" at all. Truth is, very few Torontonians even know that these community councils exist. It's a failed model. We can do better.

New York offers us a better solution. The city—which has fifty-one councillors, each representing about 165,000 people—created a local tier of government for participatory community decision-making. This tier consists of fifty-nine community boards, affectionately known as CBs, which deal with local issues like transportation, parks and public spaces. Each CB has fifty appointed members who serve as volunteers for a two-year term, as well as a full-time salaried district manager and office staff. With almost three thousand CB members across the city, people are much more likely to know someone who sits on their local board. They're also more likely to secure a position on their CB themselves and engage directly in the process. The boards hold open monthly meetings, right in the neighbourhood, providing a local gateway into municipal democracy. Citizens in each CB district are also invited to sit as public members on various committees dealing with issues such as landmarks and public safety.

New York's CB model is a step in the right direction, but there's still more room for improvement. Board members tend to be older, richer and whiter than the general population, as well as disproportionately male. Representation is improving (there's been a recent 300 percent increase in applicants who identify as Black or Latino), but the bigger problem is that all CB members are appointed by those who already hold power. That means the CBs aren't really accountable to the community itself, and they'll always be somewhat limited in their ability to challenge the status quo and effect real change. So while New York has the classroom size figured out, the selection process is definitely lacking.

Montreal offers us an entirely different—and more democratic—approach with its nineteen borough councils, each with a local mayor and councillors who are elected by neighbourhood residents every four years. These elected councils deal exclusively with community issues, such as local urban planning, parks, pools, libraries and community centres. The ratio of government bodies to the general population reveals just how local the Montreal borough councils are, and how that allows for a completely different type of accessibility than we see elsewhere:

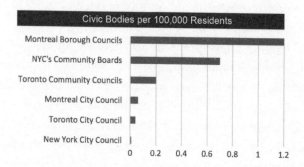

77

I recently spoke with one Montreal resident, Alex Norris, who explained the value of the city's borough council model through a personal story. In 2004, he'd been walking along Saint Laurent Boulevard, a historic commercial neighbourhood full of humble three-storey brick buildings, and was surprised to see that the local heritage grocery store had been "transformed into a worst imaginable strip mall horror." The old red bricks had been replaced by grey concrete, and a monstrous illuminated Pharmaprix sign could be seen from blocks away. "How the hell did such a thing get approved?" Norris wondered at the time. He thought the local streetscape should be protected and decided to speak out.

Instead of having to travel to Montreal's central city hall and deal with an enormous bureaucracy and a sixty-four-member council representing 1.6 million citizens, Norris simply attended a regular meeting of the local Plateau-Mont-Royal borough council. He asked questions about the renovation and discovered that the building permit had actually been issued in error. Eventually, the building owner was forced to remove the big-box-style facade and a new bylaw was approved, reducing the maximum size of commercial signage. This was local democracy in action. In fact, Norris was so inspired by the process that he decided to run for council in 2009—and he won. Citizen Alex Norris was now Councillor Alex Norris.

After hearing his story, I was curious to see for myself how the bite-size borough model affects the decision-making process, so I took a train to Montreal and attended a meeting of the Plateau-Mount-Royal council. It was like nothing I'd ever seen before, and I can describe it with two words: civilized conversation. And not just between the borough councillors, but between the politicians and members of the public. The borough councils have a question period, but it's nothing like the theatrical circus we see in Canada's House of Commons, where MPs hurl insults at each other for 45 minutes each day, but rather it's a segment of the meeting when members of the general public can ask questions. And whereas most City Councils offer citizens an opportunity to speak about an issue that is already on the agenda, the borough councils seem to allow anyone to simply walk into a meeting and ask a question—about anything. And they are expected to get a thoughtful answer on the spot. It's just one of the many democratic reforms implemented by the Montreal Citizens' Movement, which helped transform local democracy in Montreal in the 1980s.

When I told Norris that citizens in Toronto have no such opportunities, he was shocked. "You can't propose a reform?!" he asked, incredulously. Recalling his first visit to a borough council back in 2004, he pointed out that it was the question period that had allowed him to raise his issue. "I had a podium," Norris told me. It was his gateway into the democratic process. Now he sits on the other side of the room, but he still sees the value of that podium. "We're accountable to the public, not only at election time but on a regular basis," he explained. "And when [we're] being questioned critically and intelligently by the public, we come up with better policies as well. The questions we get are often very articulate. It actually helps us do our job. Even when [citizens] come and criticise us harshly, it makes us think more profoundly about the impact of what we're doing."

I noticed something else unusual about the Plateau-Mount-Royal council meeting: regular people were there. In Toronto, council meetings are attended by lobbyists, journalists, city staffers and a handful of very dedicated activists. But at the borough council meeting, the room was full of citizens who weren't the usual suspects. "They feel more comfortable expressing themselves here than they do at city hall," Norris explained. "A sense of community is built, as people with different personal histories and cultures and outlooks come together to discuss how it is we share our common space, which is the essence of municipal governance. I think one of the appealing aspects of local municipal democracy is that it's at a small enough scale, and what we do is tangible enough, that we actually can include the public in our deliberation process." Twenty-nine ordinary citizens asked questions during the meeting I attended, and each question received a polite and thoughtful answer. There was a light tone, with the mayor in particular injecting a lot of humour into his answers, eliciting frequent laughter from the audience. It felt like a group discussion, rather than a court hearing. People were enjoying themselves—an uncommon sight at a political meeting.

And the UX design was great! The borough meeting was held in the evening ("Because that's when most people are available," Norris explained), and clapping was encouraged, not viewed as some sort of physical assault against the councillors. But I don't think these UX details were the result of intentional design. Rather, these smaller-scale meetings simply lead towards a casual and accessible atmosphere. It was like being in the town hall of a small village, except we were in a monstrous city with more than 1.5 million residents. That's the magic of having a fourth tier: it creates a friendly space for ordinary people to comfortably explore and participate directly with democracy. The following day, Norris and I went for a bicycle ride in the rain, and he showed me all the amazing projects he was working on as a councillor: new parks, bike lanes and public space transformations. But it all began with an ugly sign, a borough council and a public question period.

My visit to Montreal proved to me that we can put the "local" back in local democracy, regardless of the size of the city. But it left me wondering what we can do to make other levels of government more accessible as well. If a forty-five-minute drive to city hall feeds a climate of political exclusion and disengagement, what can be said for the national governments of Canada and the United States—the second- and third-largest countries by area in the world? At fifty times the size of the average European nation, and with more than three thousand kilometres separating the national capital from some voters, is it any wonder that so many people feel disconnected from their federal government? The problem is compounded by the fact that both Ottawa and Washington exist as isolated political bubbles. While European capitals like London and Paris offer an intersection of politics, arts and business, standalone capitals like Ottawa and Washington have one single economic driver: government itself. The result, as journalist Andrew Coyne recently explained to me, is that Ottawa is "cut off from reality, hiving off the political world into a hermetically sealed company town." These governments can't be split up into smaller pieces because their whole purpose is to represent a massive area composed of regions.

But here's a fun idea: let's send our government on tour. Why do we assume that a legislative assembly has to anchor itself to one spot? Couldn't the Canadian Parliament have a meeting once in a while in Winnipeg, Montreal or Halifax? Couldn't the US House of Representatives set up shop in Houston, Seattle or Denver? The European Union does this each month. Its permanent home is in Brussels, but for four days a month, the entire legislature moves from Belgium to France. Thousands of plastic trunks are loaded onto five tractor-trailers and driven almost five hundred kilometres to Strasbourg, while all 751 parliament members and an additional 250 staff travel in a chartered train. It's called the Strasbourg Shift by some (and the Circus by others).

This monthly pilgrimage is an extreme example—and probably an excessive one (EU members have actually voted to end the practice, but all it takes is one country to veto a proposal, and France, of course, has done just that)—but it reveals that mobile government is possible. Rather than a monthly travelling circus, couldn't the Parliament of Canada occasionally visit another part of the country, just a few times each year? Members could occupy an existing provincial legislature or convention hall—a "pop-up parliament." Or why not build a couple of new legislatures? Bear with me. Let's say that we construct a brand-new House of Commons in Calgary and another in Halifax. Occasionally, our MPs and their staff would occupy these buildings, giving those who live in the East and West a sense of importance and inclusion. For the rest of the year, these satellite legislatures could serve as economic drivers for their respective regions: convention centres like no other. A typical conference venue is designed to host top-down discussions featuring a single raised podium and hundreds of passive audience seats. But with a microphone and voting interface at each seat, along with translation booths, automated speaker lists and screens for displaying motions and amendments, these new buildings would offer a unique environment conducive to large-scale participatory meetings. Not only would we be bringing government closer to the people, but we'd be creating unprecedented spaces for unions, associations, universities or corporate shareholders to experiment with bottom-up collaboration.

Democracy doesn't have to be an insiders' game. Wealthy voices, business lobbyists and political insiders will always be lurking in the hallways of power, but that's only a problem when they're the only ones there.

Introducing public lobbyists, mandatory school courses about power and resources for adults to learn democratic skills will help create a level playing field filled with informed participants who fully and deeply understand the terrain. And when cities get too large, a lower tier of community government can bring local democracy right into our neighbourhoods. Combined, these elements can transform the political arena into a place where your voice is just as powerful as the voices of those with much, much deeper pockets.

But these are just the first steps of our teardown. Our journey to creating a culture of participation has just begun.

CHAPTER 3

BETTER BALLOTS

In almost any country in the Western world, if one party takes complete control of the government against the will of the people it's called a coup and it's generally frowned upon by the international community. In Canada, however, we just call it an election and fund the whole thing with our own tax dollars. I learned about this strange phenomenon in 1993, the first Canadian election in which I was old enough to vote. When the results were announced on election night, I couldn't help noticing that the seats allocated to each party didn't seem to align with how Canadians had actually voted. Not even close. The Conservative Party had earned 16 percent of the vote, which should have translated into roughly forty-seven seats, but it got only two seats—less than 1 percent of the legislature. Meanwhile, the Bloc Québécois, which had earned *fewer* votes than the Conservatives, received fifty-four seats and was declared the Official Opposition. Most strikingly, the Liberals "won" 60 percent of the seats, a large majority government, even though most of the country *didn't* vote for them. Literally, one party took complete control of the government against the will of the majority.

During the following twenty-five years, I saw the same thing happen over and over, all across the country. I witnessed the Conservative Party of Canada win a majority government in an election where most people voted for centre-left parties. And I watched as the New Democratic Party of Alberta won a majority government, even though most Albertans voted for conservative parties. As you can see, our voting system doesn't discriminate against left or right. It betrays all voters equally, discriminating against nothing but the most basic laws of math.

But the coronation of false winners is just one of the many flaws in our voting system. Our elections also suffer from exaggerated polarization, artificially safe electoral districts that are ignored by all parties, increasingly negative campaign tactics, wild policy shifts, low voter turnout and parties that don't reflect the diversity or gender balance of the general population. All these consequences are influenced, and amplified, by our voting system.

PLURALITY ELECTIONS

The system in question is called first past the post, and it's the model used for all federal, provincial and municipal elections in Canada. While first past the post seems normal to Canadians, it's actually quite an obscure system on the global stage. In fact, among the thirty-six members of the Organisation for Economic Co-operation and Development (OECD), a group of the world's largest and most successful democracies, only one country uses first past the post for all levels of government: Canada. This inexplicable attachment to a rare and dysfunctional voting system is not only embarrassing but also incredibly damaging to our relationship with democracy. With sensible design, our elections could be a positive, friendly and inclusive exercise that people actually look forward to, rather the uninspiring, polarizing and patronizing nuisance we've learned to dread.

So what's the alternative? In all honesty, no voting system is perfect. But any alternative model would be better than the garbage system we're using now, because while every other voting model ever invented strives to achieve either a majority outcome or a proportional outcome, first past the post strives for neither. In fact, it strives for nothing. Rather, it's based on one simple rule: whoever gets the most votes wins. On the surface, this rule sounds both straightforward and fair. In fact, most Canadians would probably ask, "How *else* could you possibly declare a winner?" Well, let's start by exploring how this rule actually plays out.

Imagine a town named Northville, where a tense political battle is brewing. The town has received a federal grant to build a recreational sports facility. Some residents want to see the money invested in a new hockey arena, while others are pushing for an indoor mini-golf centre. An election is coming up, and two candidates—Harry Hockey and Gary Golf—decide to run for mayor. After a long and bitter election, Northville voters cast their ballots and vote overwhelmingly for Harry, showing clear majority support for a hockey arena.

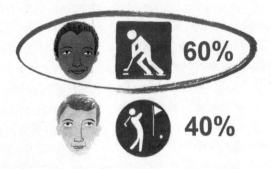

With only two candidates, this type of election actually works just fine. Having received the most votes, Harry is elected mayor. The majority of voters wanted a hockey arena, and now they're going to get it. But let's see what happens when we add just one more candidate, Helen Hockey. Now, pro-hockey voters have two options, and their 60 percent support gets split apart. Look what can happen:

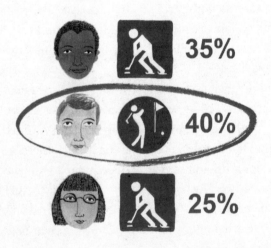

The hockey vote still adds up to 60 percent, but Gary got the *most* votes. So Northville now has a mayor who's committed to building a mini-golf course, even though six out of ten voters don't support it. That's what happens when you stick to that seemingly simple rule that whoever gets the most votes wins. If we added a fourth or a fifth candidate, the numbers would get even weirder. In Toronto, we have city councillors who've "won" elections with as little as 17 percent of the vote, because there were ten or more candidates splitting the remaining votes. The vast majority of voters didn't want the person elected, but he or she won anyway. No wonder people are feeling frustrated about politics!

The technical term for winning the most votes is a "plurality." With two candidates, Harry won a plurality of votes with 60 percent support. With three candidates, Gary won a plurality with only 40 percent. You can see why having the most votes isn't really an accurate measure of public sentiment. And not only do plurality elections distort the outcome, but they also make the entire election process a miserable experience for everyone involved. The fear of vote-splitting marginalizes candidates like Helen, who are called spoilers and discouraged from running. High-profile candidates, most often men or those with family connections, are considered to be front-runners, while other candidates are pushed out of races. This process is like an invisible primary race, narrowing the number of candidates behind closed doors. In Northville, Helen will be encouraged to drop out of the race to prevent Gary from winning. But even if she stays in the race, her supporters are now forced to consider strategic voting (where they vote for Harry because he is the candidate most likely to beat Gary). This is the norm in Canada. What could possibly be worse for democracy than a voting system that creates a disincentive for new voices to participate?

MAJORITY ELECTIONS

There's a very simple solution that easily transforms a plurality election into a majority election and fixes all these needless problems. It's called a runoff election, and you've probably seen one because they're used in many American cities and also by every political party in Canada to elect leaders and candidates in federal and provincial ridings. This is how it works: If any candidate gets more than 50 percent of the vote on the first round, that person wins. End of story. But if nobody gets a majority, then the candidate with the least votes is dropped from the race, and his or her supporters get to switch to one of the remaining candidates. In Northville, for example, Helen would be dropped from the race on the second round, since she got the fewest votes on the first count. At that point, her voters would likely switch to Harry, pulling the hockey arena's 60 percent support back together.

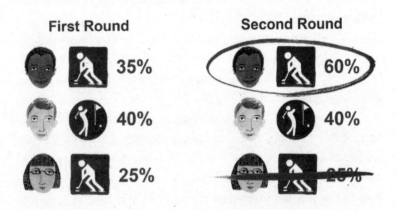

With a runoff election, Northville citizens get their hockey arena—as they should. But that's not the only benefit. As I mentioned above, plurality elections push out new voices and encourage strategic voting. Both those problems evaporate with a majority-based election using a runoff. No one will accuse Helen of being a spoiler, because in a runoff race there's no such thing. There is also no such thing as a wasted vote and risk of splitting the vote. This means that no one has to vote strategically to avoid accidentally helping to elect someone they don't like. You may have noticed that Helen didn't win the election under either system, but that doesn't mean that the outcome is the same for her. Under the runoff system, because she's not accused of being a spoiler, Helen has a chance to participate on a level playing field, develop new skills and build her base of support—all of which increases her chances of winning in the future. Under first past the post, she is less likely to achieve any of those things.

There is one more benefit—and it's perhaps the most important. In a runoff election, things get a little friendlier. Plurality elections are a zero-sum game that encourages and rewards negative campaigns and personal attacks aimed at damaging an opponent's credibility. But in a majority runoff, candidates want to both secure first-place votes *and* make sure that those who are voting for someone else will at least consider ranking them second. That creates a huge disincentive for negative campaign tactics: if you attack your opponents too hard, you could lose much-needed second-choice picks from their supporters. This shifts the focus of the campaigns back to important issues, rather than petty personal fights.

A runoff can be done in one of three ways. The traditional version uses multiple rounds of balloting, where voters are asked to come back and vote again, over and over, until one candidate reaches 50 percent. Until recently, Canada's political parties used this approach for their leadership conventions, resulting in hours and hours of evening voting and recounting that sometimes dragged on until dawn. It made for great television, a precursor to *Survivor*, with candidates kicked off the island one by one.

A simpler version (used in many American cities, as well as in France's presidential election) goes to a second—and final—round featuring only the top two candidates. The first option isn't very practical and the second approach isn't very democratic. A third way, using a marvellous thing called a ranked (or preferential) ballot, is the simplest, cheapest and most democratic approach. Just like it sounds, a ranked ballot allows you to list your choices in order of preference: 1, 2, 3, etc. In Northville, Helen's supporters would likely rank Harry as their second choice, and Harry's supporters would rank Helen second. On the second round, with only 25 percent of the vote, Helen would be dropped from the race and her votes automatically transferred to whoever was ranked second on each ballot. It's called an "instant runoff," because while there are several rounds of counting, there is only one round of voting. And if the votes are tabulated electronically, all the rounds can be calculated in milliseconds.

Every Canadian political party has now switched to ranked-choice voting using a preferential ballot. It's being used successfully for municipal elections in cities across the US, such as San Francisco and Minneapolis, and it's even being used by organizations like the Academy of Motion Picture Arts and Sciences (for best picture Oscar) and the NHL and NBA (for almost all their athlete awards). If it's good enough for them, then why are Canadian voters still being kept in the dark ages? Ranked-choice voting is as easy as 1, 2, 3, and it would create elections that are more fair, competitive, inclusive, diverse and friendly.

PROPORTIONAL ELECTIONS
While a ranked ballot provides enormous benefits, it's just the beginning. After all, we've only looked at single-seat elections so

far, such as a mayoralty race. But we don't just elect mayors—we also elect entire legislative bodies, like school boards, city councils and parliaments. Northville's ranked ballot shifted the town's mayoralty race from a plurality system to a majority system, but when we're electing a whole group, rather than a single person, the math works a little differently and the measure of fairness shifts from "majority" to "proportional."

Let's imagine that Northville elects ten city councillors, each within an electoral district or ward. For the sake of simplicity, let's assume that each ward has the same proportion of hockey lovers (60 percent) and the same vote-splitting problem: two hockey candidates and one mini-golf candidate. Under first past the post, each council seat could be won by a mini-golf candidate, even though 60 percent of the town wants the hockey arena.

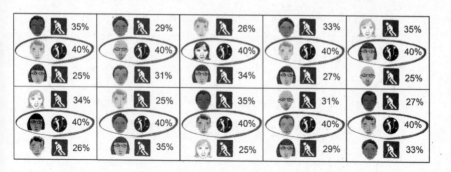

Now Northville has *ten* golf-loving city councillors, representing a population of mostly hockey-loving voters! You can see now why first past the post is so rarely used on the international stage: it just doesn't work. But what happens if we simply introduce a ranked ballot, using a 50 percent threshold? After the runoff counting, the majoritarian council would look like this:

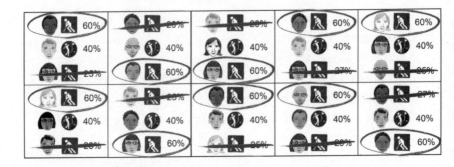

Now Northville has ten councillors who all want to build a hockey arena. Is that more fair? Yes, of course. But what about the golf lovers? Shouldn't they also get representation on council? This is where proportionality comes in. The majority system ensured that *most* people were heard. But a proportional system aims to ensure that *all* voices are heard. In other words, if 40 percent of the voters are pro-golf, then four of the ten councillors should also be pro-golf.

To summarize, here are the three main types of electoral models, and how they might play out in Northville (with grades assigned):

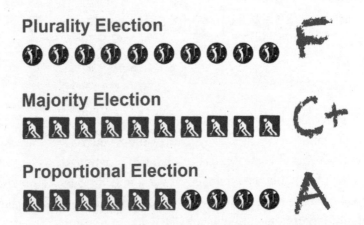

Clearly, the proportional council is the most fair. But where do those four golf seats come from? If a majority in each ward voted for hockey, how do we decide which four wards get stuck with a golf councillor?

This is where it gets fun. There are different ways to achieve proportional representation, and each model has its own benefits and drawbacks. Within the movement for voting reform, there's an interesting debate about the need for the general public to fully understand the details of these models. Some argue that people don't really need to know the mechanics, and we'll only confuse them if we try to explain how each model works. "You can drive a car," they say, "without understanding what's happening under the hood." That's true, but here's the thing: every time we get close to changing our voting system to a model that actually works, opponents of change take advantage of the fact that very few people understand the mechanics, and they use misinformation to build fear and confusion. Sure, if we were already using a proportional system, I would agree that not everyone needs to understand how it works. But if we want to *get* to a proportional system, then we'd better start focusing on how we use information, evidence and knowledge to build public support. For that reason, the following paragraphs are the most detailed and technical in this book. They explain the three most common ways to achieve proportional representation in an election. Fasten your mental seat belt.

A pure proportional representation (pure PR) system has no electoral districts at all. No wards, no ridings. Instead, each party produces a list of nominees for the entire country or region, chosen democratically by the members of the party. Then, on election day, voters simply choose their favourite party and seats are allocated from the lists, proportionate to the party's vote. For example, ballots in Northville would simply say "Hockey Party" and "Golf Party." If 60 percent of voters choose the Hockey Party, they get six seats on the council from the top of their list. The Golf Party, with 40 percent of the vote, gets four seats.

Pure PR Northville Council

Ten councillors, from lists:

Pure PR (also called list PR) is a simple system and it's used all over the world, but it has two huge drawbacks. In Canada, pure PR would entrench political parties in a way that betrays the original design of our parliamentary model (in which, historically, our elected officials are supposed to represent their voters, not their party). Technically, under our current system, nothing stops Canadians from rejecting political parties entirely and filling the House of Commons with 338 politicians who run as independent candidates. But with pure PR, there would be no way for an independent candidate to even put her name on the ballot. Political parties, which have slowly taken over our system, would become permanently dominant. The second problem with pure PR is that nobody has a local representative. Without any wards or ridings, you wouldn't be able to pick up the phone and call "your councillor" or "your MP." For both of these reasons, very few advocates in Canada or the US, if any, have proposed pure PR for our legislatures or councils. Instead, people have proposed various hybrid models, each providing an element of proportionality while preserving local representation. The two most common hybrids are mixed-member proportional (MMP) and single transferable vote (STV).

MMP, the system used in Germany and New Zealand, is an election model with two types of candidates: those running in local districts (as we have now in Canada), and those who appear on party lists. On election day, voters get a two-part ballot that asks them to choose both a local riding candidate and the party they prefer. The local seats are allocated by either first past the post or a runoff system, and then the second part of the ballot is used to fix any distortions by assigning additional seats to parties based on their proportional support. In Northville, we'd reduce the number of wards from, let's say, ten to five (by merging pairs), and the remaining five seats would be allocated from party lists. So if all five wards were won by Hockey Party candidates, but the overall party vote was 60 percent Hockey and 40 percent Golf, then the Golf Party would get four of the list seats and the Hockey Party would get one. The result is a perfect 60/40 split.

MMP Northville Council

Five ward councillors:

Five list councillors:

As you can see, you end up with a proportional government composed of two kinds of legislators: those elected as local reps and those elected from the lists. Hence the name mixed-member. Opponents argue that these party lists will be stacked with political insiders or financial donors who are being rewarded for their party loyalty. This is an absurd fear. First of all, parties would have a very strong electoral incentive to ensure that their lists are chosen democratically and transparently. Otherwise, they'd see pushback from their own members, as well as voters. Second, guess who is *already* in charge of putting names on our ballots? The same parties! Third, there are different versions of MMP, each with its own method of list-creation. So-called "open lists" allow voters to influence the order of list candidates through their ballots, while other systems create a list on election night composed of candidates who failed to win in their districts. All these models are designed to achieve a proportional outcome, while still protecting our traditional single-member ridings or wards.

The single transferable vote (STV) system, used in both Ireland and Australia, doesn't have lists at all. Instead, it uses multi-member districts, or what I like to call clusters. Wards or ridings simply get bunched together into groups that have multiple representatives. If four ridings were merged, the new multi-member riding would have four MPs for the single district. The larger the cluster, the higher the proportionality. Voters use a ranked ballot, and the runoff is similar to the majority model I described earlier. But instead of needing 50 percent of the vote to win, candidates have to reach a threshold calculated using a simple formula: $100 \div (\text{\# of seats} + 1)$. So if a ward has four councillors, a candidate needs only 20 percent support to win ($100 \div 5$). This allows smaller parties, or groups, to get a voice. In Northville, we could create two STV wards, each with five councillors. The threshold is now 17 percent ($100 \div 6$), low enough for Golf to leverage its 40 percent support to claim two of each five positions. The final results would look like this:

STV Northville Council

Ward 1:

Ward 2:

The only other twist to STV is something called a surplus transfer, which occurs if a candidate wins more votes than he or she needs. For example, if there are one hundred votes in Northville, each candidate needs only seventeen to win. So if a candidate gets twenty votes on the first round, she has a surplus of three votes. Rather than going nowhere, those surplus votes are transferred to other candidates based on the next choice ranked on each ballot. These transfers help ensure a more proportional result. The idea is that your vote should never be wasted—neither because your preferred candidate couldn't win nor because she would have won even without your vote.

So there you have it: two completely different hybrid models, one using party lists and the other using clusters of wards or ridings, but both achieving proportionality while maintaining the concept of geographic representation. There are other approaches as well, including a handful of made-in-Canada models that attempt to combine elements of STV and MMP. Each system takes a slightly different approach, but they all have one shared goal: proportional government that reflects the will of the people, or what's called voter intent.

Some PR advocates strongly prefer MMP over STV or vice versa, but in my humble opinion, they are equally marvellous.

In 2004, 160 British Columbians were randomly selected to sit on the Citizens' Assembly on Electoral Reform. Their task was to learn about voting models and propose an ideal system for the province. After five months of study, public consultation and deliberation, they recommended STV. Two years later, a similar process was held in Ontario, but this time the assembly of 206 random citizens recommended MMP. They were both right! What's notable is that neither group chose first past the post. In fact, more than a dozen government-funded commissions, reports and assemblies have recommended proportional systems in Canada including a three-year study conducted by the Law Commission of Canada which produced a 200-page report recommending MMP in 2004. Not a single major report or study has ever recommended our current system.

Proportional representation is the *only* way to ensure that every vote is treated equally. But equality of votes is not the only benefit. Just like the majority system I described earlier, the advantages of PR go much further than just the math. For example, Canada and the US are far behind other Western democracies when it comes to diverse representation in government. While there are exceptions to the rule, Canadian politicians are disproportionately white, straight and male. Canada ranks sixty-second globally when it comes to the percentage of women in Parliament, with an embarrassingly low 26 percent. Municipally it's even worse: of the largest fifty cities in Canada, only *four* have a female mayor. The data on this issue is crystal clear: the countries with the most diverse governments all use some form of proportional representation. Meanwhile, the few countries that stubbornly cling to first past the post all rank much lower.

Proportionality also affects the behaviour of candidates and elected politicians. In addition to the civility encouraged by a ranked ballot during election time, PR systems tend to produce coalition governments that have to learn how to collaborate and compromise in order to pass legislation. Imagine our politics being shaped by discussion and compromise rather than just "winners" and "losers". For example, does Northville really have to choose between a hockey arena and a golf course? Why not build a multi-use sports centre? That's the kind of outcome that can happen when you move away from binary battles towards deliberative dialogue. That should be the ultimate goal of our representative democracy: diverse leaders who work collaboratively in the interests of all. In addition, since PR elections eliminate the exaggerated pendulum swings we see in Canada, politicians have very little incentive to trigger a snap election and go back to the polls, hoping for a better result. Once a coalition is formed, it is in their interest to work together for as long as possible.

In addition to increased diversity and civility, one of the most transformative benefits of PR is a boost in political creativity. Plurality elections tend to produce two- or three-party systems that operate as a tired oligopoly, unchallenged for decades. PR, on the other hand, encourages new voices to emerge and grow, keeping everyone on their toes and in a constant state of innovation. Think of the private sector, where new ideas often come from small start-ups that disrupt a sector with an innovative approach. This process is stifled in a plurality political system, because when new parties try to form (think of the Green Party), they are attacked as vote-splitters and lose enormous amounts of support to strategic voting. And when they do achieve positive results at the ballot box, first past the post robs them of those gains. In the 2008 election, for example, almost a million Canadians voted for the Green Party, which was roughly 7 percent of the total votes and should have translated into 21 of the

308 seats in Parliament. But under first past the post, they got zero seats, an outcome that discourages their supporters from "wasting" their votes in future elections.

In those rare instances when new parties manage to win seats in Canada (think of the Reform Party), the threat of vote-splitting creates pressure to merge with a pre-existing party. That's why we have so few elected parties in Canada, and that in turn harms our democracy because, more than at any time in history, people today expect choice. From groceries to music to movie streaming, we're now exposed to a seemingly infinite amount of choice. Yet at election time, we're told the only real options are red, blue or orange. What could be more boring? In my lifetime, the number of television channels has grown from twelve to two hundred, but Canada's House of Commons has gone from just three national parties to four (the fourth being the Greens, with only one seat). Compare that with Sweden, Australia and Brazil, which have eight, twelve and twenty-eight parties, respectively, in their legislature.

"It's no coincidence that people are not participating," says Krist Novoselic, the chair of the American advocacy group FairVote. "A functioning democracy should celebrate diversity of opinion and inclusion. It can't be an exclusive club." If his name sounds familiar, that's because Novoselic was the bass player for the grunge band Nirvana, and along with Dave Grohl and Kurt Cobain, he shook the music scene to its core in the early 1990s. While celebrities often have quirky hobbies (Tom Hanks collects typewriters and Taylor Swift makes Christmas snow globes), few have become preachers of ranked ballots, threshold formulas and surplus transfers. But Novoselic's advocacy for voting reform is a direct result of his personal experience as a disruptor. In his book *Of Grunge and Government*, he explains how a handful of Seattle bands transformed the entire music industry from "big-hair bands touting a macho swagger packaged in a soft feminine look" towards "introspection wrapped in aggression and facial hair." Nirvana offered a disruptive new sound, but it was the fans who turned it into a historic musical era. "The seismic shift that occurred in rock revealed a public that was hungry for it," he wrote.

While the music scene is constantly evolving, our political parties have been singing the same square dance music for more than a century. "Just as the world of music in the '90s was crying out for 'alternative rock,' it seems that politics today needs a way for alternative political voices to play a genuine role in politics instead of being marginalized," Novoselic writes. Proportional systems achieve that goal by encouraging new voices, rewarding creativity and allowing for vote-driven disruption that forces the big parties to either innovate or move out of the way.

OUR PARLIAMENTARY CARTEL

I've described four benefits of proportional elections so far: equality, diversity, civility and creativity. But if proportionality is so much better, why are we still stuck with first past the post? The answer is incredibly simple: once politicians are elected, they rarely want to change the system that got them into power. For that reason, none of the major Canadian parties have made genuine efforts to implement proportional representation. (Some claim to support reform—but only when they aren't in power.)

Each time we get close to change, the establishment finds ways to sabotage the process. In 2005, for example, the BC government declared that the Yes side in a referendum on electoral reform needed to secure 60 percent of the vote to win. (In an amusing outcome, the Liberal Party "won" the provincial election that year with only 46 percent of the vote, yet the Yes campaign "lost"—with 58 percent.) Two years later, a similar Ontario referendum was tainted by the intentional withholding of funds for voter education, and when PEI residents voted in favour of MMP in 2016, the government simply ignored the result. Federally, the Liberal government promised in 2015 to bring in a new voting system and then backed down two years later, following a train wreck process that was designed to fail.

In addition to maintaining first past the post, the Big Three parties have also worked together for years to rig the televised leaders' debates, ensuring that new voices are excluded not just from Parliament but from public discussion. It's bad enough that first past the post robs small parties, like the Greens, of their seats. But to exclude them from the leaders' debates, even though they got hundreds of thousands of votes, is a direct attack on the most basic principles of democracy. Tony Berman, who served as the chair of the television network consortium from 2000 to 2007, publicly admitted that Green Party leader Elizabeth May was secretly pushed out of a debate by the other party leaders. He described their actions as "cynical and self-serving," but added that "at least it exposes the sham that this election debate process has become." New rules have been recently proposed for federal election debates, a glimmer of hope, but the rules have yet to be implemented. Meanwhile many provincial debates continue to exclude the leaders of smaller parties, with no cure in sight.

When we have the Big Three parties working together to push out other voices and maintain a voting system that benefits only them, this is nothing other than collusion: a political cartel collaborating to ensure that new players don't stand a chance of disrupting their dominance. These three parties each take turns with fake majorities, and it's the voters who suffer. The European

Commission (EC) describes cartels as any group that uses anti-competitive practices, such as "keeping products off the market or unfairly excluding rivals." The EC actively works to dismantle cartels because they "deny customers access to a wider choice of goods," "stifle innovation" and "cause immense damage" to a sector or economy. Sounds familiar.

Elite voices have also become quite adept at using fear to slow reform. In particular, politicians and traditionalists in the media have tainted public opinion of proportional representation with two particular myths: instability and extremism. These accusations are not only untruthful but actually the opposite of reality. I can't tell you how many times I've heard that Canada should keep first past the post because it provides us with strong, stable governments. But a quick analysis of PR countries reveals they often have longer government terms, fewer elections and more stability. (Both Germany and Ireland, for example, which use MMP and STV, respectively, have had fewer elections than Canada during the last fifty years.) Another way to assess stability, beyond frequency of elections, is in terms of legislative consistency. In Canada, which has occasional wild electoral swings between left and right, new governments often spend their first year undoing much of the work of the previous government. So what may seem like a series of consecutive "stable" governments is actually a flailing policy fishtail. This legislative instability is caused by the artificial distortions directly resulting from first past the post. Under PR, the shifts of power from coalition to coalition are more likely to be incremental and organic, reflecting gradual shifts of public opinion more accurately. If you want stability, PR is for you.

As for the fear-mongering claim that PR would give a voice to radicals and racists, this, too, is completely backwards. While

European parliaments do contain a few anti-immigrant radicals, it was the United States (using first past the post and a two-party oligopoly) that put an angry loose-cannon racist in the White House. In other words, a proportional system may give *seats* to an extremist party, but only a plurality system gives them absolute *power*. And while some claim that even a few seats can lead to power—since larger parties may be forced to form coalitions with extremists—this is a distortion of how those processes work. First of all, no party is *forced* to work with any particular fringe element. If a party wins 45 percent of the seats, they need to find just 6 percent more to form a governing coalition. Surely they're not going to pick the most extreme party to work with. Secondly, the negotiations that lead to coalition governments are complex and require compromise from all parties, as well as calculations about how their decisions will look to their own supporters—and to future voters. This moderates any deals that are made, even with extremists.

"But what about Israel and Italy?" Ugh. This is the most tiresome, overused and ridiculous question when it comes to voting systems. Opponents of fair voting often point to these two countries as examples of how PR can create unstable governments and give rise to extremist voices. The correlation is absurd. Yes, both of these countries suffer from volatile governance, and yes they both use forms of PR. But so do Denmark, Sweden, Norway and Switzerland. In fact, more than ninety other countries use PR, and it's working just fine for most of them.

What Italy and Israel have in common isn't their voting system but their turbulent histories—both are top contenders for "most invaded country in history." Lying in the middle of critical Mediterranean trade routes, Italy has suffered centuries of wars, assassinations and rebellions. More recently, Italy has served as the birthplace of both fascism and the mafia, neither having anything to do with the country's voting system. In fact, most of Italy's elections haven't even used PR! Out of forty-one elections since the unification of Italy, only fifteen have actually used a proportional system. And the worst crises they've seen, including devastating poverty that triggered the largest documented emigration in world history, have taken place under governments that weren't elected using PR.

Israel too has an unparalleled history: a narrow slice of desert inconveniently considered holy by three religions. Muhammad ascended to heaven on a horse just a few yards from where Jesus was crucified and around the corner from where Abraham tried to kill his own son. That's messy. Then you've got decades of violent terrorism triggered by two displaced peoples: Jews escaping a genocide in Europe, and Palestinian refugees who were pushed out of their own homeland. Italy and Israel indeed have problems, but pointing the finger at their voting system is misleading and foolish—in biblical proportions. If we're going to have public discussions about voting reform, let's at least get our facts straight.

While it's incredibly disappointing to see self-interested political leaders spreading these myths about fair voting, it's not just politicians who are colluding to protect the status quo. There's an entire industry of election strategists, pollsters and consultants who are also wary of change. After all, they're experts at winning elections under the current system. If the system changes, they may no longer be experts. These are the folks who often lead the No campaigns during referendums on voting reform. These backroom boys (yes, they are almost exclusively men) often argue disingenuously that we shouldn't change our voting system because ranked ballots and proportionality are just "too complicated."

Indeed, a trio of conservative political insiders launched a Canada-wide campaign in 2016 called "Keep Voting Simple" to advocate against ranked ballots or PR. Their argument is not only incredibly patronizing (they don't think you can count to three?) but also completely backwards. As we saw in Northville, the rules of first past the post may be simple, but the outcome often isn't at all. What's simple about a town with 60 percent support for a new hockey arena electing ten golf-loving city councillors? What's simple about councillors in Toronto "winning" their seats even though 75 percent of voters cast ballots against them? What's simple about a system called "first past the post" that has no post to pass? Nothing about plurality elections is simple. But *this* is simple: 40 percent of the vote should equal 40 percent of the seats. This is also simple: if 75 percent of voters don't like a candidate for mayor, he or she shouldn't win. Majority and proportional systems are simple to understand, the ballots are easy to use and the results make perfect sense. Simplicity is actually one of the greatest strengths of PR.

But you don't have to believe me—just take a look at the people who claim to prefer first past the post. While they loudly advocate for Canada to keep our "simple" voting system, they refuse to use it themselves! As I've already mentioned, when Canada's political parties choose their leaders, they use a ranked ballot. The House of Commons also uses a multi-round runoff with a 50 percent threshold when electing a new Speaker. When Toronto City Council appoints an interim councillor to fill a vacancy, it also uses a runoff—as do hundreds of councils across the country. Even the three guys behind the "Keep Voting Simple" campaign seem fine with using runoff voting in their own political parties, projects and campaigns. One of them ran multiple leadership campaigns under a ranked ballot, never once complaining that the system was somehow unfair or too complicated. Another was not only a member of the Conservative Party of Ontario when ranked ballots were used to choose a new leader—he was the party president. Their campaign to "Keep Voting Simple" is an example of astro-turf advocacy: it's designed to look like a grassroots effort, but is actually a carefully scripted, boardroom-produced marketing campaign representing the views of well-funded elite players who already wield power.

Strategists from all three of Canada's parties have played a role in obstructing reform. Most notably, the Liberal Party walked away from a campaign promise to get rid of first past the post, and majority NDP governments in five provinces have chosen to maintain the status quo. But the loudest voices opposing reform tend to belong to Conservatives, despite the fact that PR is based on free-market values such as customer choice, competition and the benefits of having new entrepreneurial voices in the marketplace. More than any other party, the Conservatives should support the idea that if the Green Party gets 10 percent of the market share (votes), then it should get 10 percent of the revenue (seats). What we've learned is that all parties tend to act in their own interest and protect the system that brought them to power.

For more than a century, our archaic voting system has delivered distorted, polarized, unrepresentative and unstable results. Switching our elections, both national and provincial, to a proportional system using transparent party lists and/or clusters of ridings would liberate our political marketplace and transform our political culture with six clear and distinct benefits: equality, diversity, civility, creativity, stability and simplicity. It can't come soon enough.

WITHHOLDING THE BALLOT

Before I wrap up this chapter, let's tear down one more thing: Who *gets* a ballot? Not too long ago, voting rights belonged to only a small exclusive group. If you didn't own property, you couldn't vote. Catholics, Jews and Quakers were all restricted from using the ballot box. Women? Nope. The journey towards universal voting rights has been painfully slow. Religious restrictions were abolished in the early 1800s, and women gained the right to vote a hundred years later. Indigenous Canadians didn't gain the franchise until the 1960s. Each reform required a political battle between those fighting for inclusion and those wanting to cling to control. We've come a long way, but there are two important groups that still don't have the right to vote, and that deserve it: permanent residents and teenagers aged sixteen and seventeen. These may sound like small groups, but together they add up to more than two million Canadians—equal in size to the populations of Nova Scotia and Manitoba combined.

The standard reasons given for this democratic exclusion is that the teens aren't ready and the permanent residents aren't citizens. Let's break down these arguments, starting with the sixteen-year-olds. Trying to figure out what age to give rights to young people is not an easy task, but let's at least try to be consistent in our approach. We already give enormous responsibilities to sixteen-year-olds, including the right to drive a car, join the military reserves and make important medical decisions. The age for sexual consent is sixteen, which means you're considered old enough to sleep with your member of Parliament but not vote for them. Sixteen-year-olds are allowed to earn money and pay income tax, yet they have no voice when it comes to how those tax dollars are spent. They are also allowed to get married—one of the most important decisions they'll ever make in their lives. If we can trust someone with a wedding ring, a two-tonne motorized vehicle, her own body and an automatic assault rifle, surely we can trust her with a single ballot.

Opponents claim that sixteen-year-olds wouldn't treat elections seriously—that they wouldn't take the time to learn about the candidates or make a thoughtful decision. But evidence suggests these cynics are mistaken. We can get a glimpse of how younger voters might behave by looking at Student Vote, a program that lets teens of all ages participate at election time with a parallel mock election using replica ballots. When Taylor Gunn, one of the co-founders, first dreamed up the project, he was advised by many that it would fail because kids wouldn't take it seriously. But Gunn ignored the cynics and pushed forward. Founded in 2003, Student Vote has now grown into a nationwide project with nine staff members and programs in more than ten thousand schools. They've conducted mock elections in every province and territory, and distributed more than four million ballots to teenagers across Canada. In the 2015 federal election alone, 922,000 students from 6,662 schools cast ballots. It's quite possibly the largest youth engagement project in North America.

But here's the most exciting thing: less than 1 percent of the ballots are spoiled. We're talking about hundreds of thousands of teenagers voting in secret, behind a screen, anonymously. A student could spit on his ballot, draw a picture of Satan or vote for Darth Vader. It's an easy opportunity for teenagers to express cynicism and apathy. But they don't. (Compare that to the 9 percent of adult voters in France who left their ballots blank in their last presidential election!) I spoke to some of the teachers who participate in the program, and the message I heard was universal: the students not only participate in high numbers, but also get passionate about the experience. "I think we really underestimate their intellect," I was told. Another teacher described how her students became completely obsessed with the televised leaders' debates. They were "hysterical" about not missing the debates, she said, and insisted on rewatching them in class. Teenagers. Hysterical. About politics. One teacher described how her students reacted when an NDP candidate attended an all-candidates' forum at the school and read his answers from a binder full of talking points preapproved by party officials. After the forum, the students talked about how disappointed they were by the candidate, and how they felt he was being controlled and "muzzled." The kids were looking for political authenticity and punished the candidate, who came in third with only 20 percent of the vote. A few teachers told me that parents have quietly confessed that the Student Vote program has affected their own behaviour. Their children not only push them to cast a ballot but even influence *how* they vote. In many cases, the teens know more about the parties' platforms than their parents do.

The apprehension about giving the vote to permanent residents is quite different. The concern isn't that they won't take it seriously, but that they will—and that their participation will somehow be harmful to society. The idea that a particular group of people can't be trusted with a ballot calls to mind claims that have been made repeatedly over the past two hundred years against every new group that has fought for voting rights. Keep in mind, we're not talking about tourists who are just visiting Canada for a few weeks or months. As the term suggests, permanent residents are people who have chosen to live in Canada, work in Canada, pay taxes in Canada and send their children to Canadian schools. They number well over a million, and not a single one of them can vote.

"But why don't they just become citizens?" you may be asking. I admit, I had the same question. It turns out, there are lots of valid reasons why a permanent resident may not have attained citizenship. For some, the financial cost alone is an insurmountable barrier. The application process can cost thousands of dollars for a family—an impossibility for those already struggling to pay the rent and buy groceries. For others, the reasons are personal and complex. For example, some countries don't allow dual citizenship, which means that an immigrant to Canada would have to renounce his original citizenship from his country of birth. That's a difficult decision for someone whose heritage and identity are bound up in his country of origin. On top of that, giving up a former passport can impact someone's ability to visit family members, claim an inheritance or collect an earned pension. Then there are administrative hurdles and regulatory burdens that can slow the process for many years. In 2016, a shortage of judges created a huge backlog in citizenship applications, meaning that people who had met all the requirements and were technically approved still had to wait months for their citizenship to be granted at an official ceremony.

What are we scared of? What makes a citizen different from a noncitizen, if they are both living here permanently and paying taxes? Do we really think that filling out a form, paying a fee, passing a test and pledging allegiance to the Queen of England makes someone more qualified to vote? If we do, then why do we not ask the same of those born here? I've never had to pass any knowledge test or pledge allegiance to Elizabeth Alexandra Mary (thank goodness), yet I'm trusted to vote. Perhaps we need to face an uncomfortable truth: that the primary reason we continue to disqualify permanent residents from democratic participation is that there lingers amongst us a widespread and deep mistrust of those with darker skin, which clouds the judgement of otherwise decent people.

The excuses for withholding the ballot from millions of people are quite shallow, but let's also look at the flip side: the strong benefits to be gained by including both groups in our democratic process. For the teens, the societal advantages are enormous.

With up to half of the residents not able to vote, these communities often get ignored by candidates as well as elected politicians. If the purpose of democracy is to empower residents to have influence over decisions that affect their lives, then we should be concerned about these neighbourhoods—especially when these are often the precise areas that are the most underserved and in need of new investments. "Parents should have the right to elect those in charge of their children's education and those charged with building the place where they've chosen to make a life," asserts Debbie Douglas, the executive director of the Ontario Council of Agencies Serving Immigrants (OCASI), a charity that works with two hundred community-based organizations whose constituents do not have access to the ballot box.

While some might suggest that teens and permanent residents don't deserve rights until they have fully embraced their responsibilities (which means teens becoming tax-paying adults, and permanent residents becoming citizens), it's quite possible that the argument is actually upside down. In other words, perhaps we're discouraging the exercise of responsibilities by withholding rights. And how do we reconcile these restrictions with the most ancient of rules: voting rights for property owners—even if they don't live there? Currently, if someone owns a house in Toronto but lives in Paris, she still get to vote for Toronto's mayor, as well as for her city councillor and school trustee. But if there are recent immigrants actually living in that Toronto house, working in the neighbourhood, paying income and sales taxes and sending their kids to the local school . . . they don't get a vote at all.

If we really think that sixteen-year-olds aren't prepared for adult responsibilities, we should raise the minimum age for driving, sexual consent, marriage and the military reserves. And if we think that citizenship tests and oaths are an important measure of someone's worth and trustworthiness, we should ask all Canadian-born residents to take those same tests and oaths. If we aren't prepared to take those steps, then we need to face our own contradictions and finally complete the 250-year journey towards universal voting rights.

All the changes I've described in this chapter—about both ballot design and ballot access—are, I believe, inevitable. There will be pioneers and there will be followers. But don't be fooled by North America's inertia. These changes are coming.

Franchise extension has been growing steadily. Twenty-six countries already allow non-citizens the right to vote in municipal elections, while New Zealand extends full voting rights, for all elections, after one year of residency, citizen or not. Here in Canada, a handful of city councils have formally adopted resolutions in support of allowing permanent residents to vote locally, including Toronto, North Bay, Guelph, Kitchener, Saint John, Fredericton, Moncton and Halifax. The 2017 report of Vancouver's Independent Election Task Force also recommended that the city's sixty thousand permanent residents be allowed to vote in local elections. In 2009, the *Toronto Star* published an editorial in support of the idea. "Right now there are entire neighbourhoods in our city that politicians don't bother to canvass because there are so few votes to be found. It corrodes our civic society if elected officials can cavalierly write off parts of our city, particularly when they tend to be the areas of greatest need," the paper wrote. "Granting permanent residents the municipal vote would give these neighbourhoods an equal voice at city hall. It would also show immigrants they are valued and that their participation in civic society is expected. The faster we integrate immigrants, the better—for them and for the city."

Federally, support is small but growing. One of the boldest efforts was made by Jay Hill, a Conservative member of Parliament, who in 2002 put forward a private members' motion calling for expanded voting rights. "Landed immigrants work, they pay taxes, their children go to public schools, they have chosen to become permanent residents in Canada and they are participants in our society," he said at the time. "Just like every Canadian citizen, their lives are affected by the decisions made at all levels of government including those before the House, decisions that will affect their present and their future and perhaps more important, their children's futures. Many eventually will become Canadian citizens. In the meantime, is it justified to deny them a say in the future of their new country?"

As for the voting age, the most common threshold in the world is currently eighteen, but it hasn't always been that way. Before the 1940s, almost all democratic countries had a voting age of twenty-one, if not higher. In 1946, Czechoslovakia was the first to lower the voting age to eighteen, and a dozen countries followed suit. During the 1970s, even more countries made the switch, including Canada, the United States, Australia and most of Western Europe. It was a slow international wave of reform that lasted about thirty years, until almost every country in the world had lowered the voting age to eighteen. Now another wave seems to be taking place. Nicaragua toppled the first domino in 1984, lowering its voting age to sixteen. Four years later, Brazil became a pioneer as well. And then parts of Germany lowered their minimum age to sixteen for municipal elections only. Argentina, Brazil, Cuba and Ecuador all followed. In 2007, Austria became the first member of the European Union to make the switch, and in June 2015, the Scottish Parliament reduced the voting age to sixteen for both parliamentary and municipal elections.

The wave is about to crash over North America as well. In 2013, Takoma Park, Maryland, a small commuter suburb of Washington, D.C., became the first American city to lower its voting age to sixteen for local elections and referendums. "Voting is habit-forming," said Tim Male, the Takoma Park city councillor who championed the change. "If you can catch people who are sixteen or seventeen and teach them that government cares about their interests, then maybe they'll hold on to that, at least as a hope or an ideal, as they get older." Like Taylor Gunn, who endured a lot of criticism when he launched Student Vote, Male received pushback when he first proposed the change. "We started pursuing the idea and heard that 'They're too immature, they won't vote, they'll treat it like a joke, I don't want to stand in line with them.'" But when the motion finally came up at a council meeting, dozens of teens attended and spoke eloquently in favour of Male's proposal. His motion won, six votes to one, and the next election was held with the new rules. The results were staggering: sixteen- and seventeen-year-olds voted at a rate three times higher than the grownups! And those teens seem to have stayed engaged, even after election day. "The best thing about it," Male told me, "is that sixteen- and seventeen-year-olds now email me and call me, and ask for things. They feel like they have representation, and they reach out."

Reforms to our voting system are coming as well. Slowly but surely. Just three years ago, I had the honour of working on an Ontario campaign that secured Canada's first legislation that allows cities to use ranked ballots (with either a 50 percent threshold or multi-member STV).

Out of 444 municipalities in the province, only one (London) decided to try it out. That's an innovation rate of about 0.2 percent. But it's a baby step. London city council is now the first government anywhere in Canada to abandon first past the post. Since then, Kingston and Cambridge have held referendums about switching to ranked ballots. I had the pleasure of working on the Yes campaigns, both of which we won. Citizens in Maine also recently voted in favour of switching over to ranked ballots for all state elections—a first for any state or province in North America.

Canadians are ready for change and hungry to learn more about alternatives to the status quo. I see it in classrooms, when I lead workshops on voting reform. And I saw it on election night in 2015, when I appeared on CBC to explain the failures of first past the post using bar graphs made of Lego, then watched as my ninety-second interview gained hundreds of views on Facebook, then thousands, then tens of thousands, hundreds of thousands and, finally, millions. In fact, within twenty-four hours this short and playful clip became the most watched CBC political video of the whole year.

We spend so much energy and time focusing on who is running in our elections and who is winning. But rarely do we step back and ask, "Are we doing this right?" The voting system is everything. It can change who runs, how they campaign, how we vote, who wins and how our legislatures operate after each election. The stakes are high, and so important. There will always be political insiders wanting to cling to our existing rules. And those who have won elections under the current system will fight to keep things just as they are. That's why electoral reform will always be a grassroots, bottom-up process, pushed forward by people like you.

VOTING SYSTEMS OVERVIEW

	Proportional		Majority	Plurality
	Mixed-member proportional	Single transferable vote		
Grade	A	A	C+	F
Also known as	Additional member system (UK)	Ranked choice voting (US)	Instant runoff voting, ranked choice voting, alternative vote	First past the post, single member plurality
Abbreviation(s)	MMP	STV	IRV, RCV, AV	FPTP
Strives ...	to make all votes count.		to make most votes count.	for nothing.
By using ...	party lists.	ranked ballots and multi-member districts (clusters).	ranked ballots.	nothing.
Threshold to win	100 ÷ seats	100 ÷ (seats+1)	50%	Random
Increase in diverse representation	Best	Better	Good	Terrible
Encourages civility and positive campaigns	Yes	Yes	Yes	No
Legislative stability	Yes	Yes	Yes	No
Encourages collaborative government	Yes	Yes	A little	No
Used in	Germany, New Zealand	Australia, Ireland	San Francisco, Minneapolis	Canada

PLURALITY BALLOT

Choose one candidate:

GOLF, Gary ◯

HOCKEY, Harry ✓

HOCKEY, Helen ◯

RANKED BALLOT

(For majority or proportional runoff)

Rank your choices:

GOLF, Gary ◯

HOCKEY, Harry ②

HOCKEY, Helen ①

TWO-PART BALLOT FOR MMP

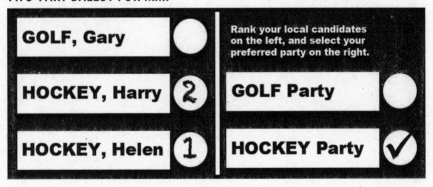

GOLF, Gary ◯

HOCKEY, Harry ②

HOCKEY, Helen ①

Rank your local candidates on the left, and select your preferred party on the right.

GOLF Party ◯

HOCKEY Party ✓

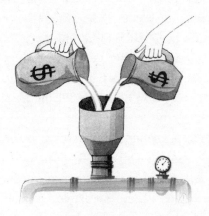

CHAPTER 4

BRIBES, WINKS AND NODS

It's not hard to imagine a stadium filled with tens of thousands of young people, cheering wildly. But before 2015, it would have been difficult to imagine them cheering for anything other than a pop star or sports team, let alone a dishevelled seventy-four-year old man ranting about campaign finance reform. Yet that's exactly what happened when Bernie Sanders crossed America like a rock star, waving his hands in the air while declaring, "We need to get big money out of politics and restore our democracy to combat a corrupted political system controlled by deep-pocketed special interests and the billionaire class." Sanders was tapping into a fear of many citizens across the Western world: that our elections barely matter anymore because a handful of very wealthy people behind the scenes have much more influence than we do. This sense of political hijacking feeds our growing cynicism towards politics in general, and Sanders figured out how to turn that cynicism into both anger and hope, mobilizing passionate citizens from coast to coast.

Here in Canada, corporate influence on democracy is as old as our political system itself. Our very first prime minister, Sir John A. Macdonald, resigned in disgrace after newspapers revealed that he'd not only accepted a bribe but actively pursued it. A political "donation" of $360,000 had apparently been made in exchange for a promised multi-million-dollar contract to build Canada's first transcontinental railroad. The public backlash was swift, leading not only to Macdonald's resignation but to the collapse of his Conservative government. (It's mildly amusing that Macdonald's face adorns the Canadian ten-dollar bill, given that he was kicked out of office for illegally soliciting and accepting cash. That's kinda like commemorating sprinter Ben Johnson by putting his face on bottles of stanozolol.)

Bribery is still a part of Canadian politics today, at all three levels of government. (To learn more, Google any of these phrases: MFP scandal, Airbus affair, Charbonneau Commission or Gomery report). But stories of politicians or political staffers explicitly breaking rules for their own self-interest represent only the tip of an iceberg and are arguably a distraction from the bigger picture. The primary problem we're facing isn't criminal activity but rather the fact that excessive private influence has become a normal and legal part of our system. To put it more bluntly, our political system has evolved into a sophisticated enabler of mass institutionalized bribery. In just the past couple of years, for example, we saw an enormous public outcry against "cash for access" fundraisers, where wealthy donors schmooze with ministers and parliamentarians in exchange for a hefty fee. The parties of Justin Trudeau, Ontario premier Kathleen Wynne and BC premier Christie Clark in particular were publicly shamed, and each was pressured to introduce legislation designed to limit or minimize these kinds of exchanges.

You'd think that 150 years after Macdonald's Pacific Scandal, we'd have this figured out. Instead, we seem to be going in circles in a kind of a political Groundhog Day. (Notably, the 1873 Pacific Scandal and the 2016 cash-for-access fiasco were both exposed by *Globe and Mail* reporters, six generations apart.) Despite decades of promises and reforms, powerful corporations continue to wield enormous power in our legislatures and our city halls. So why is it so hard to get big money out of politics? The best analogy I've heard to describe the problem is that water always finds a way. In other words, you can build a dam on a river, but eventually the water will flow over it or find another route around it. Money, too, has an uncanny way of finding its destination, even when obstacles are placed in its path.

Some jurisdictions in Canada have implemented regulations that attempt to restrict the flow of political donations. You can think of that as a valve, limiting how much water gets through. The valve can be turned off completely by placing an absolute ban on certain types of contributions. In 2004, for instance, Jean Chrétien's Liberal government banned all corporate donations, shutting one valve. But just because a company can't donate directly, that doesn't mean its CEO, directors or lobbyists can't donate personally, as citizens, achieving the same result. That led us to the cash-for-access problem, where company representatives were paying money to get face-to-face meetings with cabinet members. Similarly, Toronto City Council banned corporate donations in 2009, but according to a 2016 *Toronto Star* investigation, some of the donations that used to come directly from companies now simply flow through alternative (and less transparent) channels including family members. Porter Airlines, for example, used to contribute money to municipal candidates using corporate cheques. After the ban, the *Star* investigation found that $11,100 was donated to city hall candidates by Porter president and CEO Robert Deluce, along with his wife, daughter and son—all using personal cheques. In 2006, Liberal leadership candidate Joe Volpe received $108,000 from family members connected to executives of Apotex Pharmaceuticals. He later returned $27,000 that was shown to have come from children under the age of eighteen, including a fourteen-year-old and two eleven-year-old twins (each of whom donated $5,400, the allowed maximum). Water finds a way.

If there was one single water line connecting companies to politicians, we could simply turn it off with one twist of the valve. But as we've seen, the water can simply flow through another pipe. And there are *lots* of pipes—a messy labyrinth with multiple routes connecting each source and destination. From a private company, outgoing water can travel through board directors, family members, employees or professional lobbyists. It can also flow through third parties such as industry associations or political action committees. And the incoming water often doesn't flow directly to politicians but travels through political parties, riding associations, nomination races or leadership campaigns. When we connect all these detours together, we end up with dozens of possible ways for water to reach its intended goal.

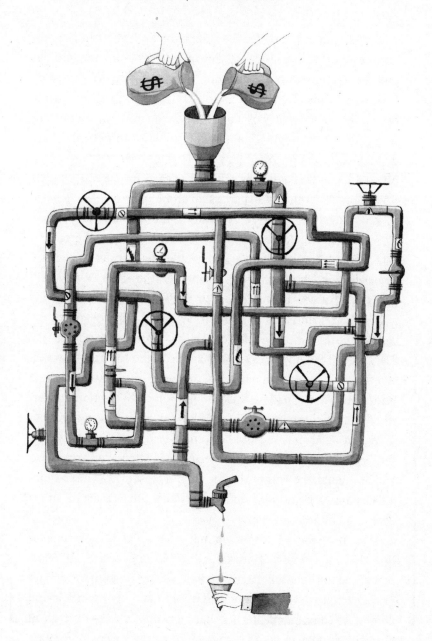

With so many routes for the water to travel, you can see how hard it is to try to control the flow of corporate money into our political system with valves alone. That's why many campaign finance reforms often focus not on how much money is flowing but on the transparency of the flow. Like the water meter on your home, disclosure regulations force candidates to publicly share detailed information about how much water they have and which pipes it came through. Remember the cash-for-access scandals I mentioned? Of the three parties involved, only one (the Ontario Liberals) agreed to ban these shady gatherings and completely close that particular valve. The other two parties (the federal Liberals and the BC Liberals) simply added new rules to increase disclosure and transparency. Essentially, they said, "We're still going to sell access to politicians, but we'll put a water meter on it."

Disclosure can be helpful, but it depends on the details of the regulations and what people do with that information afterwards. The City of Toronto, for example, has disclosure rules that force all candidates to reveal the names of their campaign donors. But the information isn't made available until after the election is over, which renders it quite useless in terms of helping voters make an informed decision. And unlike some disclosure systems, which require donors to reveal their occupation, employer and board appointments, the Toronto program (and most in Canada) require only a name and address. That makes it difficult to track the funds back to an alternative source.

So we need more information, but we also need an overhaul of how that information is presented. Disclosure records are enormous, and the onus is currently on voters to decipher them. A mayoral election in Toronto might have as many as five thousand donors, so you can imagine how hard it would be to go through all that data and try to figure out which companies were attempting to influence which candidates. The city also collects enormous amounts of detailed information about which lobbyists speak to which politicians about which subjects. But both of these data sets are so large that no one really looks at them—and more importantly, no one is connecting the dots between them. Some information can have value on its own, but other kinds have meaning only when cross-referenced with another data set. You know those nutritional charts on packaged food? Those lists consist of three separate pieces of data: the number of nutrients/calories in the package, the recommended daily intake (RDI) for each and the serving size. That's all good data to have, but what makes it really effective and practical is that Health Canada forces food manufacturers to cross-reference all three pieces of data on one simple label. Imagine if you wanted to buy a box of cereal and had to check three websites to find out the nutritional value. One website tells you how much iron is in the whole box, another tells you how much iron you need each day and a third tells you how many bowls of cereal are in each box. Prediction: no one would look at any of the websites, and it would be as if the data didn't exist. And that's exactly how Toronto's current lobbyist registry and campaign disclosure records work.

Here's a real-life example of what I'm talking about: A company called Allvision recently submitted an application to install eight massive digital billboards on a major highway in Toronto. The proposed signs not only pose a safety threat to drivers, but also break multiple regulations because of their size, location and brightness. The project would also set a major precedent, since the highway is currently billboard-free. City staff recommended against the application, and the city's sign advisory committee rejected it as well. City councillors were presented with all the facts about safety, neighbourhood impact, the lack of community consultation and incorrect information used in the application . . . but they voted in favour of the signs anyway. Why would councillors ignore data, science and proper democratic process? The lobbyist registry offers some clues. It turns out there were more than 150 meetings between lobbyists and city councillors regarding this specific application. Here are the records for two lobbyists alone:

Lobbyist Paul Sutherland met with the following councillors: Paul Ainslie (twice), Michelle Berardinetti (twice), Shelley Carroll, Josh Colle, Gary Crawford, Frank Di Giorgio (four times), Doug Ford (five times), Mark Grimes, Norman Kelly (twice), Giorgio Mammoliti (twice), Peter Milczyn (four times), Denzil Minnan-Wong (twice), Frances Nunziata (twice), David Shiner and Karen Stintz. He also met with Amin Massoudi (Doug Ford's executive assistant), Earl Provost (the mayor's chief of staff—five times), Mike Makrigiorgos (Councillor Cesar Palacio's executive assistant), Paul Saracino (political staffer), Sheila Paxton (political staffer), the deputy city manager (twice) and the manager of the city's sign unit.

Lobbyist Daniel Bordonali met with the following councillors: Paul Ainslie, Maria Augimeri (twice), Ana Bailão (six times), Michelle Berardinetti (twice), Shelley Carroll, Raymond Cho, Josh Colle (five times), Gary Crawford (three times), Vincent Crisanti, Janet Davis, Glenn De Baeremaeker (twice), Mike Del Grande (twice), Frank Di Giorgio, Paula Fletcher, Doug Ford (five times), Mark Grimes (twice), Doug Holyday, Norman Kelly (twice), Mike Layton (twice), Chin Lee (four times), Peter Leon, Josh Matlow, Mary-Margaret McMahon, Peter Milczyn (seven times), Denzil Minnan-Wong, Frances Nunziata (three times), Cesar Palacio (twice),

John Parker (twice), James Pasternak (twice), Anthony
Perruzza (twice), Jaye Robinson, David Shiner, Karen Stintz
(six times) and Adam Vaughan. He also had seventy meetings
with senior political staff (aides, executive assistants, chiefs of
staff, policy advisers, etc.).

Allvision spent tens of thousands of dollars on lobbyists, trying as
hard as possible to influence the process. But now let's connect the
dots. A quick look at the lobbyist registry reveals that those same
lobbyists, acting as ordinary citizens, just happened to donate
thousands of dollars to the same councillors they were lobbying:

Contributor	Amount	Contributor Type	Candidate	Office
SUTHERLAND, PAUL	$300.00	Individual	Pantalone, Joe	Mayor
Sutherland, Paul	$150.00	Individual	Hall, Diana	Councillor
Sutherland, Paul	$25.00	Individual	Mammoliti, Giorgio	Mayor
Sutherland, Paul	$2,225.00	Individual	Mammoliti, Giorgio	Mayor
Sutherland, Paul	$150.00	Individual	De Baeremaeker, Glenn	Councillor
SUTHERLAND, PAUL	$20.00	Individual	Pantalone, Joe	Mayor
Sutherland, Paul	$300.00	Individual	Filion, John	Councillor
Sutherland, Paul	$150.00	Individual	Saundercook, Bill	Councillor
Sutherland, Paul	$150.00	Individual	Stintz, Karen	Councillor
Sutherland, Paul	$300.00	Individual	Ford, Doug	Councillor
Sutherland, Paul	$150.00	Individual	Nunziata, Frances	Councillor
Sutherland, Paul	$150.00	Individual	Augimeri, Maria	Councillor
Sutherland, Paul	$150.00	Individual	Moeser, Ron	Councillor
Sutherland, Paul	$250.00	Individual	Thompson, Michael	Councillor
Sutherland, Paul	$150.00	Individual	Milczyn, Peter	Councillor
SUTHERLAND, PAUL	$150.00	Individual	Kelly, Norm	Councillor
Sutherland, Paul	$150.00	Individual	Perruzza, Anthony	Councillor
Sutherland, Paul	$250.00	Individual	Palacio, Cesar	Councillor
Sutherland, Paul Harry	$200.00	Individual	Bussin, Sandra	Councillor

Contributor	Amount	Contributor Type	Candidate	Office
BORDONALI, DANIEL	$500.00	Individual	Pantalone, Joe	Mayor
BORDONALI, DANIEL	$200.00	Individual	Pantalone, Joe	Mayor
Bordonali, Daniel	$150.00	Individual	Stintz, Karen	Councillor
Bordonali, Daniel	$150.00	Individual	Oomen, Nancy	Councillor
Bordonali, Daniel	$150.00	Individual	Nunziata, Frances	Councillor
Bordonali, Daniel	$150.00	Individual	Di Giorgio, Frank	Councillor
Bordonali, Daniel	$250.00	Individual	Thompson, Michael	Councillor
Bordonali, Daniel	$150.00	Individual	Milczyn, Peter	Councillor
Bordonali, Daniel	$150.00	Individual	Del Grande, Mike	Councillor
BORDONALI, DANIEL	$150.00	Individual	Kelly, Norm	Councillor
Bordonali, Daniel	$250.00	Individual	Palacio, Cesar	Councillor
Bordonali, Daniel	$150.00	Individual	Beaulieu, Kevin	Councillor
Bordonali, Daniel	$1,000.00	Individual	Ford, Rob	Mayor
Bordonali, Daniel	$200.00	Individual	Ford, Rob	Mayor
Bordonali, Daniel	$200.00	Individual	Berardinetti, Michelle	Councillor
BORDONALI, DANIEL	$150.00	Individual	Ainslie, Paul	Councillor

These numbers aren't large, but you can be sure donations like these wouldn't be happening if there wasn't a benefit for donors. At a bare minimum, they are counting on privileged access to decision-makers. If a lobbyist catches the eye of a candidate at a fundraising event, even if the ticket was only a hundred dollars, there's a wink and a nod that translates into "I might be calling you for something. I hope you'll answer the call. I'm on your team." The contributors are simply keeping their networks warm.

It took me a few hours to dig through the lobbyist records and campaign donor data to connect the Allvision dots. But why aren't we already doing this kind of cross-referencing automatically? The first step is to make sure that disclosure records are being released as a proper digital data set, rather than a useless PDF. That way, anyone could access the information through an open data portal and create their own charts, lists, analyses and so on. Even better, government IT staff could write some software code that would automatically correlate every single donation to the existing lobbyist records. This would be an incredible resource for voters and journalists during an election, but it could also be used between elections. Just before each vote in Parliament or at a city council, a list would be published online showing not only which politicians were lobbied on that topic, but how much money they accepted from those lobbyists or other people associated with their client (including family members). Coincidentally, Toronto's lobbyist registry and Canada's mandatory food labelling legislation were both introduced in the same year (2007), but only one requires the data to be cross-referenced to give it context. So essentially, we have all this amazing disclosure information about big money in politics, but it mostly goes unnoticed. No one is reading the water meters.

CLEAN FUEL

Beyond valves and meters, there is one more remedy that can help reduce (or even eliminate) corporate influence in politics. But first, allow me to tweak the analogy. Rather than imagining political money simply as water, let's think of it as fuel. The water analogy explains *how* it flows, but a fuel analogy explains *why* it flows and why the problem is so persistent. Election campaigns are expensive, and that money has to come from somewhere. Campaigns need fuel—fuel for advertising, printing, polling, office rent and staff salaries. Rich folks have fuel. Large companies have fuel. We'll never be able to eliminate the desire to influence the political process. But we can reduce the need for fuel. After all, quite often it's actually the politicians who are pushing for these transactions, not the donors. Back in 1872, it was Sir John A. himself who wrote these fateful words to business magnate Hugh Allan: "I must have another ten thousand; will be the last time of calling; do not fail me; answer today." More recently, it was revealed that each cabinet minister in Ontario was given an annual fundraising quota, to be secured through private cash-for-access events. Former US secretary of state John Kerry once said, "The unending chase for money I believe threatens to steal our democracy itself." (He openly uses the word "corruption" to explain the current climate, explaining, "I mean by it not the corruption of individuals but a corruption of a system itself.")

So if we reduced the thirst for fuel in the first place, we would severely reduce the ability of donors to leverage their wealth into power. One simple approach is to place strict limits on how much candidates can spend on their campaigns. You can think of these spending limits as a restriction on the size of the fuel tank. With less need for fuel, there would be less need to solicit contributions. But the most important cure is not valves, meters or the size of the fuel tank—it's displacement. Any liquid can be displaced by another liquid. If we can fill campaign tanks with a cleaner fuel, there will be no room left for private money.

If you think about it, political candidates probably don't want dirty fuel in the system any more than you or I do, because big money comes with strings attached. Whether those strings take the form of an explicit agreement (translation: a bribe) or the more innocent wink and nod, they place expectations—and perhaps limitations—on the future actions of the politician. If you were a politician, wouldn't you prefer to feel truly independent rather than beholden to those who are owed favours? And if you were a candidate, wouldn't you prefer to focus on your campaign rather than the unending chase for money? We'd be doing *everyone* a favour (except the corporate donors, perhaps) by finding clean campaign fuel.

So how does this clean fuel work? There are a few ways. In Canada, if you contribute money to a federal party you can claim it on your tax return, which serves as an incentive for ordinary people to make donations. The City of Toronto has a more direct subsidy, offering a 75 percent rebate on all small donations. If you give a hundred dollars to a candidate, you'll get a cheque from the city (about a year later) for seventy-five. Candidates don't need to seek as much money, since the fuel tank is now partially filled with public funds. One drawback of this approach is that the refund is delayed, which discriminates against lower-income donors. (Even if you know that your hundred-dollar donation will end up costing you only twenty-five, you still need to have that hundred dollars available in the first place.)

A more fair way to implement a public subsidy is to use grants rather than rebates. A matching grant offers candidates a one-to-one subsidy—so if I give fifty dollars to a candidate, his or her campaign will get another fifty dollars directly from the government. This system, used in the US for presidential primary elections, allows people to leverage a small donation into something larger. Even better than a matching grant is a multiple match. A program in New York City multiplies the first $175 of each contribution at a 6:1 ratio. In other words, if you give ten bucks to a candidate, the government gives him or her another sixty.

According to a report co-authored by the Brennan Center for Justice and the Campaign Finance Institute, New York's rebate program has completely changed the culture of campaign finance in the city. Before the program came into effect, only 30 percent of the city's census districts had donors who gave $175 or less to a council candidate. But by 2009, with the introduction of the rebate program, that number had tripled, to 90 percent.

It's also important to note that the jump in participation occurred mostly in neighbourhoods with higher poverty rates and higher concentrations of minority residents. "Small donor matching funds help bring participants into the political process who traditionally are less likely to be active," says the Brennan report. And the impact is clear: the first NYC election that used the new system produced the city's first African American mayor. The system has also been credited with electing the first Dominican American, Asian American, Asian American woman and African American woman from Staten Island, as well as the first third-party candidate in thirty years. In 2009, for the first time, New York City elected a council with a majority of members from communities of colour. (New Yorkers like the rebate system so much that they recently voted in favour of expanding the program during a referendum in November 2018. Moving forward, the matching grant will be offered at an 8:1 ratio, for the first $175 of each donation.)

As you can see, rebates, credits and matching grants reduce the reliance on big donors and introduce a healthy dose of cleaner fuel into our elections. Yet none of these models are perfect. All three require donors to have some disposable income up front, and they all end up distributing public subsidies based on the political preferences of a small group of people (only about 1 percent of the population makes political donations). If we're going to subsidize elections with clean fuel, we should use a system that allows anyone to participate regardless of income, and we should ensure that the distribution is reflective of the broader public, rather than just those who are most engaged.

This leads us to the two final forms of public finance: the per-vote subsidy and Democracy Dollars. Per-vote subsidies are an annual allowance given to a political party, based on how many votes the party got in the last election. In 2004, the Canadian government introduced a per-vote subsidy that delivered annual funding to all parties at a rate of $1.75 for each vote received in the prior election. This is one of the most democratic approaches to public election financing, because *all* voters (not just 1 percent of the population) help direct the funds. But this system too has its problems.

First and foremost, per-vote subsidies have a bad habit of getting cancelled. Seven years after Jean Chrétien introduced this source of clean fuel for Canadian elections, the entire program was cancelled by Stephen Harper. North Carolina had a similar program, called "Voter Owned Elections," and it too was eliminated in less than a decade. Most recently, a per-vote subsidy was introduced in Ontario by the Liberal government in 2016, but then cancelled two years later by the Conservative government, who labelled it a "taxpayer-funded slush fund." The second problem is that per-vote subsidies incorporate strategic voting into the funding formula. It's bad enough that smaller parties are harmed at the ballot box by strategic voters who don't want to "waste their vote" in a first-past-the-post plurality election. With a per-vote subsidy, it's not just their vote that doesn't go to their preferred party—it's their financial contribution. Third, the model uses old data. For four years after an election, parties get public money based on their support in the previous election. Even if its support falls drastically, a party will still get ongoing funding based on old information. Likewise, if a smaller party begins to grow and attract new public support, that change isn't reflected in the funding until the next election. So the parties that were popular four years ago always get the most money to spend on the following election, which perpetuates the status quo and punishes new voices.

This leaves us with the final version of clean fuel displacement, and my personal favourite: a bold experiment taking place in Seattle using coupons called Democracy Dollars or Democracy Vouchers. Four coupons, each worth twenty-five dollars of public money, are mailed to every voter to give to the candidate(s) of their choice. This system puts complete control of the public subsidy into the hands of all voters, on a level playing field. It

In New York City, with a 8:1 **multiple matching grant** system, you'd write a cheque for only $11.00. The government would cover the rest, $88.00, paid directly to the candidate.

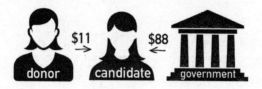

In Seattle, you wouldn't have to write a cheque at all. You'd just give all four of your **Democracy Vouchers** to the candidate. Your upfront cost would be zero.

Seattle has completely changed the way that money influences elections by transforming political subsidies into a universally accessible program. According to a post-election analysis by the Win/Win Network and the Every Voice Center, the shift was dramatic and on par with the results seen in New York. In 2017, Seattle's first time trying this new system, the number of campaign donors tripled and reached an all-time high. An estimated 84 percent of the donors were new to the political process, and donors were much more reflective of the general population (with more donations coming from youth, women, people of colour and low-income residents). The previous election was dominated by big money, and less than 50 percent of total donations came from small contributions. But in 2017, that number jumped to 87 percent.

Injecting clean tax-funded fuel into election campaigns shouldn't be controversial. We already publicly fund almost every aspect of elections anyway: the printing of ballots, hiring of election staff, purchase of tabulation machines, rentals of voting stations and so on. Every single part of our elections is funded by you and me—except for the most important part: the actual campaigns! Whether we're using rebates, grants or vouchers, the more clean fuel we can get into the pipes, the better.

But until we've switched over to fully subsidized election campaigns, we still have to figure out how to minimize the damage caused by dirty fuel. And for this, I suggest that that the most logical remedy has always been right in front of us, albeit obscured by traditional thinking. It can be spotted only by turning our assumptions upside down. That's exactly what two American academics, Bruce Ackerman and Ian Ayres, have done by proposing that we could purify our campaign fuel by turning off all the gas meters. They suggest that donations—just like ballots—should be completely secret. No disclosure at all. To anyone. The idea is that since wealthy donors make contributions to politicians hoping to get something in return, what would happen if the politicians themselves couldn't confirm where the money was coming from? What if the intended recipient couldn't figure out which pipe the fuel was coming from? I admit that when I first heard about it, the idea seemed completely crazy. But the more I think about it, the more I realize that Ackerman and Ayres have stumbled upon a strange truth: even transparent political donations are unethical.

Imagine that you took a university course and found out later that a few of the students were giving cash "donations" to the professor. Would you trust that those contributions had no effect on their marks, or yours? What if it was your kid's high school class, and you found out other parents were giving a monthly "contribution" to the teacher? That would seem completely unfair and immoral, because the teacher has an obligation to maintain impartiality. The same would go for any public employee, such as doctors or judges. It would be crazy to accept a system that allows patients or defendants to offer money, because it would put those professionals in a conflict of interest. Why, then, have we come to think it's perfectly kosher to openly, publicly and transparently contribute money to the election campaigns of politicians whose job is to impartially represent *all* voters?

Here's why this is so important: Big money isn't just about the so-called 1 percent. It's also about the combined effect of the top 20 or even 50 percent. While the super-rich can easily influence elections with their deep pockets, middle-class voters also distort policy in their favour by being the only ones who can afford even small political contributions. It's the lowest-income earners who suffer the most, which is why our anti-poverty programs are consistently underfunded. Do you know why I have so much insight into the winks and nods that take place at political fundraisers? Because I've done it myself. As a political activist, I'm deeply aware of how important it is to maintain active and trusting relationships with politicians. So if I'm invited to a fundraiser, I go. And when I make eye contact with the candidate, I too am saying, "I might be calling you for something. I hope you'll answer the call. I'm on your team."

Transparent donations have another major flaw: they perpetuate the status quo because donors are hesitant to support new political challengers, which could trigger reprisals from incumbents. I've never given money to a candidate I didn't respect. But I've probably withheld donations from a candidate I liked because I was worried it might harm an existing relationship with a sitting politician. Secret donations would work against the status quo by providing cover for those who want to challenge people already in power.

Ripping all the fuel valves off our financial pipes may seem like a far-fetched idea, but not too long ago, anonymous voting was also a radical idea. Voting used to happen in public until secret ballots were first introduced in Australia in 1856. Britain didn't implement the change for another fifteen years. All of Canada's provinces held their elections with public and transparent votes before introducing private voting booths, following Australia's lead. Ackerman and Ayres are simply calling for an evolution of the secret ballot, extending the idea to financial contributions as well. They call it a secret-donation booth and have proposed a very detailed process that ensures complete untraceable anonymity. It's an extreme proposal, no doubt. But it's the best I've seen.

The other option, of course, is to go to the opposite extreme, taking transparent disclosure to never-before-seen levels. A few clever political activists in the US have proposed introducing NASCAR-style uniforms for politicians, revealing the "sponsors" who fuel our democracy. The larger the contribution, the larger the logo. It's crazy, but it sure would shine some light on corporate power, and it would serve as a powerful incentive for politicians to think twice about who they accept money from.

Here's the bottom line: capitalism may be a great system for producing wealth, but it's a failure when it comes to equal distribution of that wealth, which means that as long as people are allowed to legally contribute money to politicians, the voices of those with more income will be amplified and we'll continue to see government decisions that serve their interests. Admittedly, the problem is much worse in the United States, where the Supreme Court has absurdly ruled that corporate political donations are a form of free speech—thus ensuring that almost any attempts to curtail corporate interference in elections will fail. But here in Canada, we have our fair share of political interference and dirty fuel—all within the parameters of existing laws.

Small fuel tanks and appropriate valves are crucial mechanisms that can help us track and reduce the influence of private wealth on our elections. But to solve the root problem and gain the greatest long-term benefits for democracy, we need to displace corporate funding with massive injections of clean fuel. In the meantime, we desperately need to connect the dots between donors, lobbyists, associates and family members. And if we're not prepared to force politicians to embrace a shame-based system of wearable disclosure, then it's time for us to seriously consider outlawing traceable political donations—of any kind.

One year after Bernie Sanders filled those stadiums by delivering passionate speeches about getting big money out of politics, the "billionaire class" had officially moved its head office from Wall Street into the White House. This may seem like a setback, but really it's just a more transparent version of what's been happening all along: private money has always been fuelling our politics. Important changes and reforms have been made, but their impact has been minimal in comparison to the transformation we need. So we have a choice: we can keep spinning our wheels or

CHAPTER 5

IT'S MY PARTY (AND I'LL CRY IF I WANT TO)

"Soul-crushing and demoralizing." That's how a friend of mine, a well-respected community leader, described her experience trying to get involved with a political party in Canada. Jenn became a member at twenty-five and was eventually elected to the party's provincial council, where she brought forward proposals to boost member participation, such as producing educational materials about how the party works. Rather than welcoming her suggestions, the members responded to Jenn's enthusiasm with suspicion and hostility. She described the party as "stunningly toxic," with a strong emphasis on centralized control and a "siege mentality" that treated any new ideas or dissent as "antithetical to solidarity." She said that positions within the party were rewarded based on loyalty and had been occupied by the same people for decades, creating an insider club that felt unwelcome to new voices. "One of the ways that control is maintained is by making the process of getting involved at the local level as difficult and unfriendly as possible," Jenn told me. During her four years on the provincial executive, she and the fourteen other members never went around the table to introduce themselves. Her job there was to fall in line, not to bring her own voice. "The pressure to not rock the boat is immense," she said. When party members tried to bring forward controversial ideas at a convention, for example, the establishment organized loyalists to line up quickly at the microphones, keeping others away. They're called mic muffins. It gets even worse. Jenn described the party leaders as "high-functioning psychopaths who understand power and intimidation" operating within "a culture that selects for individuals who can withstand and thrive in a low-trust, high-acidity environment."

Of course, Jenn's harsh words are the perspective of just one person—perhaps an isolated, disgruntled outlier. I wanted to assess the prevalence of her experience, so I recently posted this simple question on Facebook: "Have you ever joined a political party? If so, rate your experience: 10 being fulfilling and 0 being traumatizing." More than a hundred people responded, and the most popular answer was "0." Then again, social media often attracts negative voices, so maybe we should dismiss these opinions as well. But here's a perspective that's impossible to ignore: "After fifteen years in daily politics, I am less of a fan than I ever was of political parties. I've come to believe that parties do more harm than good." That quote is from Graham Steele, who not only served as a member of the Nova Scotia legislature but was the minister of finance. Here's another perspective, from the leader of Canada's Green Party, Elizabeth May: "If I were inventing democracy from scratch I would not have invented political parties. In their current form, at their worst they represent an impediment to independent thought."

When party members, volunteers, ministers and leaders are all saying the same thing, it's probably a good idea for us to listen. Parties are one of the most important parts of our political system, the natural entry point for electoral engagement. If a chess club or Frisbee league was described as "stunningly toxic," it would be tragic, but harmless to society at large. Political parties, however, aren't just social clubs. By bringing together like-minded people who share certain goals and beliefs, political parties offer an avenue to shape policy, choose candidates and help promote their values. Parties produce the social spaces in which political communities can flourish. When those spaces evolve into insider cliques, fearful of new voices, the results are not just tragic—they're disastrous.

To address this crisis, it's important to acknowledge that the poisonous culture of our parties is not random and does not take place in a vacuum. There are elements built into the system that intentionally centralize power and alienate anyone who isn't part of the inner circle. Similar to the teardown of government processes I've carried out in the first four chapters, here too we can identify the mechanics of exclusion and dismantle them one by one.

Let's start at the top and take a look at how political parties treat their own elected politicians. We currently elect 338 members to the House of Commons, each representing a geographic district, and together they're supposed to speak for the diverse political views of the nation, including yours and mine. But a groundbreaking book titled *Tragedy in the Commons: Former Members of Parliament Speak Out about Canada's Failing Democracy* gives us a troubling glimpse into how our Parliament actually operates. The authors of the book, Alison Loat and Michael MacMillan (co-founders of Samara Canada, a non-partisan think-tank), borrowed a technique from the private sector, where businesses often conduct exit interviews with departing employees, asking them to reflect on their years at the company in the hope of gaining helpful suggestions to improve the workplace. While exit interviews take place in almost every sector, no one had ever thought of doing it for politicians—at least not until 2009, when Loat and MacMillan began interviewing former members of Parliament from all five parties. As the title of the book suggests, the message they heard wasn't pretty. Straight from the mouths of those who've served as honourable members came a picture of disappointment and frustration. Anecdotes about child-like behaviour during Question Period or the toxicity of partisanship would not surprise most Canadians. But there was one common thread that might indeed surprise voters: Despite holding the highest level of elected office in the country, most of the MPs felt that they had no voice. Instead, they felt "controlled," "manipulated" and even "bullied" by the offices of their respective party leaders.

Loat and MacMillan explain that our political culture "renders MPs impotent," leading to an "absence of power" for our elected representatives, and that "discipline is so tight that members must restrict their public comments to speaking points the party has provided." These sentiments were echoed by former MPs from across Canada, who said that party leaders have "dictatorial powers," that Parliament "is at risk of being redundant and irrelevant due to increased power in the hands of the executive," that "the job of an MP now is to show up for the party, not for their constituents," and that they were often pressured to act "like a trained seal."

These are literally supposed to be the most powerful people in the country, representing ordinary Canadians in our Parliament each day. If our MPs don't have a voice, then neither do we. How can any citizen or party member feel empowered and engaged if our own MPs feel like trained seals? Centralized control defeats the whole idea of having parties in the first place—which is to bring like-minded people together to work collaboratively towards legislative goals. If we can't get our parties to respect their own caucus members (elected MPs), then we'll have no hope of getting them to respect their larger membership.

Centralized power within party caucuses in not an automatic or inevitable outcome. According to Leslie Seidle, a research director with the Institute for Research on Public Policy, of all the world's modern democracies, none "has heavier, tighter party discipline than the Canadian House of Commons." It wasn't always like this. Our system was actually designed explicitly to empower individual MPs and to limit the power of the prime minister. In fact, as Steele points out, "The concept of 'premier' or 'first minister' is hardly acknowledged in the Canadian Constitution." Before 1970, parties weren't even listed on our ballots! It was just a candidate's name and occupation: Peter Jones, barber; Sally Smith, teacher. The emphasis was on the candidate, not which party she was with or who her leader was. In our parliamentary system, the prime minister is supposed to behave as "first among equals," but over time, the party leaders have become more powerful, and they've repeatedly changed the rules to gain unprecedented control over the government and individual MPs.

To be fair, members of Parliament have to balance three different (and often conflicting) pressures, which Loat and MacMillan describe as "the triangular relationship between constituency wishes, personal opinion and party loyalty." That's a tough balance to maintain, and of course if an MP is elected under a party banner, then allegiance to that party should have significant impact on his decisions. What we've lost is the triangular balance: it's become 100 percent party loyalty. If we want to end the tragedy in the Commons, we must decentralize political power by giving more influence to MPs. The first step is to understand how party discipline works in Canada, and how it's so effectively enforced by the party whips who ensure obedience in the House of Commons. (The political use of the word "whip" is disturbing, especially since it comes not from the leather strip itself, but from the term "whipper-in," defined in the *Oxford Dictionary* as "a huntsman's assistant who keeps the hounds from straying by driving them back with a whip into the main body of the pack." No subtlety there.)

Theoretically there are supposed to be two kinds of votes in the House: whipped votes and free votes. But records from Parliament indicate that almost every single vote is whipped. Canadian MPs occasionally vote independently, but in the last Parliament, even the most free-thinking MPs voted against their parties only 2 percent of the time. In the UK, that number is 20 percent. So what is it about Canada that has led to such strict party discipline? The answer can be found by compiling and dissecting the assortment of threats used by whips to "encourage" MPs to vote a certain way. Then, through targeted reforms, we can disarm whips by minimizing or eliminating each of these threats.

We can begin by restoring local candidate nominations. Party members in each district are supposed to nominate a candidate, whose name then appears on the election ballot. Some nomination meetings attract only a few dozen people and others attract hundreds, but the idea is the same: the decision is being made by local members. Beginning in 1970, however, party leaders in Canada were given the ability to overrule local nominations and veto the democratic voice of the membership. This change not only disempowered local party members but became one of the mechanisms used to keep elected MPs loyal and obedient. If they wanted to run in the next election, they had to fall in line. Party bureaucrats also use tricks and loopholes to influence the outcome of these votes and outmanoeuvre their own members. Tensions and rivalries between local members and central party bureaucrats have become common. "A well-run nomination battle can be one of the most inspiring events in politics," Loat and MacMillan note, "with the potential not only to transform the winner from citizen into politician but also to transform slightly interested citizens into engaged political participants. But at its worst, the nomination process is a manifestation of the negative perceptions that people tend to have of politics—an opaque, manipulative and even cruel game that turns both citizens and candidates away from the democratic process."

Another way that prime ministers keep MPs obedient is by dangling the hope of a promotion to cabinet. This doesn't really work in the UK because the average size of the governing party's caucus is 350 MPs and there are only twenty cabinet positions. So if you're a British MP, your chance of getting promoted to cabinet is 1:17. With such little hope, you're more likely to act independently and less likely to worry about whether you're impressing the prime minister. But in Canada, the average size of the governing caucus is only 164 (because our Parliament is half the size, and also because we have more parties in the House of Commons), yet our cabinet is inexplicably larger, fluctuating between thirty and forty. These bloated cabinets even include ministers who don't actually have a ministry! (They used to be called minister without portfolio, but that was eventually changed to the less embarrassing minister of state). So in Canada, instead of a 1:17 chance of getting into cabinet, you've got a 1:4 chance. Hey, not bad odds! Cutting our cabinet in half (bringing it in line with the UK) would reduce by half the government whip's ability to use promotion promises as a tool of persuasion.

A third tactic used by whips, believe it or not, is seating assignments. Evidently, MPs really care about where they sit! (Who knew?) In his Samara exit interview, one MP said he was "punished" by being sent to "a seat back by the rearmost curtain," while more loyal MPs were given seats near the front row. And here's another control tactic: if MPs need to travel out of town to a meeting or conference, they have to get permission. If you've been naughty (say, by thinking independently or trying to represent your voters), you might not be allowed to go on that trip. Both of these tactics remind me of grade school, where a teacher may send a disruptive student to the back of the class or withhold a hall pass. Rather than infantilizing our MPs, we could simply remove all these decisions from the hands of party whips or leaders. Seating could be assigned randomly, alphabetically or geographically. Travel budgets could be assigned by an independent treasurer accountable to caucus.

One more tactic that is used by leaders and their whips to keep MPs in line is the threat of expulsion from the party or caucus. This too is an incredible distortion of the British-inspired Westminster system, in which the party leader is supposed to be accountable to his or her caucus—not the other way around. The great irony of this power shift is that it may have been inadvertently caused by attempts to *increase* democracy. For half a century following Confederation, each leader was chosen by his party's caucus. Then, in 1919, leadership conventions were introduced, and party members from each district, called delegates, began to gather to choose their leader. This actually first happened by accident when Liberal leader Wilfrid Laurier planned a national policy convention, but then died unexpectedly from a stroke shortly before the gathering took place. The party decided to go ahead with the convention and use it as an opportunity to choose a new leader. This convention approach spread to other parties and was used for seven decades, until the members began to push for even more internal democracy. Slowly, the parties switched to a one member, one vote (OMOV) system, which allows *all* members to vote—not just the delegates who get sent to a convention. The provincial Parti Québécois pioneered the trend in 1985, and the rest of the country soon followed.

On the surface, these changes seem designed to boost democratic accountability within each party. More voters = more democracy, right? Not necessarily. While well intentioned, the switch to member-elected leaders has contributed greatly to the concentration of power within each party and within the House of Commons. When the leader was chosen by the members of caucus, he or she was accountable to those members. Those two things were inextricably linked. When we broke one, we broke the other. Not only does the caucus no longer choose the leader, but now the leader can choose and remove caucus members! All the power has shifted into the leader's office.

Of all the countries with democracies based on the Westminster model, Canada is the only one that has party leaders chosen directly by members of the public. I envy those other countries because, as backwards as it may seem, our party members would actually have *more* control and influence (through their district associations and MPs) if they didn't also choose the leader. In fact, a growing number of parliamentary observers and experts, including columnist Andrew Coyne and former Speaker Peter Milliken, believe that party leaders should once again be elected by, and accountable to, caucus. (The same could apply to every province as well, where the local legislatures have many of the same problems we're seeing in Ottawa.) Myriad simpler reforms could also give more power to MPs. For example, parties could maintain a membership vote for leader while also creating a mechanism that allows a majority of caucus members to trigger a new leadership race. They could also place decisions about removing an MP from caucus into the hands of the entire group—not just the hands of the leader.

Some of the reforms I've proposed may seem to contradict each other. One increases party members' power by giving them control of their local nominations, while another removes their power to choose their party leader. But the proposals are driven by the same motivation and achieve the same goal, which is to reduce the concentration of power in the leader's office and ensure the highest level of accountability (party leaders accountable to MPs, and MPs accountable to their local members).

Change won't be easy, though, because once again, those who stand to lose power will do everything they can to stop any attempt at reform. Conservative MP Michael Chong recently made a valiant effort with a private members' bill called the Reform Act, which aimed to restore local control over nominations and give MPs the collective power to remove members from their caucus and dismiss their leader. In 2013, I was invited to serve as the national campaign director for the Friends of the Reform Act, and I worked closely with Michael to ensure that the bill would pass. Private members' bills rarely survive parliamentary debate, but Chong was determined to push his through, and he worked with MPs from all parties to make it happen. The party leaders predictably stalled the bill for months and successfully pushed for amendments that weakened its strength. But thanks to immense public pressure, the

Reform Act was unexpectedly adopted by both the House of Commons and the Senate, and it became law in June 2015. The parties, however, quickly found loopholes in the legislation and essentially ignored it. Not much has changed.

The saddest part about all this is how much talent is wasted by the systematic silencing of our elected representatives. Loat and MacMillan observed "a perplexing disconnect: strategic and independent-thinking men and women who had apparently lost all sense of independence and initiative once subsumed under the party brand." Former MP Keith Martin told them that "the system works against innovation, works against independent thought, works against representing the constituents." Comments like this inspired Loat and MacMillan to ask two important follow-up questions: "If MPs are disenchanted with their own parties, then how can we expect regular citizens to engage with those same parties at all? And if they claim the party leadership pushes them away from constructive politics, is it any wonder that so many Canadians can't even be bothered to cast a vote?"

Here's another question we should all be asking: What's the point of having a legislature with 338 seats if only party leaders are expected to have any influence? It's time to fight for the other 333—to reclaim their voice, and ours.

DUMBING DOWN THE WORLD

But the way that parties treat their MPs is just the beginning. There's another group of people who get treated even worse: voters. Evidence suggests that Canada's major parties don't like or respect regular people. I've witnessed it from the inside. Fear and disdain of the masses is in their DNA. The souls of our parties are spiritually damaged, leaving them to operate within a cynical world view that results in a form of condescension unrivalled by any other type of social organization. For example, I recently joined all four major parties, just to see how they communicate with their members. The messages, most of which simply badgered me for money, were written with a tone that made me cringe:

> David,
>
> I've got two sets of numbers in front of me:
>
> The first is how many more donors we need to cross 90,000 on the year—and set a new record. As of five minutes ago, that's just 3,053.
>
> The second is a calculation specifically for you, David, and how much you need to give before tomorrow's deadline to maximize the tax credits you can get back. That number is $5.

I have no problem with automated personalization at the top of an email ("Hello Dave"). As a political organizer, I use that trick all the time. But I'd never pretend that I'm actually writing a personal email, just to you, about you. Especially not one like this:

> David,
>
> I have a confession to make.
>
> Sometimes when I'm at the office late going through donation records, I listen to Taylor Swift. While jamming to "Shake It Off" for the umpteenth time, I found this—can you check it out, and let me know if it's correct?
>
> Record for: **David**
>
> Election year support so far: **$0**

I would also never dream of sending a fake forward to my lists. I despise fake forwards.

> David,
>
> I got an email from Tom this morning asking about tonight's goal.
>
> **Can I tell him you're on board?**
>
> Anne
>
> National Campaign Director, Canada's New Democrats
>
> —— Forwarded message ——
>
> From: Tom Mulcair
>
> Subject: Checking in
>
> Anne,
>
> I know our team has a big goal to hit before midnight. How's it going so far?
>
> It's great to know we've got supporters with us every step of the way.
>
> Hopefully we can add even more before the day is over.
>
> Keep me posted.
>
> Tom

I've saved the best for last.

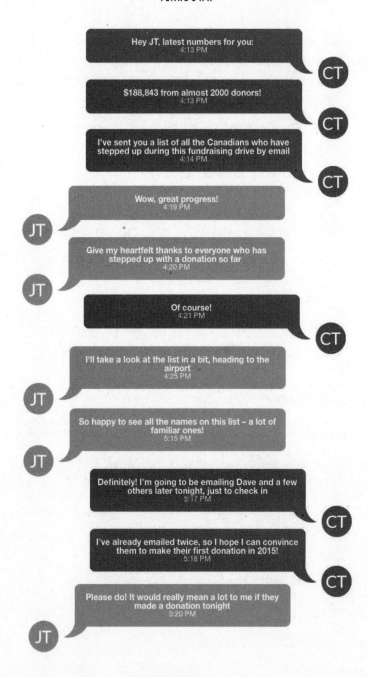

Hi Dave,

See above. I just wanted to share the conversation I had with Justin Trudeau with you. He wanted me to check in with you.

Thank you,

Christina

Senior Director of Fundraising

If only there were a hint of humour, some suggestion that they're mocking themselves or light-heartedly embracing a self-deprecating approach to fundraising. But no. There doesn't seem to be any hint. If you ever get a message like the ones above, I urge you to write back and use whatever profanity you think is appropriate. When adults treat adults like imbeciles, they don't deserve your donations—let alone your vote. But these silly emails aren't the problem— they're just a symptom of an elite political culture that has little respect for ordinary people. Sadly, in their attempts to communicate with the simple-minded masses (me and you), it is the parties themselves who end up dumbing down the world.

Think of the ridiculous rallies they hold for the television cameras, each one a tightly stage-managed and scripted performance lacking spontaneity, creativity or authenticity. I worked in the central NDP office during the early 2000s, and during the Leaders' Tour, we'd arrange these rallies in each city. I watched as the rules gradually became more strict as each campaign unfolded. First we had rules against handmade signs. You know, the things passionate people create with a marker and hold up proudly as a way of saying, "I'm an actual individual person with a particular point of view, and I want everyone to know why I'm here." Eventually, we didn't even allow candidates to bring in their own official signs.

These were nominated NDP candidates who had taken time off from their own campaigns to support the leader's event, and yet their signs were confiscated at the door. Only the leader's signs were allowed.

But then things got worse. And weird. Over the past decade, the evolution of the political placard has stooped to unimaginable new lows. During elections, each campaign prints thousands of identical placards and hands them out at rallies. They all measure 11 by 17 inches. They are all two colours, usually white text on a darker background. And most importantly, they all express something that is unbelievably, inconceivably, inexplicably mundane. And increasingly, with only two words: Strong Leader. Strong Plan. New Mayor. Better City. These placards were one of the many reasons I stopped working for political parties and attending partisan rallies. When you see thousands of people all waving the exact same sign, you quickly feel like you're part of a cult, not a social movement. It's both the message and the monotony that makes the whole event seem incredibly awkward.

Cardboard, markers and paint represent the democratization of mass gatherings. Handmade placards allow participants to feel that they're more than a mob of clapping morons, that they're contributing something unique to the cause, and that their own thoughts and creativity are valued. And to an outside observer, handmade placards show that the room is full of actual thinking human beings. On the flipside, mass-produced two-colour, two-word placards are an embarrassment to our species and a cultural crime. Handing out thousands of these meaningless cards and asking everyone to wave them wildly is one of the quickest ways to demoralize a crowd, discourage future participation and transform a rally into a mockery of what a political gathering can actually feel like. If you work for a party, don't hand them out. If you're a rally participant, don't hold them up.

Recently, just for fun, I applied the Pathetic Placard tactic to a single day of my own life—a Saturday that included pancakes in the morning with some friends, a birthday party and an evening concert. Throughout the day, I tried to make people feel more excited—just like our parties do.

There's another element to partisan rallies that feeds cynicism: teleprompters. There are few things less inspiring than watching a politician pretend to speak off the cuff while reading a pre-written speech off a tilted slab of glass. These automated politicians are rarely able to connect with an audience the way a freestyle speaker can. As CBS correspondent Mark Knoller wrote in 2009, "The danger in teleprompter use is that the speaker will be more focused on reading the words than in conveying a sense of understanding about what he's saying." Politicians who use two teleprompters (one on each side) have been repeatedly mocked for their ping-pong delivery. Former vice president Walter Mondale once referred to teleprompters as "idiot boards." Yet painfully scripted politicians have become so common that I can remember clearly the four times in my entire life that I've witnessed an elected leader deliver a full speech in a manner that seemed to contain genuine thoughts originating in the moment. (If you're curious, those leaders were Colombia's Enrique Peñalosa in 2001, Brazil's Lula da Silva in 2003, Bob Rae in 2013 and Naheed Nenshi in 2016). Even Jack Layton, who had an incredible skill for speaking off the cuff during Toronto City Council meetings, was carefully scripted once he became a federal party leader.

The lack of authenticity can be detected in a televised speech, but the real impact is felt by those who are in the room. When a political speech is delivered at a rally or convention using a teleprompter, what could be an exciting moment is transformed into bland second-rate theatre. Of course, we also don't want to set a standard that only allows confident public speakers to enter politics. But those who aren't as comfortable could simply read from printed notes, which would at least be more genuine than pretending to be spontaneous while using a one-way mirror. And even those speeches should contain some blank spots so the speaker can at least experiment with a little improv. There's no reason to sacrifice all spontaneity just for the sake of risk aversion. Voters are hungry for authenticity and want to see real people sharing real thoughts. If mainstream parties don't embrace authenticity, they'll continue to bleed support to vacuous celebrities and clowns who have the courage to be spontaneous. This is simple: politicians who want to connect with voters and inspire their own volunteers need to learn how to talk to them first.

A FULL PULL

But the biggest crimes committed by our parties are not carried out in Parliament, at rallies or in my inbox. They are committed at our doorsteps. You see, with traditional platforms such as newspapers and network TV shrinking each year, parties have to work harder to reach the general public, and knocking on doors is one way to do that. While most people are unlikely to read through a party's entire platform or attend policy meetings, they just might chat with a neighbour for a few minutes about issues and policy proposals. For democracy to thrive, voters must be informed about the options available, so community conversations are a crucial part of the process. The crime is that none of the parties actually do this. Yes, they absolutely knock on doors, but the interaction at the doorstep is hollow and vapid—by design. I learned this eighteen years ago, when I worked on my first election campaign. Michael Valpy, a well-respected journalist, was running as a federal candidate for the New Democratic Party in my Toronto neighbourhood, and I signed up to volunteer shortly after his nomination. A week later, I was offered a paid administrative job in the main campaign office, providing me a front-row seat to the inner workings of an election campaign. I felt nothing but deep admiration for Valpy, my co-workers and our team of volunteers, but the campaign methodology I was exposed to left me feeling cynical.

I was hoping the campaign would be about issues and policy. I'd naively assumed that our volunteers would be trained on the specifics of the NDP platform, and that we'd develop the skills to become persuasive messengers on people's doorsteps. Instead, I learned that contemporary campaign strategists have very little faith in one-on-one persuasion, and instead have an obsession, almost religious in nature, with the practice of GOTV, or get out the vote. According to the GOTV gospel, it barely matters how many people you persuade. All that matters is how many people you "pull" on election day. Here's how one political insider, former NDP strategist Bill Tieleman, has described it: "Let's say the Conservatives are polling 40 percent of the vote, NDP at 35 percent and the Liberals at 25 percent . . . with 100,000 eligible voters in the riding. With 40 percent, the Conservatives should have the most votes and win—but wait. If the

NDP gets 50 percent of its voters to the polls and the Conservatives and Liberals only 33 percent, the NDP will have 17,500 votes versus the Conservatives' 13,200 and the Liberals' 8,250—and win the riding easily. That's the 'GOTV surprise.'"

As a result of this approach, party volunteers aren't trained to explain the platform, persuade the voter or answer questions (in fact, they're often discouraged from answering questions or spending too much time at any one doorstep). Instead, they're given a single mission: find out who each person is voting for. Armed with clipboards and printed lists of every voter, party volunteers knock on doors and ask, "Can [insert candidate's first name] count on your support on election day?" Then they record the voter's response. This is called "identifying the vote," or "voter ID." Later, back at the campaign office, another volunteer enters all this information into a massive database. On election day, teams are sent out with printed lists of those who promised to support their candidate, and they knock on those assigned doors, reminding people to vote. Meanwhile, other volunteers are inside each polling station, keeping close track of who's voted and who hasn't, again using printed charts. The "outside" volunteers regularly cross-reference their lists with the "inside" volunteers, updating their records with a ruler and pen. If an identified supporter has been reminded but still hasn't voted, the volunteers go back to that doorstep to remind her again . . . and again . . . and again. The party will keep knocking on that door until the person votes. That's called "pulling the vote." I call it harassment.

Imagine if companies behaved this way. Sure, they collect data on us, and yes, they're getting increasingly sophisticated with targeted online advertising based on our preferences and shopping behaviour. But they don't verbally ask us if we plan to buy something, and then harass us until we follow through!

Knock, knock! "Good evening, Mr. Meslin. You told us that you'd buy a new pair of Levi's jeans, but we noticed you haven't purchased them yet. We knocked on your door earlier today, but we thought you might need another reminder. Have you bought them yet?"

But here's the absurd part: not only is repeatedly pestering people on election day kinda rude, but studies reveal that it has little to no effect. Knocking on doors during a campaign and talking to people is of course a great idea, and evidence suggests that making personal contact with voters can increase a candidate's support substantially. But keeping track of every single voter and then staging an elaborate exercise of coordinated harassment seems to raise a campaign's results by somewhere between 0 and 0.5 percent, which makes Tieleman's "GOTV surprise" story not just unlikely but outrageously delusional. Yet the GOTV fable is told over and over by campaign strategists from all parties, as if they all went to the same religious after-school program as kids. They've put all their faith in the GOTV gospel, and they dedicate their volunteer resources not to persuading voters but to compiling data on them.

Allow me to be blunt: the emperor has no clothes. Over the past three decades, while parties and their GOTV gurus have allegedly mastered the fine art of "identifying" and "pulling" their supporters to the polls, election turnout has actually gone *down*—dramatically. GOTV is a scam of the largest proportions, and the negative impact it has had on our political culture is enormous. But before I describe the harm caused by GOTV, let me explain why I think it's become so prevalent. After all, if it doesn't work at all—as I'm suggesting—then why does every single party continue to do it?

Well, the reasons are many. First, GOTV provides a beautiful simplicity to a campaign, in terms of methodology and structure.

Trying to figure out how to persuade thousands of people, how to inspire them, how to give them hope . . . that's a complicated recipe. It's almost impossible to teach, and there's no clear path. Campaign managers want a checklist and a roadmap, and GOTV provides both. GOTV also provides a quantifiable metric. Hope and inspiration, on the other hand, are impossible to measure. The final ballot count on election day provides each campaign manager with a concrete measure of his or her success, but waiting for that result requires a lot of faith, patience and confidence. What if those campaign managers want to track their progress along the way? What if they need emotional reassurance that they're doing a good job as commander in chief? GOTV provides that reassurance with colourful charts and graphs that showcase their growing numbers, each day. Campaign managers love it. GOTV also serves as a marvellous black hole for volunteers. You see, parties prefer to use a top-down approach to both policy and messaging, tightly controlling who says what and when. We've already heard from MPs who feel controlled and scripted by their own parties. If they don't trust their own caucus members to serve as ambassadors to the public, can you imagine how terrified they must be of having random volunteers knocking on doors and saying something that might be off message? This leaves campaigns with a dilemma: how do you distract dozens, if not hundreds, of volunteers and make sure they aren't trying to talk to voters about issues? GOTV is the answer. Give them clipboards or tablets, and send them out to collect data. In the absence of trust, GOTV is a great way to keep everyone busily occupied. In a way, voter ID and GOTV are just part of the largest and most elaborate scavenger hunt in the world. Forget about Pokémon GO. GOTV is the largest outdoor virtual reality game transforming otherwise rational adults into obsessive gamers racing against time.

A fourth factor that keeps the GOTV myth alive is the enormous amounts of money invested in it each year. Hundreds of people make a living consulting about GOTV, teaching it, designing software for it and implementing it. This industry produces a loud parade of well-funded preachers. And GOTV is engrained into the cultural fabric of modern election campaigns. Or more accurately, it *is* the fabric on which all other stories are woven. All things electoral are about, for and because of GOTV. Parties even have their own mythology about how they discovered this incredible mathematical phenomenon. In England, GOTV is called the Reading system, after a particular Labour campaign in 1954, while New Democrats in Canada excitedly tell tales about the Riverdale model, based on a fabled by-election in 1964. (At the Valpy campaign office, pinned to a bulletin board, was a little pocket-sized booklet explaining the Riverdale model, eerily reminiscent of Mao's *Little Red Book*, which coincidentally originated in the same year as the sacred Riverdale campaign).

There are five reasons why I believe GOTV has become an irrational cult-like focus of all modern election campaigns: simplicity, reassurance, distraction, money and mythology. Now here are two reasons why we should care: voters and volunteers. Voters suffer under GOTV-focused campaigns because they're treated not as reasonable people who want to hear about issues or contribute their own ideas but as fools who likely won't even remember to vote. Each voter ID door-knock is a wasted opportunity to engage and inform. (Some parties refer to identified voters as "marks," which is appropriate, since the term "marked man" is defined as "a person who is singled out for special treatment, especially to be harmed.")

But campaign volunteers suffer even more. A voter can simply close the door, shake his head and carry on with his day. But a campaign worker is stuck with her scavenger hunt clipboard for hours, days or weeks. The real loss becomes clear when you begin to imagine what those volunteers could otherwise be doing with those hours. I fantasize about election campaigns with policy workshops that explore the history, context, evidence, arguments and counter-arguments for all the major proposals in the party platform. I imagine a group of trained messengers who can then go to community meetings and explain the platform while also recruiting new volunteers. I dream of canvassers knocking on doors and saying, "What issues are important to you?" instead of asking, "Who are you voting for?" The intellectual void that is GOTV turns away volunteers who actually want to engage in political discourse and try to persuade their neighbours through respectful discussion. I'm living proof of this: I was so disappointed with the GOTV methodology I saw on the Valpy campaign that I haven't volunteered for a local partisan campaign during the ensuing twenty years. I just can't do it. It's soul-crushing.

Here's another twist: the alleged goal of voter ID is to boost political engagement on election day in favour of a particular candidate, but the math doesn't add up. If you consider all the hours spent on voter identification, data entry, database management, inside volunteers, outside canvassers and so on, you'll find that it would actually take less work overall to simply knock on every single door on election day and remind *everyone* how and where to vote, and of course, to make a final pitch for your candidate. Let's call it a full pull. No clipboards required. If you think of it that way, you begin to realize there's a dark side to GOTV. Campaigns aren't producing lists of identified supporters to make it easier to remind them to vote on election day. They're making those lists to ensure that their volunteers don't accidentally remind an opponent's supporter or an undecided voter. Essentially, GOTV is an elaborate effort to *reduce* the number of people who are being reminded to vote. Rather than being about increasing participation, identifying votes is part of a highly sophisticated campaign of selective exclusion. In that sense, GOTV campaigns are, arguably, the largest coordinated vote suppression effort in the history of modern politics.

Experienced campaigners may scoff at the idea of a full pull. "We don't possibly have enough volunteers to pull every voter!" they will say. That may be true under the current political climate, where parties have few members and even fewer volunteers. But they should factor in all the potential volunteers who aren't participating at all—like me—because they've been pushed away. If the soul of campaigns hadn't been hollowed out by GOTV practitioners, there would be a lot more enthusiastic volunteers. (Some parties have even resorted to paying to fill the volunteer gap, hiring GOTV canvassers to carry out the mind-numbing task of identifying votes in priority districts. The NDP calls these staff Poll Cats, which is odd considering that a polecat is a masked member of the weasel family with a skunk-like smell.) And how many people do they really need anyway, if all they're doing is knocking on doors with a quick reminder about voting? A typical postal worker covers about five hundred households a day, and each of those households has an average population of three. That means that on election day, in order to knock on *every single door* with a quick reminder about voting, campaigns need to recruit only ONE volunteer out of every fifteen hundred people. If you can't recruit 0.07 percent of your district to volunteer for your campaign, then you're doing something terribly wrong.

Here's the punchline: the people each party is trying so hard to avoid pulling are being pulled anyway! The NDP spends weeks preparing lists to make sure their volunteers don't remind a Liberal to vote, but the Liberals are pulling those same people. And the Conservative voters who are so carefully avoided on election day by the Liberals are being dragged to polls by the Conservatives. With all decided voters being pulled, no one is really accomplishing anything through this complex process of strategically avoiding opponents' supporters. It's just layers and layers of tragic farce, a multi-million-dollar live performance of slapstick comedy.

I'm not opposed to lists and databases—they are an organizer's best friends. In any election campaign, lists are essential for tracking volunteers, donations, requests for lawn signs or questions from voters. And there's nothing wrong with wanting to get out your vote on election day! But you don't need to harass people to achieve that. And you don't need to track them, or even know who they are. You just need to give them a reason to vote, through genuine attempts at respectful persuasion, followed by a full pull. Modern campaigning's cult-like obsession with voter ID is political poison, alienating a growing number of volunteers and voters.

Before I wrote this section, I dropped into a volunteer training session for a major election campaign in Toronto to see if anything had changed since my first experience in 2000. The well-attended introductory session focused on how to build trust with voters by telling short personal stories, how to identify votes and the importance of pulling identified votes on election day. Over a two-hour period, not one single moment was spent talking about the issues or the campaign platform.

Here's the bottom line: voters don't really need to be reminded—they need to be informed and inspired. The obsession with lists is pushing away young volunteers and reducing voter participation. If campaigns focused more on issues, rather than simply building a network of coordinated harassment, they would be doing themselves—and the rest of us—a huge favour.

IT'S BETTER TO BE A MEMBER

Mic muffins. Whips. Fake forwards. Pathetic placards. Idiot boards. Weasels. Scavenger hunts. If we want to reboot our political parties, there's clearly a lot of work to be done. How do we transform institutions that have become steeped in cynicism, fear and risk aversion? If you want to be a part of that change, the first step is simple: join a party. That doesn't mean you have to become a fiercely partisan, banner-waving lunatic. It just means that you support the general values of a party and want to be part of shaping that party's platform, strategy, team and future. You can even be a member of a party while still collaborating with like-minded people from other parties (more on this in the next chapter). But if you don't sign up as a member, then you can't effect change from within.

Party membership in Canada is currently at an all-time low, estimated to be around 2 percent—one of the lowest rates in the world. To be honest, I'm not convinced that the parties are very concerned about it. In fact, I'm quite sure they like it that way. After all, our parties invest little to no money in member recruitment. They spend millions of dollars on advertising every year, on the radio, on TV, in print and online, and countless more on those full-colour leaflets that get distributed to households during campaigns. These ads contain empty slogans, negative attacks, photos and maybe a hashtag. But have you noticed that they never say "Join our party" or "Become a member today"? You'd think that they'd take advantage of the opportunity to recruit volunteers. Yet I can't remember ever seeing a single piece of partisan literature promoting party membership. In fact, the only reason I've tuned into this strange absence is because one nationwide organization has recently begun using the slogan "It's better to be a member" on all its ads. That organization is Virgin Mobile. When I began to see this slogan everywhere, it dawned on me that I'd never once seen something similar on an NDP, Liberal, Conservative or Green ad. The exception is during local nominations or leadership races, when candidates themselves will recruit new members to help them win. But from the central party, public recruitment of new members is almost unheard of.

This is a trend I've been watching for quite a while. Back in December 2000, after the Valpy campaign wrapped up, I noticed that we didn't do any proactive follow-up with our volunteers. We had a party on election night, packed up our office the next day and that was it. It was like a circus leaving town without a trace. I was curious to find out if this was common practice or an anomaly, so three weeks after election day, I looked at all 301 NDP campaign websites across the country to see how they were reaching out to their volunteers and supporters. Sixty-four sites had not been updated at all. They were still asking for money, for election volunteers, even for votes. They offered nothing. Sixteen websites had been updated with a simple "thank you" message but no reference to further action or opportunity. One website actually said, "Thank you and see you next time," as if there were nothing else to be done for the next four years. Twelve sites had disappeared completely. Ten years later, I recreated the experiment, this time looking at all the major parties. I coordinated a team of volunteers who tracked eighty-nine campaign websites (from the Toronto area) before, during and after election day. One month after the votes were counted, 25 percent of the sites had vanished completely, 55 percent had no information whatsoever about joining the party and only 13 percent invited viewers to attend a meeting. Volunteers also tracked candidates' Facebook pages, and they found that following the campaign, not a single one posted an invitation to join the party or attend a meeting. In 2014, Samara Canada carried out a similar but much larger project looking at more than 1,300 riding association websites across Canada. Only 6 percent listed the names of the local leadership team, less than 5 percent had information on meeting schedules and less than 1 percent had information about how to become a candidate.

Despite the lack of outreach and recruitment, a few thousand people do indeed join these parties each year. But when they do, they're not exactly welcomed with open arms. I've been tracking all the emails I've received since I joined all four major parties six months ago (for research purposes). One party invited me to a nomination meeting to help choose a candidate for the upcoming election, but there was no information about how to register as a candidate myself. I wrote back, asking how the process works—but I was informed that the nomination period was already over! They'd hand-picked a candidate, refrained from informing their own members that nominations were even open and then invited us all to vote for their single candidate. (FYI, this is how elections are conducted in North Korea.) Another party invited me to the annual general meeting, which I believe was a genuine effort to engage members, but their UX design (see chapter 1) was a disaster. They used an abbreviation in the subject line (breaking the first rule of plain language), and there were no graphics or colours in the message itself (breaking the first rule of effective marketing). There wasn't even a single exclamation mark! So the invite sounded and looked boring. I attended the meeting anyway, only to find the outside door locked and no signage directing people where to go. I had to flag someone down to open the door from the inside, and then wait for someone else who'd been to a meeting before and knew where the room was. The meeting itself followed a bureaucratic structure, with no explanation for new guests about what was happening or why. It was an insiders' meeting for insiders. This may not have been their intent, but it was the result.

I also received a few invitations to events where I was expected to bring my body but not necessarily my mind. These included national conventions (where the parties need a big crowd for the leader's speech), gatherings to watch a televised debate and a few parades. Over six months, I received no more than a handful of emails that made me feel like a party genuinely wanted to hear my thoughts. Meanwhile, over that same time period, I received 214 emails asking me for money. These fundraising messages were bright, loud, colourful and saturated with exclamation marks. On one single day, I received—I kid you not—fourteen fundraising messages from the Liberals and NDP alone. Curiously, the Conservatives didn't send me any emails at all but relied on phone calls and snail mail. Of the eleven letters I received in the mail, eleven asked me for money and zero described further opportunities for involvement. The ratio was the same for their phone efforts. Overall, the message I received is that the parties were very interested in my wallet and my ability to fill crowd shots at a parade or convention, but little else. It's quite understandable. Centralized and stable control of any organization is much easier without engaged members. Community-driven participation could quickly lead to unwanted policy proposals or even a challenge to the current leadership.

Back in the NDP head office, a decade ago, I learned how fearful the party bigwigs were of their own members. I remember sitting around a map of Toronto with my co-workers and talking about ridings where we hadn't yet nominated a candidate. Riding after riding, the same question was asked: "Does anyone know anyone who could run there—maybe a friend or family member?" I responded with another question: "Have we emailed our members in these ridings to see if anyone wants to run?" The others looked at me like I was crazy. When the membership is excluded from the most basic processes, like candidate selection, it's little wonder that party membership is so low. As former Liberal MP Keith Martin confesses in *Tragedy in the Commons*, "We're not giving people any reason to join a political party."

I want to be very clear about something: I'm not blaming individual people for the misdeeds of their political organizations. Party volunteers, especially at the local level, are some of the most dedicated and passionate citizens you can find. It's the culture of the parties that we need to dissect and overhaul. It's a culture of exclusion, and it's built into the DNA of all parties, driven by both fear and cynicism. And to be fair, their fear isn't completely unfounded. In a first-past-the-post system, we tend to see only two or three major parties, and they are all what we call "big tent" organizations, meaning that they are essentially informal coalitions of groups representing a wide political spectrum. The New Democratic Party (and the Democratic Party in the US) includes everyone from moderate progressives to far-left anti-capitalists. And on the other side of the spectrum, the Conservative Party (and the Republican Party in the US) offers an umbrella for those who identify as progressive fiscal conservatives, as well anti-government libertarians, pro-gun activists and a whole array of folks who are opposed to gay marriage, sex education or abortion. Understandably, leaders within those parties are scared of their own members because each party has an extreme element with views that are inconsistent with a moderate message. This is one of the reasons that nominations are controlled and volunteers muzzled.

This problem of big tent parties that artificially bring together people who actually have little in common would evaporate with proportional representation. Parties on the left would split into factions that represent varying degrees of socialism, while those on the right would fragment into organizations that can more practically represent the diverse interests of people who are currently forced under a broad "conservative" umbrella. This would have a couple of enormous benefits. First, parties would spend much less time fighting internally. Almost every leadership race we see turns into a battle between the left and right factions of the party. This is a result of incompatible factions being forced together in the first place. Second, parties would no longer be scared of fringe elements within their own ranks because those folks would no longer be members.

But the most important way that proportional representation would affect party culture is by creating an environment in which the old parties could simply die—at last. Without fear of vote-splitting, new parties would emerge—parties that are more innovative, youthful, creative and bold. I spoke earlier about the need to break up the gang of partisan dinosaurs by allowing new parties to disrupt the sector. In addition to offering more choice for voters, these new parties would also be more inclusive and participatory. You can't have an insiders' club at the local level if your party is brand new and actively recruiting volunteers and candidates in hundreds of ridings. Turnover and renewal are crucial for any ecosystem to thrive. In a forest, the nutrients from dead trees feed the saplings on the ground. With PR, we'd have a healthy turnover, with older parties—rigid in their ways—naturally replaced with new growth. And that would make our entire political culture more interesting and inviting.

But we don't have proportional representation, so you're pretty much stuck with the existing oligopoly for the time being. The parties don't want you to join them, and that's precisely why you should. You'll have to dig deep to find out how to get involved, how to get elected onto the local district association and how to play a part in decision-making and policy proposals. You might have to ruffle some feathers, and you might experience pushback from the existing leadership. If we are ever going to change our political parties, it will happen only because people who are committed to that transformation took the time to fill out a membership form and get involved. You won't be alone. There are people in every party, every day, trying to open the doors and make the process more collaborative. In particular, younger members are often leading the way on reform. Help them out.

In *Tragedy in the Commons*, authors Loat and MacMillan neatly sum up the current status of our partisan institutions, writing, "The stark reality is that most Canadians no longer like, trust or join national political parties." The situation is intolerable. Rather than creating spaces for political community, our parties are feeding apathy and cynicism. We can and must transform these organizations and reclaim our democratic space. It's not an easy task, but it's crucial. Without a teardown, we're sentencing ourselves to decades of the same old problem: a cartel of condescending parties stifled by their own inertia and fear.

CHAPTER 6

BLOOD SPORT

Imagine landing your dream job, showing up for your first day of work and being completely ignored by your new colleagues. That's what happened to Graham Steele, the former finance minister of Nova Scotia. After winning a four-way race to secure the NDP nomination in the riding of Halifax Fairview, and then winning the seat itself with 58 percent of the vote, Steele took his seat in the legislature. But when he rose to speak for the first time, representing the ten thousand residents of his riding, he found "that no one in the room, absolutely no one, was listening." Although Steele thought the actions of his fellow politicians, "in any other gathering of grownups, would be shockingly bad manners," he soon discovered that the silent treatment was actually relatively good behaviour for his colleagues. His tell-all exposé, *What I Learned About Politics*, describes a "parody of democracy" in the provincial legislature, where the most common type of interaction between politicians is to "heckle, interrupt and insult." He observed that "the last thing on their minds is mature consideration of someone's argument," and sadly confessed that "visitors to the gallery often go away shaking their heads in bewilderment."

Steele's experience is not an anomaly. After interviewing eighty former members of Canada's legislature, the authors of *Tragedy in the Commons* labelled our Parliament the Kindergarten on the Rideau. This wasn't just their opinion but the unanimous opinion of the politicians themselves. One former MP compared the legislature to a zoo, while another described "partisan drivel" that "poisons the atmosphere of the chamber." According to Green Party leader Elizabeth May, in her book *Losing Confidence*, "Question Period has sunk to the lowest levels of rudeness and incivility in living memory.... There is no cooperation. There is no effort at consensus. The House has become toxic through excessive partisanship and collective amnesia has wiped away the sure knowledge that it does not have to be like this." She describes in detail the "infantile questions," "egregious behaviour," "cruel tone," "sexist taunts" and "disrespectful heckling" that have come to dominate parliamentary debate. And we treat this as if it's normal. With hundreds of adults being paid to act like angry toddlers, Canada's House of Commons is essentially the largest and most expensive daycare in the country.

Chances are, none of this is shocking to you. We've simply become accustomed to verbal warfare as a substitute for thoughtful conversation—and not just in Parliament but in our provincial legislatures and our local city councils. Our militaristic approach to politics takes complex issues and recklessly transforms them into simplistic polarized teams: right versus left, urban versus suburban, drivers versus cyclists, environment versus business. This team-sport mentality has four results: First, legislation is often ideologically driven rather than evidence-based. Second, we have fishtail policies that flip back and forth between binary views, depending on who is in power. Third, actual dialogue is replaced with political theatre that reduces all our politicians to the intellectual equivalent of hockey goons. Fourth, voters increasingly turn their backs on the whole circus, not out of apathy but in disgust.

Is it too idealistic to imagine another approach? Rather than battlegrounds populated by players with inflexible opinions, could our councils and legislative bodies serve as arenas of conversation? I confess, I sometimes have doubts. I watch my young son playing video games, passionately immersing himself in medieval battles (*Clash Royale*), modern warfare (*Call of Duty*) or futuristic laser fights (*Star Wars*), and it makes me wonder if perhaps our militaristic approach to politics is an unavoidable consequence of human nature. Maybe we're just attracted to the thrill of fighting. Then again, there's *Minecraft*—an odd video game that's simply about building things. When you play *Minecraft*, you're not trying to "win" and you don't have to kill anyone. Rather, it's an infinite and complex virtual sandbox. Most importantly, you can collaborate. My son and I have built castles, underground subway systems, gardens and bridges. Here's the most interesting part: *Minecraft* is the second-best-selling video game of all time. Although it was only introduced in 2009, it's already surpassed the net sales of long-time favourites like *Grand Theft Auto* (launched in 1997) and *Super Mario Brothers* (1985).

We probably shouldn't make sweeping conclusions about human nature by comparing video game sales. And I can tell you that when my kid plays *Minecraft*, he'll occasionally go on a rampage, killing as many zombies, creepers and skeletons as possible. But the success of both war games and building games serves as a reminder that while we like to fight, we also have the capacity to be energized by acts of creative collaboration. We can be drawn in either direction and can thrive in either environment. I should also point out that the best-selling video game of all time is *Tetris*—a puzzle. If political compromise is the art of seeing how people's perceptions and needs differ and then finding a way to arrange all those needs and ideas into one coherent shape, then all *Tetris* lovers should be easy recruits for a new kind of politics. We're hard-wired to enjoy problem-solving, building and collaboration. The question is: Can we take these traits that lie within us and somehow allow them to come alive in our democratic spaces? That shouldn't be too much to ask.

The first step towards moving beyond the team-sport partisanship that gets in the way of good policy-making is to stop blaming politicians. While we often hear cheap slogans about "kicking the bums out" or "draining the swamp," evidence suggests that the problem is much more complex. In *What I Learned About Politics*, Steele writes: "The fact is that our politicians are us. There isn't a better, more perfect, more angelic version of us. The people who are elected to office used to be us, and once they're in office they respond in human ways to the pressure of the job. You would do the same if you were elected. Yes, you would. And if you think you wouldn't, you'd be one of those bright-eyed politicians who didn't know what they were getting into."

Steele tells a story about sitting in the legislature and watching the leader of his party, Premier Darrell Dexter, answer questions from the leader of the Opposition, Stephen McNeil. Suddenly Steele realized that he'd heard the exact same back-and-fourth discussion before—when *his* party was the Opposition. "Stephen was using the same words, the same tactics and the same arguments that Darrell had used," he writes. "And Darrell was giving the same replies that the Conservatives had given to him when he was the one posing the questions. . . . It struck me then forcefully that there was hardly any point to who sat in my chair or who is on which side of the house. None of us was dealing with the real issues."

The MPs interviewed for *Tragedy in the Commons* held a similar view. "Our exit interviews suggest that politicians seem to deplore their own public behaviour," Loat and MacMillan write. "They fear it's turning people away from politics. So why not change? If they regretted it so much, why didn't they stop?" In *Losing Confidence*, Elizabeth May explains that politicians seem to act out of character, and that their surroundings somehow transform them into juvenile thugs. "People who would not ordinarily be crude . . . become the worst version of themselves."

It seems that ruthless, adversarial opposition is built into our system by design. In that sense, thinking you can fix the problem by electing better politicians is like trying to fix your smartphone's shattered screen by replacing the batteries. Our elected representatives are just one part of the system and, depending on their environment, they can be pulled towards creativity or battle. Towards *Minecraft* or *Call of Duty*.

In his memoir, Steele notes that in the Nova Scotia legislature, "fifty-one grown-ups act in ways that, if repeated in their private lives, would end their personal relationships and, if repeated in other workplaces, would get them fired." True, but if an *entire* workforce was behaving badly, a smart employer wouldn't fire everyone. Instead, she'd try to figure out why her workplace was bringing out the worst in her employees, and then make whatever changes were necessary. In the political workplace, our terminology, procedures and even the physical spaces used for debate are all structured to maximize conflict. So rather than trying to "kick the bums out," we should be looking at what we can change about our political spaces to bring out our best.

CIVILITY BY DESIGN

If you were asked to design a legislature in a manner that guaranteed conflict and hostility, you'd likely end up recreating Canada's House of Commons. It's like a sports arena or battlefield, with our MPs organized into two groups and facing each other from opposite sides of the room. One group is literally called the Opposition. Thanks to the seating arrangements and terminology alone, a hostile fight is all but guaranteed—before a single word is spoken.

It's bad enough that our elections are full of militaristic terms like "war room," "boot camp" and "trenches." Perhaps these phrases can be forgiven, since our elections are essentially battles with winners and losers. But once the ballots have been counted and our elected representatives enter the legislature, why continue with battlefield terminology and procedure? Hard-core traditionalists will wail with emotional pain at any suggestion of tampering with the centuries-old tradition of Her Majesty's Loyal Opposition. To them, any change to our political system is sacrilegious, as if the British Westminster system of governance were handed to us by God, its rules etched onto tablets carved from the Canadian Shield.

Traditionalists speak of "adversarial representation" and "rituals of confrontation" as indispensable and untouchable treasures. This is rubbish. These folks are rust on the gears of history—champions of inertia and mediocrity. To them I say, don't chain yourselves to our history: its purpose is to inform, not to command. This is particularly true when you consider that the term "opposition" wasn't even intended to be used in the manner we use it now. Two centuries ago, when a young British Parliament was slowly emerging from a long history of absolute monarchy, it was considered treasonous for a member to challenge the executive. What slowly developed was the idea that MPs did indeed have the right to oppose—not an obligation to *constantly* oppose, but simply the right to oppose if and when necessary. The term "loyal opposition" was a playful phrase that acknowledged the new and radical idea that an elected representative could be both critical of the government and loyal to the Crown at the same time. But since then, the concept of a parliamentary opposition has transformed into the nonsensical idea that the second party's role is to challenge the government's every move and simply act as an alternative government in waiting. What a colossal waste of talent and a missed opportunity for discussion between human beings with different perspectives. Why are we paying 338 people a salary of $172,700 each, simply to act as knee-jerk supporters or opponents of legislation? This is precisely what voters are so sick of: the inefficient and childish battlefield that our politics has become.

Traditionalists will quote John Diefenbaker, who said in a speech titled "The Role of the Opposition in Parliament" that "the reading of history proves that freedom always dies when criticism ends."

are generally more independent than members of cabinet. Unfortunately, after this multi-partisan dialogue has taken place, the party leaders will often kick their own members off a given committee and replace them with MPs who have been given detailed and divisive marching orders. A simple reform proposed by multiple former politicians is to allow all committees to fulfill their work for the entire legislative session by preventing party leaders from interfering with their membership. Once again, we have evidence that politicians want to work together—they just need the right environment for that to happen.

There's also a need to dramatically redesign the physical spaces of governing. For example, one of the best ideas I've heard to fix the tone of our legislature is to break up the mob. Instead of assigning seats based on parties, with a party on one side yelling at another party on the other side, why not mix them up? This proposal, a *Motion for Randomized Seating in the House,* was introduced in the House of Commons in 2012, also by Bruce Hyer. "The mindless tribalism has always bothered me," he said at the time. "We would no longer be sitting in hockey teams, with our coaches dying to send us over the boards for a brawl. We'd get to know them as people."

Canada wouldn't be the first to try this. There are at least three countries that don't arrange their national parliaments based on party affiliation. Both Norway's Storting and Sweden's Riksdag, for example, have seating plans based on geography rather than party. Former Austrian foreign minister Bruno Kreisky once wrote: "In Sweden, for the first time, I was able to observe a well-functioning democracy. Those holding different political views were treated with the utmost respect; they were not regarded as opponents, if only because in the Swedish Parliament the seating of delegates was not arranged according to party, but by the regions from which the representatives came. Thus, Social Democrats sat next to Conservatives, Communists next to Liberals, peasants next to industrial workers; they came from the same region, they were 'Landskap' in Swedish, and had often been friends since childhood."

The Icelandic parliament, the Alþingi (pronounced "all-thing-y"), has used random seating for a hundred years. At the beginning of each legislative session, each member reaches into a box of numbered balls, just like a Bingo draw, to determine where he or she will sit. I asked Thorstein Magnusson, deputy secretary general of the Alþingi, about the benefits of this approach, and he told me, "Heckling is more forceful when members are together in one group. Randomized seating has contributed to greater acquaintance between members of different parties than otherwise would be the case."

We have few examples of non-partisan seating arrangements in North America, but one of the best case studies is Toronto City Council, which has no official parties. I asked Councillor Joe Mihevc to explain the impact that randomized seating has on civility in the chamber. He said: "Politics is about many things, including working out ideological differences and building trusting relationships, where people agree on some issues and disagree on other issues, all within a context of understanding and respecting differences. It may seem superficial, but the seating plan at council allows for these trusting relationships to form. When you sit beside someone for meeting after meeting, people with different views often see the good reasons behind a difference of opinion. That often leads to a different conversation and a creative solution. It makes council more of a human place."

I asked Joe what he thought the council would be like if the right and left factions sat in groups on opposite sides, as they do in Parliament. "This would be disastrous for council," he told me. "It would polarize municipal politics needlessly." Precisely. Randomized seating could also increase the independence of MPs, allowing them to represent their constituents more effectively, rather than just toeing the party line. "Right now, we are all lined up," said Hyer. "If one of us stands up contrary to the wishes of the leader or the party, everybody notices instantly." But with random seating, he noted, "When you vote your constituents' wishes or your conscience, it will be less obvious that you have voted differently than the other members of your party."

Randomized seating is just one of many reforms that would change the physical nature of our political spaces. During one of my visits to Calgary's City Hall School, I was told that having kids in the building actually makes the adults behave better. Simply by being in the presence of curious and observant children, everyone was more aware of their actions. While reforms tend to focus on ritual and process, we should never underestimate how our physical surroundings affect our behaviour.

———

There's one more proposal I'd like to add to my mix of remedies: professional help. Isn't it strange how we incorporate trained mediators and facilitators into so many aspects of our lives, except perhaps the most important deliberative space? Companies in North America spend more than a billion dollars each year on team-building exercises designed to increase trust and understanding among their employees. Workplace conflicts of all kinds are solved with the help of external mediators who help navigate paths towards compromise. And of course at the smallest level, millions of us have recruited the skills of marriage or relationship counsellors to help us learn how to love each other. So if we use trained mediators for our workplaces and our homes, why don't we do it for government? If two loving partners need professional help to learn how to listen to and understand each other, what the heck did we expect would happen if we tossed 338 MPs into a room and asked them to make complex decisions on behalf of an entire country?

Of course, our legislatures and councils do have a Speaker or Chair, but neither is expected to play an influential role. Under *Robert's Rules of Order*, the procedural guide used by our governments, the Speaker or Chair serves as a passive referee overseeing a legislative battle and then declaring a winner and a loser. By focusing exclusively on the principle of majority rule, *Robert's Rules* ensures that minority voices are ignored and consensus is explicitly *not* a goal. What I'm proposing is entirely different: an active yet impartial facilitator. A marriage counsellor for Parliament!

Some might be concerned that such a moderator would carry too much power in a legislature or council chamber. Could he truly remain neutral? Of course he could. That's exactly what professional facilitators do. It's their job, and they're certified to do it. We have people right here in Canada who have the skills and training to play an impartial yet active role in a discussion. In fact, coincidentally, the International Association of Facilitators is based in Toronto!

If you're still concerned about opening the legislature to an unelected voice who might use Jedi mind tricks to influence the outcome of debate, here's a less controversial idea: train politicians to talk to each other. A good friend of mine, Annahid Dashtgard, is the co-founder of a company called Anima Leadership, whose trainers and coaches weave together practices from science, psychology and social systems to help clients in the following areas:

- organizational health and human systems architecture
- diversity, power and anti-bias research
- emotional intelligence and mindfulness tools
- relational leadership and bridging difference
- conflict transformation and dialogue skills
- leadership coaching

This kind of training is not cheap, quick or easy. But Anima insists that the investment pays off. "Research consistently shows that organizations that have a healthy culture and inclusive workplace perform head and shoulders above others," the company claims. Clients agree. Anima has been hired by almost every kind of organization you can imagine in all three sectors: public, private and non-profit. From tech companies to schools, police forces to hospitals, and even government agencies. But there is one kind of organization that has made no effort to train its leaders: the decision-making bodies that regulate almost every aspect of our lives. Other than our own legislatures, no employer places people into positions of power with absolutely no preparation or training.

Anima's motto is "When people are in environments where they matter and belong, the extraordinary becomes possible." Wouldn't it be nice to live in a world where the words "government" and "extraordinary" could co-exist in the same sentence or thought? I asked Annahid what she would do if she were hired to train a new crop of recently elected politicians. What would the program look like? After some thought (actually, it was the longest pause of all my 120 interviews, which shows how intentional and self-aware her thinking is), she described a plan:

> I would do basic across-the-board mandatory training in social, emotional and psychological skills, looking at the conscious and unconscious mind, looking at how powerful the unconscious mind is, how powerful emotions are, what it means to be triggered, how we lose control in those moments, and how to manage ourselves before trying to manage others. Current neuroscience says that our primal brain or unconscious mind is infinitely more powerful than the conscious thinking part of ourselves. What we feel—our instincts, needs, biases—motivate everything that we say and do. Helping people understand the way our minds work, and how it motivates what we do, actually give us more control.
>
> I'd break them into groups of thirty, to actually have room for relationship-building and conversation. The groups would be multi-partisan. There would be three days of training—but spaced apart, not all at once. The first day would be on emotional social skills: self-awareness, self-management, and also relationship-building among people in the room. I think these skills are the foundation of good leadership, period. And most people don't have them. The second day would look at bias and inclusion, and the third day would focus on critical conversations: how to disagree in a way that we retain our own humanity and avoid dehumanizing the other side.
>
> We'd offer as much thoughtful social and emotional infra-structure as there is currently training around policies, *Robert's Rules of Order* or how to operate your office computer. I'd really build the relationships so that when they're in the Parliament,

it's harder to be so easily dismissive. If I'm connected to you on some emotional level, it doesn't mean I'm not going to disagree with you, but how I disagree is going to show up in a different way.

If these investments were made, the impact would just be mind-blowing. Government would finally be able to actually harness collective intelligence, rather than some dominant personalities continuing to replicate the familiar. This is the piece that would start to dismantle a lot of the ways that power is abused.

All of this flowed from Annahid's mind like a river. Here's a person who knows, intimately, how to help people learn to talk and listen to each other. Knowing that these facilitation and training programs exist, it's inexplicable that workshops like the ones she describes aren't already a mandatory part of representative government. Before politicians start making critical decisions that affect millions of people, they should learn about each other in a really deep and personal way. They need to understand each other's motivations, hopes, dreams, fears, strengths and weaknesses because those are the underlying forces that will influence their actions.

Some people will think this kind of emotional intelligence training is flaky. But it's not—it's science. Here are some flaky ideas: Force all members of Parliament to live in shared housing where they take turns cooking for each other. Hotbox the entire legislature. Start every meeting with leaders saying something nice about another party. Schedule pre-budget ayahuasca ceremonies. Those are radical ideas! But there's nothing even remotely radical about training people to listen to each other and understand their own emotional strengths and weaknesses. Anima's work is so effective, in fact, that the company has been contracted to design and implement peace-building projects for communities in conflict in Europe and South America. Nothing flaky about that.

I first met Annahid twenty years ago, in the weeks leading up to a protest in Quebec City. Along with twenty thousand others, we would be travelling in buses to speak out against the Free Trade Agreement of the Americas, which threatened Canada's autonomy to implement environmental and labour standards. We heard in advance that organizers planned to erect a massive security fence to keep us far away from the negotiations, so we held a press conference in Toronto featuring respected cultural leaders who criticized this fence as an unnecessary and provocative security measure. (My job for the press conference was to rent and install an actual chain-link fence in the room, a theatrical prop that stood between the speakers and the media.)

Once we arrived in Quebec City, protesters divided themselves into three zones: a safe green zone for sanctioned protest, an orange zone for unsanctioned yet peaceful protest and a red zone for those who wanted to physically challenge the fence (and were prepared to get arrested). Annahid and I both spent most of our time in the green and orange zones, but when a group of radical protesters broke off from the sanctioned march and began to walk directly towards the fence, we were drawn to the impending clash. Soon enough, the fence had been knocked down by a small army of anarchists and union leaders, but their momentary revolution was quickly pushed back by an actual army equipped armed with tear gas, rubber bullets and water cannons. To be honest, I don't know what anyone thought would happen if the fence actually came down. Would we take over the negotiations? Write our own international trade deals? No one had planned that far ahead. It was just about taking down the fence. Still, the symbolism felt intoxicating.

Two decades later, Annahid a mother and I a father, our activism has definitely mellowed. I don't regret being in Quebec City, donning a gas mask and challenging that fence. Public protest can be a powerful way to bring attention to an issue, energize a group and empower those who feel voiceless. But at the same time, I can't help wondering if we were buying into a divisive "us versus them" mentality that we'd been exposed to through so much pop culture. Were we playing a live-action political version of *Call of Duty*? Maybe the chain-link in Quebec City was a distraction from a more complex and fortified barrier: the deeply engrained emotional fences that obstruct dialogue, reinforce polarity and prevent us from achieving the sustainable and just future that is within reach.

An American philosopher once said, "If you want to make the world a better place, take a look at yourself and make a change." How do we, as voters and citizens, feed the political hostility we see—and resent—in government? Rather than showing our representatives what civil discourse could look like, we often settle into social echo chambers where like-minded friends simply reinforce our own views. As a community organizer, I often find my initial instinct for a campaign is to identify an enemy and then plot a battle plan to defeat them. Polarization is an effective and simple way to tap into people's anger. But in recent years, I've been experimenting with ways to break down political walls, adopt non-adversarial tactics and encourage cross-partisan engagement. I've invited far-right conservative journalists out for lunch. I ran an online marketing campaign highlighting car owners who support bike lanes. I started a multi-partisan rock band at city hall (this revealed not only that socialists and capitalists can collaborate under the glare of stage lights, but that Mike Layton can sing a mean "Highway to Hell"). I've worked for the New Democrats, collaborated with a Conservative MP, helped develop policy for a Liberal government and delivered a keynote address at an Ontario Green Party convention. I was even called a "promiscuous endorser" in a local newspaper after publicly backing three city council candidates who were all running for the same seat.

I've marched in the streets many times, and I'm sure I will again. And I recognize that sometimes oppositional tactics are required—especially for marginalized communities that are so often excluded from decisions that affect their lives. But despite many fond memories of tense street protests, I feel that the most subversive and radical work to be done is the tearing down of emotional and cultural walls, rather than physical ones. Operating as a multi-partisan activist and collaborating with people who usually don't work together has been incredibly rewarding. It's a different type of intoxication, fuelled not by adrenaline but by overcoming the structural obstacles that so often stand in the way of teamwork, personal growth and real change.

LAUGHTER BEHIND THE CURTAIN

At this point, you may be confused. I championed the benefits of disruptive competition in chapter 3, but now I'm preaching harmonious collaboration. And in chapter 5, I encouraged you to become a member of a party, while now I'm encouraging you to be non-partisan. But there is no contradiction. In fact, the seeming incompatibility between these ideas gets to the core of the transformation that needs to happen: the birth of a new political culture that fosters the organic coexistence of competition and collaboration. It sounds like a naive goal, but I've seen it in practice and it's a beautiful thing. And I've found it in the strangest place: corporate conferences! Specifically, I'm talking about trade associations, which are behind-the-scenes private-sector groups that shatter the most common stereotypes of the free market by bringing competitors together to collaborate, share ideas and pool resources.

I've seen ReMax, Royal LePage and Sutton agents hang out together at the Canadian Real Estate Association convention. I've seen senior executives from McDonald's, Pizzaville and Tim Hortons sit in workshops together at the Canadian Franchise Association conference. And you know those companies that sell eyeshadow and shampoo at tea parties in living rooms? Even they get together, through the Direct Selling Association—Avon, Arbonne and Mary Kay, all working together as a team. Most surprisingly, they all seem to enjoy it! These execs spend most of the year participating in cutthroat capitalist competition, desperately trying to undermine each other and steal as much market share as possible. But for one weekend, they put the performance on hold. And during that intermission, behind the curtain, they share meals, participate in team-building exercises and laugh. A lot. The mood is oddly joyous, and the toxic animosity we find in our political culture is absent. "It's often said," journalist and economist Andrew Coyne once told me, "if airlines behaved the way political parties do, and they ran ads saying, 'My opponent's planes crash a lot,' no one would fly on any of them." In the private sector, he explained, "there is a self-policing dynamic. There's an understanding that while we're competing, we're also all in this together. In politics, this same realization has not kicked in."

I believe we can create the same kind of collaborative behaviour among competing political parties, but it has to begin at the grassroots, with individual people like you. It's a bottom-up cultural shift that encourages people from different parties to be friendly, respectful and collaborative. To be transpartisan is to entirely habits are currently so shallow that people like me, who dream of human beings having conversations with each other, are considered radical.

What stands in our way is not really tradition, as much as *selective* tradition. After all, adversarial parliaments are hardly traditional in North America. From a bird's-eye view of history, our polarized legislatures can be seen as a modern experiment—not a historic treasure. Rather than seeking tradition from the past two hundred years, why not reach back a little further—maybe a thousand? Centuries before academics began coining terms like "emotional intelligence" (1964) or "deliberative democracy" (1980), many of North America's Indigenous nations were practitioners of both. While Europe was stuck in the Dark Ages, the five founding nations of the Iroquois Confederacy were developing the Kaianerekowa, the Great Law of Peace, which describes an elaborate system of participatory governance complete with a bicameral legislative process, universal rights, referendums and rotating spokespersons. "Hostilities shall no longer be known between the Five Nations," declared the Kaianerekowa, calling for an open and inclusive immigration policy that extended hospitality to refugees from other nations and granted them "equal rights and privileges in all matters." At the same time, Europeans were launching the genocidal Crusades. When nations of the Confederacy were burying their weapons on Turtle Island, the Catholic Church was busy experimenting with new tools to torture people. And while the Great Law of Peace was codifying gender rights and granting powerful authority to the Clan Mothers, Europeans were literally burning witches. But the most interesting aspect of the Kaianerekowa, and a clear contrast to Western culture, is its emphasis on political civility and what we now call emotional intelligence. "The Chiefs of the League of Five Nations shall be mentors of the people for all time," the law states. "The thickness of their skin shall be seven spans, which is to say that they shall be proof against anger, offensive action and criticism. Their hearts shall be full of peace and good will, and their minds filled with a yearning for the people of the League. With endless patience they shall carry out their duty and their firmness shall be tempered with a tenderness for their people. Neither anger nor fury shall find lodging in their minds and all their words and actions shall be marked by calm deliberation."

Endless patience. Tenderness. Calm deliberation. These are completely foreign concepts in our modern political culture, which is based on aggression and conflict. And these aren't just ancient traditions but are still being practised today. For example, the Kahnawá:ke community, just south of Montreal, uses a sophisticated participatory consensus model that organizes participants into three groups. While two of the groups take part in a back-and-forth facilitated amendment process, the third observes and gives feedback at the end. If all three groups don't agree, the process begins again.

In Kahnawá:ke, "the decision-making process is not an adversarial one," writes assistant professor and community leader Kahente Horn-Miller. "It relies on calm deliberation, respect for diverse views, and substantial agreement." In a 2013 paper, "What Does Indigenous Participatory Democracy Look Like?" she describes the difficulties and benefits of deep democracy: "Participation in a consensus-based decision-making process is a unique experience and requires a change in thinking. Often, the initial feeling amongst participants is skepticism that everyone present might be able to agree on something. However, participants involved in the consensus process often express feeling surprise and relief once a decision is reached."

The Kahnawá:ke model is a far cry from the "majority wins" approach that European cultures embrace. Remember, in chapter 3, when the proportional election gave the town of Northville a council that truly reflected its wishes (six hockey councillors and four golf councillors)? That's representative, but if the council itself uses *Robert's Rules* and binary yes/no votes, then the hockey councillors will win every vote and the golf councillors won't really have any influence at all. No election system on its own can guarantee collaboration. To achieve consensus, we need to look not only at how we elect our representatives but also at the process they're expected to use once elected—and the skills they need to communicate with each other.

Taiaiake Alfred, a professor of Indigenous governance at the University of Victoria, offers a powerful vision of consensus in his book *Peace, Power, Righteousness: An Indigenous Manifesto*: "Our traditions demand a higher standard of conduct—in fact, a completely different conception of the leader's role—than do the conventional corporate models that dominate business and politics in mainstream society. Simply put, for us it is not enough to know how to gain, hold and use power. Like my forebears, I believe that leadership consists in invoking the power of reason and that the human capacity to achieve harmony is best developed through pacification and persuasion."

Sadly, many Indigenous communities in Canada no longer use consensus models. Part of the colonial assault on their culture included the forced transition to a Western-style governance model. The participatory model used in Kahnawá:ke is rare, but Alfred is calling for an overhaul of Indigenous democracy to reflect traditional values by rejecting "divisive electoral politics and Western-style institutions." He adds, "The kind of revival we need cannot be accomplished under *Robert's Rules of Order*." Although his message is about reforming Indigenous governance, Alfred hopes that the rest of Canada will also consider learning from our country's most ancient traditions—what he calls the "Indigenous contribution to the reconstruction of a just and harmonious world."

On a visit to Nova Scotia, I had the pleasure of dining at the home of former Liberal Party leader Danny Graham, and our long discussion drifted towards the theme of civility, with a focus on both the barriers and the possibilities. He shared a story from his time as the leader of the Opposition that illustrates the uphill struggle facing anyone who wants to reform the system from the inside. Graham spoke favourably at a press conference about something the government had just done, and afterwards a veteran journalist warned him that the political reporters had discussed giving him less coverage unless he was more negative. The media loves a good fight, and journalists rarely cover positive collaboration. In this way, they're creating an incredible distortion of who we are. The same thing happens in the comment threads of news articles, which are full of anger and hostility—they can leave you feeling hopeless about humanity. But it's common knowledge that political groups hire anonymous writers to post hostile comments and feed the flames of adversarial politics. If we see nothing but conflict in the news and comments threads, it leaves us with a distorted view of who we are and reinforces our belief that we aren't capable of listening to each other.

Our cultural resistance to political collaboration is strong. We have language not only to encourage hostile behaviour but also to punish good behaviour. For example, if a minority government works together with a smaller party to pass legislation, the smaller party is said to be "propping up" the government. The term has a clear negative connotation—it implies that one party is offering power and legitimacy to another party that isn't worthy of support. This kind of language is designed to shame collaborators, just as those reporters attempted to shame Danny Graham into being more adversarial. But despite his experiences, Graham is hopeful. He points out that regardless of what our governments get up to, we have a worldwide reputation as a pleasant and polite people. In fact, with political arenas across the globe increasingly dominated by partisanship, animosity, anger and aggression, Graham sees a clever opportunity for Canada. "Wouldn't it be wonderful," he says, "if Canada, poster-child for civility, was able to turn it around?"

Let's make this our challenge. We don't have to continue to use the same broken systems that we inherited from our parents' and grandparents' generations. We've proven, repeatedly, that our species is able to evolve politically and adopt new practices of governance and power-sharing. For centuries, political disagreements were resolved on battlefields and decision-making power was wielded by those with the strongest armies and sharpest swords. Then a slow journey took us from tyrannical monarchy to representative government. But while we replaced bullets with ballots, we never really moved beyond the battlefield. Let's push our evolution forward, shifting conflict to conversation. Rather than tolerating mob-driven verbal warfare and ruthless tribalism, we have the capacity to transform the House of Commons, our provincial legislatures and our city councils. Our political spaces should feel energizing, extraordinary and sacred—not through Victorian rituals, but through stunningly authentic dialogue based on respect, curiosity, humility and patience. Anything less is an absolute betrayal of what we're capable of and what we so desperately need.

CHAPTER 7

TAKING THE REINS

Enough about politicians. We've looked at how we elect our representatives, who funds their campaigns, how their behaviour is affected by political parties and how they interact with each other once in office. But what about the rest of us? Is our role as citizens only to cast a ballot once every few years, then simply sit back and watch?

Increasingly, people are thirsting for more influence and more power—between elections. Younger people in particular, who've grown up in a crowd-driven world, are accustomed to responsive systems that operate from the bottom up. Politics is ripe for a massive decentralization of decision-making: a shift in power away from elected gatekeepers and towards participatory models that empower millions of ordinary people every day.

For example, have you ever wished that you had more control over how the government spends your hard-earned money? Imagine if you could participate directly in your local government's budget process, proposing your own spending ideas and voting on expenditures? That was the premise of participatory budgeting, a bold project launched in the Brazilian city of Porto Alegre in 1989. A small portion of the local government budget was placed in the hands of ordinary citizens, as an experiment in direct democracy. Three decades later, tens of thousands of (mostly low-income) Porto Alegre citizens continue to participate each year, allocating roughly $200 million (over 20 percent) of the city's total budget. Participatory budgeting—or PB, as it's affectionately known by its supporters—has now spread across Brazil and beyond. The first North American experiment sprouted in Chicago in 2010, when Alderman Joe Moore initiated a PB project in his ward. All residents over sixteen, regardless of citizenship or voter registration status, were invited to research, propose and select projects to be funded with Moore's $1.3 million local budget. In that first year more than sixteen hundred citizens cast ballots, and eight years later the project continues to grow, with residents recently proposing and approving funding for new trees, new streetlights, alley lights and park improvements (including two chess tables and fencing on a basketball court). "The participatory budgeting elections have exceeded even my wildest dreams," Moore wrote in an open letter to constituents when the results came in. "They are more than elections. They are community celebrations and an affirmation that people will participate in the civic affairs of their community if given real power to make real decisions."

PB experiments are now popping up all across the United States and Canada. The largest is in New York City, where sixty-seven thousand residents recently voted on community proposals to allocate $38 million across twenty-eight council districts. Boston has added a twist by allowing teens to decide how to spend $1 million of the city's budget—the first youth-led PB process in the US. Thousands of youth (some wearing T-shirts that said "I've been managing millions since I was a teenager") gathered at Idea Assemblies across the city, producing hundreds of proposals. The approved projects included public art walls where local artists could showcase their work ($60,000), Chromebook laptops for local high school classrooms ($90,000), a skate park feasibility study ($50,000) and improved lighting in two parks ($110,000). Here in Canada, Halifax city councillors Waye Mason and Jennifer Watts have taken PB youth engagement to a whole new level by abolishing age requirements and allowing "anyone who can hold a pencil" to vote. "People participate as family units," Watts explained to me, "enabling people at a very young age to engage in a decision-making process about their community and give very direct feedback about what was important to them. Young kids were the ones who were the most diligent in their voting."

Canadian PB experiments are unfolding in cities across the country, as well as at the provincial level. But these pilot programs are small and usually involve only a tiny fraction of the capital budget. Expanding these experiments into larger permanent programs would be incredibly transformative, especially if they also began to explore the other side of the equation: revenue. It's one thing to decide how your money is spent. But what about influencing how much you're taxed in the first place? You might assume that if we gave too much budget control to voters, they'd simply vote against all taxes and financially suffocate our public services. I would argue that not only is this a terribly pessimistic view of the average person, but it also represents a complete misunderstanding of people's relationship to money. The truth is that people have proven over and over that when presented with the option to give away their money, on their own terms, they do it—happily. In fact, most North American families are in debt because they spend more than they earn. People *love* spending money. The problem with taxes is that people have no control over how that money is spent and little understanding of where it actually goes—both of which inevitably lead to resentment. Catchphrases like "cash grab" or "gravy train" paint government spending as wasteful and of no benefit to our daily lives. I'll happily give Apple twelve hundred dollars because I know I'm going to get a shiny MacBook Air in return. The price tag doesn't seem like a "cash grab"—it's just a purchase. But when it comes to government spending, we clearly see the price tags (sales tax, income tax, property tax) but sometimes forget all the things we get in return: schools, hospitals, roads, clean water, libraries, courts, airports, fire trucks, police stations, food safety and parks.

I recently heard of a creative solution to our cultural disconnect between taxes and services: put price tags on everything! Imagine fire hydrants, bus stops and playgrounds, each with a price tag showing the actual cost to build and operate it. Participatory budgeting offers a similar result (without making our cities look like department stores) by giving residents the opportunity to experience the tough choices that politicians have to make. Buy toys for the local daycare or plant a tree? Fix the sidewalks or the swing sets? By building a deeper understanding of where our money goes and how government spending affects our daily lives, we can minimize simplistic arguments about "gravy trains" and open the door to more meaningful discussions about taxes.

But the most exciting thing for me about PB is how it seems to be attracting an outsider crowd. When I attended a PB showcase in Brooklyn, I was immediately struck by the volunteers who were

standing at tables or booths promoting a particular funding proposal. They didn't seem like the usual suspects—the "activist" crowd.
Jennifer Watts echoed this sentiment, explaining that PB has
attracted people who would never come to a regular public meeting,
and even people who don't vote in general elections! Coincidentally,
while writing this chapter, I happened to notice my brother-in-law
Matthew wearing a button that said "Ward 33 Participatory Budget.
Ask me about PB!" A church pastor, Matt is heavily involved with
his community, but he'd never before attended any kind of formal
political meeting. PB was his entry point, and it could be for millions
more. As they say, "He who pays the piper calls the tune." PB lets
citizens call their own tune, building better neighbourhoods while
also boosting engagement, financial literacy and trust.

DO US A FLAVOUR

Getting citizens directly involved with budgeting is great, but
governments do a lot more than manage finances. What about
legislation? Could an ordinary citizen have a direct impact on
developing policy or drafting laws? Here, too, there are successful
experiments that reveal a whole new way to approach politics.
One of my personal favourites is a unique system that allows
citizens in Montreal to directly influence the policy agenda at city
hall. While it can be frustrating to see your elected representatives make a decision you don't agree with, it can be even more
frustrating to see them entirely ignore an important issue—as if
it didn't even exist. That was the situation facing Montreal's
urban agriculture community, a group of activists trying to bridge
the gap between nature and cities, back in 2010. While surveys
revealed that 50 percent of Montrealers were already doing some
form of local agriculture at home, there was no support for the

idea from city council. Several non-profit groups wanted to work with the city to expand urban agriculture and to revisit some problematic laws, including one banning backyard chickens. They repeatedly sent letters asking how to get involved and who they should talk to, but all they received in response was what Montreal activist Gaëlle Janvier referred to as a *lettre morte*, or a "dead letter," which is a hollow response that essentially says nothing. It was a brush-off.

Urban agriculture was growing rapidly in the city, but city hall itself was disengaged from the issue and non-responsive to citizens. Out of sheer frustration, a group of young urban agriculture activists decided to make some noise to get the city's attention. They held a press conference in front of city hall featuring two special guests of honour: a pair of contraband chickens, illegally smuggled into the city from a nearby farm.

The spectacle attracted a flood of journalists, video cameras and TV trucks, but councillors continued to ignore the issue. The activists tried other stunts as well, such as delivering baskets of locally grown fruit to the council chambers, but nothing seemed to get the attention of the politicians. In any other city, these activists might have simply given up. But Montreal has a unique political tool that allows citizens to directly influence the agenda at city hall and force a discussion on an issue. Under the rules of the Right of Initiative, groups can compel the local government to respond to a topic by gathering the signatures of 5 percent of the population (age fifteen and over). The city will then be forced to hold a fully funded public consultation on the issue, produce a formal report and publicly respond to the report's recommendations.

Here's how it's described on the city's website: "The Right of Initiative is a tool that allows you to propose for consultation any idea or innovative project that's important to you and to others. Your elected officials are required to carefully review the results of such public consultations and clearly explain any decisions they may make as a result. Unlike existing consultations that generally concern projects already under way, this tool gives all citizens the right to propose and submit for public discussion new propositions that represent the support of the community."

Janvier and her activist colleagues decided to try it out, even though no one in the city had ever successfully compiled enough signatures. They would need to collect fifteen thousand hand-written signatures within ninety days. To do that, they mobilized teams of volunteers and spread out across the city. With a decentralized campaign, dozens of helpers and no one keeping a daily tally, they accidentally ended up with more than twenty-five thousand signatures—almost twice as many as needed!

Once the signatures were submitted, the city complied with the request and the consultation was planned. Everything suddenly changed for Janvier. City staff became enthusiastic about the process and the topic itself. Dialogue was now taking place between her group and the city, something that was simply not happening before. As required by the legislation, the Office of Public Consultation wrote a comprehensive report and delivered it to council's executive committee. The report contained more than one hundred submissions from the public, as well as official reports from each of the city's nineteen local borough councils (see page 77).

At that point, the official process was over. The executive committee could have simply ignored the issue. But the hard work of the community activists had paid off and the city created a permanent committee on urban agriculture, including a city councillor and Janvier herself, representing a coalition of grassroots neighbourhood groups. And for the first time, the city created an urban agriculture mandate within city hall, with dedicated staff members within the department of sustainable development.

Nine years later, chickens are still illegal in Montreal. There are a few pilot projects in a handful of neighbourhoods, but progress has been slow. Some of the activists feel jaded and claim that the committee report was mostly ignored. But the petition process helped unify the community, engaged tens of thousands of citizens and finally put the issue on the map. "When you think about it, we informed twenty-five thousand people what urban agriculture is, and what a public consultation is," Janvier noted. "When we asked people to sign the petition, a lot of people said, 'What the hell are you talking about?' We were on an education campaign for three months, and that had a dramatic impact. People know what urban agriculture is about now. Five years ago, that was not the case." The signature-gathering process also triggered awareness in the media and in the minds of politicians. "Urban agriculture was the most talked about subject in the news," Janvier said. "The media covered the whole process, and the politicians became educated as well. Before, elected officials had no clue what we were talking about. All of a sudden, everyone was talking about it, and [politicians] needed to have an opinion on it. So they informed themselves, and had to know about the subject and talk to the media about it. The city is now working on fruit trees, bees, and access to space. My sense is that the door is open now."

———

Montreal's Right of Initiative may have opened doors, but in Manitoba, a member of Parliament has pioneered an even bolder experiment that allows citizens to not only put an issue on the map, but to collectively draft actual legislation to be introduced in the House of Commons.

Once a year, each MP is invited to put forward a private members' bill about any topic. Usually, MPs will choose an issue close to their hearts or one that an advocacy group has asked them to take action on. But in 2014, Larry Maguire, MP for Brandon-Souris, a rural riding in the southwestern corner of Manitoba, created the Strengthen Canada Project. Sort of like the Lay's "Do Us a Flavour" program, which invites millions of customers to propose new potato chip flavours, Maguire's initiative asked the residents of his riding to submit ideas for private members' legislation. This wasn't a playful exercise or a mock parliament. Maguire was placing real power directly into the hands of ordinary people, and the winning proposal would be introduced in the House of Commons as real legislation, just as the winning Lay's flavours are made into real potato chips. "I believe our democracy can be improved if Canadians are provided more opportunities to have their voices heard," Maguire wrote. "I would like you to submit your ideas that will make a positive difference in the lives of Canadians—and who knows—might just become law!"

Nearly one hundred ideas were submitted by local residents. These were then narrowed down to eleven finalists by a group of political science students, as part of their coursework. The finalists included the following ideas:

- adopt proportional representation in Canada
- study the idea of making people automatic organ donors unless they specifically opt out
- ban the use of neonicotinoid pesticides in Canada
- ask the government to introduce a tax credit for those who vote in federal elections
- create mandatory labelling for all genetically modified ingredients

These are proposals for actual legislation, coming not from the prime minister or a cabinet minister or a senior member of the bureaucracy, but from ordinary people. It's a revolutionary model. "Not only did individuals have to come up with the ideas," Maguire explained to me, "they also had to present their case and defend it at a town hall and answer questions." Maguire's office partnered with Brandon University students, who offered research time and helped the finalists with their town hall presentations. The winning submission, calling for a study on how the federal government can assist provincial governments in standardizing electronic medical charts, was proposed by Dr. Jay Winburn, and the bill was formally introduced in the House of Commons on March 30, 2015.

Although it was not adopted by Parliament (private members' bills rarely are), Winburn still feels great about the process. He described himself as "not a very political person" in a conversation with me. "I had never done anything like this before. I've never been a member of political party. It was a new experience for me. I just think this is a real issue that the country needs to face." But because his proposal was kind of wonky and technical, he definitely didn't expect to win the contest. In fact, he was surprised that anyone even showed up to the town hall. "I would have thought that people would rather have been at home watching TV. But the room was full." I asked him why he thought the process was so successful, and he pointed out that it was a rare opportunity to engage in politics in a non-combative and non-partisan manner. "I think we all hate elections because it's all negative. But this was an entirely positive process." Winburn found personal benefits from the process as well. "It crystalized a lot of things in my own thinking," he explained. "To put the bill together, I had to more formally think about things that were important to me but I had only thought about in the abstract." In other words, the process itself forced him to become a more deliberative citizen. "If the only time we get to express our citizenship is at a ballot box," he said, "I think that we're not really part of the process. This involves citizens thinking more about what's actually important to them."

BEYOND BREXIT

Montreal's citizen-triggered consultations offer a way to force a dialogue when politicians are turning a blind eye, and Larry Maguire's crowdsourced legislation experiment opens the door to increased participation, awareness and education. But neither of these models actually put real decision-making legislative power into the hands of the people. Dr. Winburn's proposal went nowhere in Parliament, and Gaëlle Janvier admits that Montreal's Right of Initiative is limited in its ability to produce rapid policy change. "The downside of it is that in the end, the public consultation is just a public consultation," she says. "The powers are still in the same hands."

This brings us to the most common form of direct democracy: the referendum. There is no reason why, once elected, politicians need to act as our representatives for all decisions, rather than delegating some of those decisions back to us. Referendums allow citizens to take the reins and vote directly on legislation that affects them. The people become the legislature. But there's a catch. Any attempt to decentralize power brings with it a trade-off between quantity and quality. People gathered in a small group (a legislature or council, for example) have the opportunity to listen to each other, learn from each other's perspectives and perhaps find common ground. But when a group gets too large, its members are less likely to be exposed to meaningful dialogue or learn from each other. In 2016, Google announced that the search phrase "What is the EU?" was trending in the UK within hours of Britain's unexpected vote to leave the European Union. This sparked an important discussion about the effectiveness of referendums and whether or not average citizens are informed enough to vote on complex issues. The answer is: it depends. The inevitable trade-off between quantity of participants and quality of the conversation can be either mitigated or amplified, depending on the design of the referendum itself. Here are seven design features that can make or break the effectiveness of a public vote:

1. The biggest mistake is to hold a referendum on the same day as a general election. Ballot questions are often ignored by the media and by voters if they're mixed in with campaigns

for mayors, councillors or parliamentarians. But with a stand-alone ballot, both voters and journalists are more likely to pay attention.

2. The length of the process is equally important—a deliberative process can't be rushed. The shorter the campaign period, the less likely citizens will be informed and engaged.

3. A well-funded education campaign is crucial for any referendum process. Ideally, some kind of neutral body will be funded to provide balanced information for voters. Ireland does this with its independent Referendum Commission, and in California, the secretary of state distributes a Voter Information Guide containing summaries of each proposal, statements by supporters and opponents, rebuttal statements and non-partisan analysis.

4. Advocacy groups can also be encouraged or created to promote each option on the ballot. However, referendum campaigns are often won by whichever side spends the most money, so it's critical to have reasonable spending limits and a publicly funded subsidy for all those campaigning.

5. The source of the ballot question can influence people's votes as well. A question proposed by a government, for example, can quickly turn into a divisive confidence vote about the government itself. People may vote No just to send an angry message. (Brexit may be a good example of this, as well as the 2015 Vancouver referendum on transit funding.) A much better approach is for the question to be proposed by the people themselves. In Switzerland, for example, citizens have eighteen months to collect one hundred thousand signatures to trigger an automatic national vote on any topic. Twenty-seven American states (and British Columbia) also have some form of direct democracy legislation. But

the most effective way to develop a referendum question is through a process called a citizens' assembly or citizens' reference panel. This approach was pioneered in British Columbia in 2004 to recommend a new electoral system. A group of 160 ordinary citizens were chosen at random (like a jury) to spend twelve weekends learning about voting systems, two months consulting with the public and two final months deliberating and preparing a recommendation. Seven months later, 58 percent voted in favour of their proposal. Voters knew the proposal was coming from their neighbours, not from the government or any special interest group.

6. Another interesting innovation is to offer three or more options on the ballot, rather than a traditional binary yes/no vote. Prince Edward Island did this for its 2016 referendum about electoral reform, offering voters five options and asking them to rank them in order of preference.

7. A reasonable vote threshold, typically 50 percent, should be used to determine victory.

Those are the seven key decisions that affect the value of a referendum process: timing, duration, education, funding rules, source of the proposal, number of options and threshold for victory. If these criteria are managed properly, the outcome is a healthier democracy. Of course, these same criteria can be used to intentionally sabotage the process as well. Remember the 58 percent Yes vote in the 2005 BC referendum? Well, the government had set the victory threshold at 60 percent, so the Yes side "lost" despite receiving 260,000 more votes than the No side. Another great example of choreographed sabotage occurred in Ontario's 2007 referendum on electoral reform. The source was good (also a citizens' assembly) and the threshold was fair (50 percent). But the government decided to withhold funding for educational materials related to the issue. On top of that, the vote was held on the same day as a general election and was almost completely ignored by the media. One month before the vote, polls revealed that 47 percent felt they knew nothing at all about the proposed voting system and another 41 percent said they knew "a little," leaving only 12 percent who felt informed about the issue. The entire process was designed to fail. Predictably, in this intentional vacuum of information, voters chose the No option.

We can do better than that. In his 2015 paper "Referendums and Deliberative Democracy," University of Toronto professor Lawrence LeDuc writes: "If the overtly partisan motives that drive many referendum campaigns can be limited or controlled, if better question wording and availability of information can lead to greater clarity, and if citizens can be more fully engaged over a longer period leading to higher and more inclusive rates of participation, there is every reason to believe that direct democracy can become more deliberative in practice. Under such an ideal model, citizens would be more positively disposed towards their institutions and processes of governance, because they would be more fully engaged."

Amen. And keep in mind that referendums don't always have to be about major issues such as gay marriage, drug legalization or new voting systems. There are countless decisions currently made by our governments that could and should be delegated to us—the people who actually live and work in our neighbourhoods. The main thing holding us back is our own lack of faith in each other. There is a commonly held perception that the general public simply can't be trusted with decisions beyond a general election. I hear it all the time. For example, Toronto City Council recently had a heated and divisive debate about whether to rename a community sports stadium after Rob Ford, our controversial former mayor. Many members of council, including the current mayor, were in favour of the proposal, while others were strongly opposed. As the vote drew nearer, newspapers wrote editorials both in favour and against, and people in both camps frantically wrote letters to the editor and drafted petitions. I felt baffled by the entire process and posted this simple question on Facebook: "Regarding Rob Ford Stadium (and all public spaces), why not let the people who USE the space decide what it's called? Democratize it."

This is not only a reasonable suggestion—it's the only reasonable approach. Why should a decision about a small local stadium be made by people who have never set foot in it? (With politicians in charge of naming our schools, stadiums and airports, it's no wonder they often end up naming them after politicians!) The only people who should participate in naming a local stadium are the people who actually live near it or use it. But my Facebook post received a lot of negative feedback. Can you guess what the most frequent comment was? Two words: Boaty McBoatface. This is, of course, the infamous winning entry in the #NameOurShip contest, which was intended to crowdsource a name for a new research vessel in England. Of the hundreds of names proposed, the most popular was Boaty McBoatface—a result that is now frequently used as evidence that ordinary people can't be trusted with ordinary decisions.

It's sad how easily we buy into such a self-deprecating view of ourselves. Let's quickly dissect the true Boaty story. First, this fable didn't happen in a vacuum. There is context here, which is that we're rarely asked for our opinion on anything. So when people hear about an unusual chance to vote on something, it's really darn exciting and an opportunity for childish fun that can quickly turn into a viral sensation. But if we were accustomed to democratic participation in our daily lives, then silly proposals like

Boaty McBoatface would have no meaning and no legs. Second, hundreds of thoughtful names were submitted. The Natural Environment Research Council could have internally chosen a list of finalists (leaving out silly proposals), and then let people vote on those. That's exactly how the Toronto Raptors were named. And here's the twist: I got my hands on the actual voting data, and it turns out that only 31 percent of voters actually chose Boaty McBoatface! Just like the Northville election in chapter 3 that resulted in the election of Gary Golf, the #NameOurShip contest was also a victim of first past the post distorting the intent and expression of voters. Most of the other entries to the contest were smart, creative and thoughtful. Among the top ten was Katharine Giles (to honour an expert in global warming who'd recently died in a cycling accident), Poppy-Mai (a tribute to a young child who'd been diagnosed with a brain tumour) and Henry Worsley (honouring a British explorer who'd died in 2016 while attempting to complete the first solo crossing of the Antarctic). All the organizers needed to do was use a ranked ballot, on which voters would list as many names as they wanted, in order of preference, and then go through a runoff with multiple rounds of counting. Despite its infamous reputation, Boaty McBoatface does not serve as evidence that people are stupid. Quite the opposite, it provides us with hard evidence of my entire thesis: stupid systems with stupid rules will deliver stupid results.

I dwell on this story only because it's indicative of a much larger trend: mocking ourselves. From Brexit to Boaty, people are increasingly buying into the myth that you shouldn't be trusted with any decision-making power. This defeatist view is holding us back from so many opportunities to liberate our voices. Here in Toronto, we used to have referendums all the time. Local residents would vote every year on tax issues, election reform and even public improvement projects like bridges and streetcar lines. But it's been decades since we've experimented with any form of citywide participatory decision-making. Rather than moving democracy into the future, we're actually moving it backwards. We've handed over the reins entirely.

To be clear, I'm not a fan of replacing government with direct democracy. There are those who would like to get rid of politicians entirely and replace our legislatures with a mobile app that would allow all of us to vote on any policy or budget proposal. In sheer numbers, this shift could trigger a massive boost in participation and would represent the largest decentralization of power we've seen in centuries. But the trade-off I mentioned earlier would be catastrophic, and our already low quality of deliberation would likely tumble even further. The more people involved with a particular discussion, the less likely they are to hear each other's views. Only a small number of people gathered in a room can make eye contact, listen to each other, and work towards common ground and maybe even reach a consensus. If you think back to chapter 6, all my proposals to reduce adversarial politics were focused on human contact and physical proximity. If we replaced our legislatures with an app, we'd also be eliminating the physical spaces that hold hope for facilitated civil discourse between informed citizens. Direct democracy, as a replacement for legislatures and councils, would give us more democratic width but less depth. It would be a step backwards based on a gross miscalculation that measures political engagement by volume alone. But the other extreme—giving away all our power to politicians—is equally foolish. There's ample room for us to experiment with the rigidness of our current representative model.

Politicians on both ends of the political spectrum are increasingly adopting rhetoric about revolution and "giving power back to the people." But unless they're talking about changing the decision-making process itself, they're full of hot air—and they're part of the problem. We need to push back against slogans and replace them with clear proposals that will decentralize government decisions through new and innovative forms of direct democracy. Participatory budgeting, citizen-triggered consultations, crowdsourced legislation and deliberative referendums are all practical ways to increase participation and innovation while reducing apathy and cynicism. Because the best way to give real power to ordinary people is to place the reins of government directly into their worthy hands.

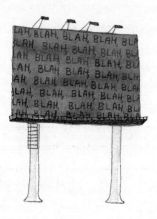

CHAPTER 8

STREET NEUTRALITY

"Net neutrality is the freedom to say, watch and make what we want online without interference from internet service providers. There is a plan to destroy net neutrality. It's up to us to stop it."

This call to arms was sent out by Mozilla, the non-profit grandmother of internet stewardship, after the US Federal Communications Commission (FCC) proposed new policies that threatened the democratic nature of the online world. Net neutrality is a set of rules assuring that the internet is a level playing field—that CNN doesn't load any faster than Sally's Neighbourhood News. The largest internet providers have spent millions of dollars lobbying governments to end net neutrality, because they want to create a wealth-based tiered internet that will allow them to charge CNN a premium for faster speeds while slowing down, or "throttling," other sites. Mozilla's advocacy is part of a wide and growing movement to protect net neutrality. Proponents include TV political comedian John Oliver, who asked his viewers to send letters of opposition to the FCC through a special website: GoFccYourself.com. (Millions of messages were sent within hours of his plea.)

But while groups across North America are pushing for fair access to the internet, there's another platform—equally important—that we've completely neglected. The visual environment in our own physical public spaces has been abandoned and is now almost exclusively controlled by private interests.

Commercial billboards are ubiquitous. They grow like weeds—on top of buildings, on walls, in parking lots, along our highways and in our town squares. But unless you happen to have hundreds of thousands of dollars to purchase advertising, this visual space is off limits to you. On top of that, strict regulations and cultural norms stifle the creation of community-driven art or visual political expression, leaving us with a monocrop of commercial garbage. Polling consistently shows that most people dislike billboards, yet they've become such a common part of the landscape that we've simply grown accustomed to the nuisance. Besides, they seem harmless enough. With all the problems in the world—poverty, hunger, violence—who cares about a bunch of ugly signs?

But billboards aren't just visual pollution. They have enormous impacts we rarely think about, some of which directly affect our democratic culture. First, they ensure that one single unifying message dominates our public spaces: *Buy more stuff*. Just as your decorating choices at home say something about you, the design of our shared public spaces reflects who we are. What does it say about us—and what does it teach our kids—when the largest and loudest messages in our communities are only about consumerism? Our own surroundings reflect a distorted depiction of our values, feeding our self-doubt about the possibilities of democracy and citizen engagement. On top of that, the ads themselves are often designed to make us feel lousy about ourselves by tapping into our insecurities. It's a one-two punch: first they try to convince you that you're inadequate or somehow damaged (your teeth aren't white enough, you have bad breath, people notice your dandruff), and then they offer you a product to fix your "problem." What impact do all these messages have on our collective mental health? In a world where so many of us are already dealing with self-doubt about our bodies, why would we hand over our public spaces to an industry that's committed to making us feel like garbage?

Second, billboards cheapen a city because we don't tend to put ads on nice things. Packages of spaghetti and tubes of toothpaste are covered in logos. Your kitchen stove may have a logo, but it's likely quite small and subdued. Your sofa does not have a logo. Neither do your nicest clothes. The more precious something is to you, the less likely it's visually commercialized. Your car has a logo, but it's smaller than a mouse. A giant commercial logo across the side of a car or a couch would make it look trashy and second-rate. When the Toronto Transit Commission wraps an entire streetcar in vinyl advertising, it's transforming a glorious urban icon into a forty-five-ton mobile spaghetti package. A few advertising companies have actually tried to offer people cash in exchange for affixing vinyl ads to their personal cars. Not surprisingly, these ventures went nowhere because people take pride in their cars and don't want to cheapen the appearance. Shouldn't transit riders get the same respect? Shouldn't our streets?

But the issue that is most often overlooked is that billboards erode our sense of collective ownership and social identity. What makes your neighbourhood unique? Probably the small businesses, public art, local architecture and historic landmarks. Billboards do the opposite: they create a monolithic aesthetic, with the exact same mass-produced ads placed in thousands of locations across North America.

Billboards run counter to the incredible diversity we find in our neighbourhoods. In a city like Toronto, where we pride ourselves on how many languages are spoken, how many countries of origin are represented and how inclusive we are as a culture, our billboards seem out of touch. They're exclusively English and the models predominantly white. The women have long hair, the men short. You won't see a turban, hijab, kippah or cross. You won't see a wheelchair, a crutch or a hearing aid. You won't see two men holding hands. How many people have stood in Yonge-Dundas Square, looking up at the flashing digital ads, and not seen themselves reflected back? What an oddity that our central town square doesn't portray the very people who walk through it.

Billboards may have an urban feel, but it's cookie-cutter urbanism. They can make us feel like visitors in our own spaces. Imagine if someone walked into your own home, took all the art off your walls and replaced it with a bunch of commercial signage. This is precisely what we've done to our streets. Each billboard erected in public space serves as a reminder of who really wields power in our society. Like dogs marking their territory, billboards emit a message of spatial ownership and control.

This erosion of our sense of belonging is important because of this simple truth: when we know something belongs to us, we take care of it. We invest energy, money and time in our homes, our bodies, our cars, our bikes and our clothes, simply because we know they lie

within our personal sphere of ownership. So one of the simplest things we can do to boost political engagement is to remind people that the public landscape belongs not to the government or to commercial enterprise, but to all of us. It's *your* space. When we privatize the visual environment in our public spaces, we achieve the exact opposite goal.

PULLING WEEDS

If we want to see our public spaces live up to their name, it's time for us to view billboards for what they are:

> **in·va·sive spe·cies** (noun) Something alien whose introduction or spread adversely affects the surrounding habitat, is likely to cause harm and aggressively out-competes other species.

Billboards are introduced by outside forces and drown out all other voices. The Toronto Zoo website explains that invasive species not only "have negative impacts on biodiversity" but can eventually "form monocultures that replace all diversity within an area." Nothing could more accurately describe the impact that commercial advertising has on visual expression in our communities.

So what do we do? How do we reclaim our public spaces and clear the clutter? The Nature Conservancy tells us, "The best way to fight invasive species is to prevent them from occurring in the first place." Some communities are doing just that. Four American states (Vermont, Maine, Hawaii and Alaska) have banned billboards entirely. The city of Oakville, Ontario; the Plateau-Mont-Royal borough in Montreal; Victoria, Texas; the French city of Grenoble; and the city of São Paulo, Brazil, have all banned billboards. São Paulo even removed its pre-existing billboards—all fifteen thousand of them! A ban is the most honourable approach, because it treats billboards for what they are: pieces of corporate garbage that offer no value to anyone except those who own them.

I spoke with Plateau-Mont-Royal borough councillor Alex Norris, who pushed for the billboard ban in his district. He pointed out how strange it is that cities often have much stronger regulations for storefront signage than they do for billboards. "If we believe in buying local and supporting our local merchants and our local economy," Norris told me, "then the least we can do is not discriminate against our own merchants by imposing more severe regulatory burdens on them in terms of commercial signage than we do on large national and multinational advertising corporations." But his main concern was the impact billboards were having on the character and uniqueness of Montreal's neighbourhoods. "A sense of place is a very precious thing," he explained, "and when you allow big industrial billboards . . . that dominate the landscape, you're taking away from the sense of place." Of course, since the borough adopted the ban, its lawyers have spent years fighting in court with the three largest billboard companies (Pattison, Astral, CBS Outdoor), which are challenging the ban with their own legal teams.

Lawyers and lobbyists play a big role in the outdoor advertising industry, for two reasons. First, billboard companies have a product that no one actually likes, so that requires a lot of creative lobbying at city hall. Second, the profit margins on billboards are colossal, allowing these companies to spend heavily on influencing the political process. Their lawyers fight against new laws and enforcement, while their lobbyists find clever ways to leverage legal loopholes or incentivize politicians to secure exemptions to the rules.

More than any other industry, outdoor advertising has learned how to use lobbyists effectively. A 2013 *Toronto Star* investigative report analyzed data from the city's lobbyist registry and concluded that billboard companies were the most active lobbyists. These professional persuaders are smart, strategic and effective. Sensing that public opinion is slowly turning against them, they've been shifting their political approach. Rather than simply asking for permission to install more ads in public space, they are now offering to make large cash donations to the city or providing other supposed community benefits as an incentive.

One recent example of this would be the privatization of street furniture, a term that refers to all the functional objects appearing on our sidewalks, including benches, garbage cans and bus shelters. In Toronto, this story begins in 1999, when a smart company named Olifas Marketing Group (OMG) offered city council thousands of free garbage cans. In exchange, all OMG wanted was permission to put advertising on the cans. The sign bylaw, of course, doesn't allow advertising to be installed directly on our sidewalks, so the company was asking for an exemption. But OMG couldn't simply offer the city millions of dollars in exchange for that exemption. Imagine how that would have looked! The optics would have been terrible because everyone knows that policy shouldn't be for sale. But because OMG offered "free" street furniture, no one saw it for what it is: a company getting special treatment in exchange for financial incentives. Institutionalized bribery.

City council approved the deal (hey, free garbage cans!), and suddenly thousands of new mini billboards began to appear on sidewalks across the city. OMG knew the public might not like the sudden avalanche of commercial advertising, especially in areas that had always been ad-free (including parks, schoolyards and residential streets), so the company adopted a clever approach that I call incremental intrusion. For the first few weeks, the new bins had no ads at all. Instead, they were covered with posters of an enormous sunflower and messages designed to make you feel good. Half of them said "Be Vibrant" and the other half simply said "Feel Good." I'm not joking. The new cans were bright, shiny and friendly. We got used to them. But slowly, the "Feel Good" posters were taken down and replaced with advertising. It happened so gradually that no one even noticed. This was the single largest expansion of outdoor advertising, and privatization of the commons, in the history of Toronto.

The new garbage cans might have been provided for free, but the city quickly learned an age-old economic lesson: you get what you pay for. Customers have leverage and influence in any financial transaction, but when you get something for free, you're no longer the customer. OMG's customers weren't the politicians at city hall or the taxpayers, but the companies paying for the ads. Under this new financial model, the advertising was more important than the garbage can. So the free bins were themselves pieces of garbage, built with the structural integrity of an empty pop can. They began breaking down as soon as they were installed, metal doors flinging open and blocking the sidewalk or a bike lane. And the bins were often installed perpendicular to the curb, which blocked pedestrians but made the advertising more visible to drivers. These weren't really garbage cans with ads on them at all; they were billboards with lousy garbage cans attached. After the tin OMG bins fell apart (literally), the company proposed a new design that had two-metre-high illuminated billboards attached. They invested in and lobbied hard for prototypes that were installed across the city. In my role as the advocacy director of the Toronto Public Space Committee, I helped coordinate a campaign against the proposal, which we eventually defeated.

But the OMG experiment was just the beginning. What happened next was the Coordinated Street Furniture Program, a phenomenon taking over streets across North America. Under this program, cities are convinced to sign long-term contracts that privatize their benches, bus shelters, bike racks and garbage cans—all managed by a single advertising company. Toronto's twenty-year contract with Astral Media, signed in 2007, provides free street furniture, plus millions of dollars in direct payments, in exchange for loosening the rules that used to prevent commercial advertising from appearing on our sidewalks and in our neighbourhoods. The city has even bent the rules further recently, allowing Astral to install commercial video screens right beside people's homes.

Like cheap toys from a dollar store, the Astral bins have also been a disaster—even worse than the original OMG bins. The foot pedals cracked, the recycling stickers wore away and the plastic doors never seemed to lock properly and were constantly swinging into pedestrians. Now Toronto is on its fourth generation of private garbage cans: a newly revised Astral design made of metal. But those bins are already falling to pieces. Astral spokespeople insist that they're trying as hard as they can—and bizarrely blame the failure of their garbage bins on the fact that "there are moving parts." Compare all these sad broken bins to our glorious cherry-red Canada Post mailboxes: government-owned, ad-free receptacles that always work perfectly. I've literally never seen a dent, crack or broken lock on a mailbox. Not once in my life. Even with "moving parts."

But with the financial success of the street furniture contracts, advertising companies are now looking at more ways to persuade city councils to weaken municipal laws with new forms of financial incentives. Sometimes the ads and the so-called community benefits are physically attached to each other (think of bus shelters or the original OMG bins). But in other cases, an advertising company will offer to pay for something that's completely unrelated to the ads—a brilliant practice I like to call bundling. They'll take a bad thing that nobody wants (billboards) and bundle it together with a good thing.

For example, Outfront Media recently applied for permission to install a large flashing digital billboard in a residential area. The proposed sign, with its flashing digital ads that rotate five thousand times a day, breaks every part of the existing bylaw: too wide, too tall, too bright. No one would want one of these near their home. But Outfront offered to donate a slice of its profits ($40,000 a year) to a local skating arena. So now if a councillor votes against the billboard, he or she is essentially voting against kid's hockey too. What's really frustrating is that the city has a donations policy that is explicitly designed to ensure that "donations occur at arm's length from any City decision-making process." There's a good reason for this: offering money in exchange for special treatment is a form of bribery. The donations policy states that "applicants seeking an approval, permit or license shall not concurrently offer or make voluntary donations to the City or an agency, board or commission for community benefits," and that "there is a blackout period in planning approval processes during which discussions about voluntary donations for community benefits are not permitted and voluntary donations may not be offered, solicited, or accepted." Yet the exact opposite happened in this case: the cash revenue was offered to the city-funded arena by the billboard company at the *very same meeting* where councillors granted multiple exemptions to the sign bylaw. When I filed a complaint with the city's integrity commissioner, she ruled that no rules were broken because the ten-year-old policy regulating donations and community benefits astonishingly doesn't include a definition of "donations" or "community benefits." Without clear terminology, no one can actually break any rules. It's the wild west.

The sad irony of all this is that while advertising revenue, donations and community benefits may seem attractive to councillors and taxpayers alike, they actually add up to a handful of toonies per citizen. The idea that we can't collectively pay for our sidewalk benches or skating rinks without commercial assistance is absurd. Here's a great story: Back in 2001, a company named Tribar proposed mounting an enormous digital billboard on Toronto's iconic Bloor Viaduct bridge, overlooking the Don Valley. It would be aimed at the cars driving on the parkway below, but it would also illuminate the entire ravine, including the nature trails, the bike paths and the Don River itself. Ad companies had been trying to install signage on the parkway for years, but the city always said no. So Tribar created the ultimate bundle: if the city gave permission to install a two-storey television screen above one of North America's largest urban green spaces, the company would (are you ready for this?) contribute $3.5 million towards the construction of a suicide barrier on the same bridge. When the proposal was presented at city hall, the two items were bundled together, so if you were against the video screens (which I was, of course), then you were portrayed as also being against the suicide barrier. Politically, it was a nightmare

Often they are actively interfering in the legal enforcement of existing bylaws. In Toronto, for example, there are dozens, possibly hundreds, of large corporate billboards that simply aren't supposed to be there. No permit. No permission. In 2005, I coordinated a collaboration between the Toronto Public Space Committee and a class of urban planning students at Ryerson University to conduct an audit of signage compliance. The students compiled a list of every billboard in one midtown area and then, with the support of local councillor Joe Mihevc, asked city staff a very simple question: Do these billboards have permits? What they found was shocking—the city had permits on record for only 42 percent of the signs. Later that same year, I was hired by Councillor Mihevc to work as his executive assistant, and one of my top priorities was to deal with the illegal signs. Rather than trying to get dozens of billboards removed at once, I decided to test the waters. On behalf of the councillor, I filed a formal request asking for the removal of two particular signs that were in a residential area, standing in front of (and blocking the view of) a grove of trees.

What happened next is almost unbelievable. City staffers confirmed to our office that the billboards were illegal, and they informed us that the signs would be dismantled. "Our contractor is in the process of having the signs removed," they assured us. "The contractor has had to contact Hydro to have the electrical wires for lighting removed from the billboard prior to work commencing. This should happen today or tomorrow at the latest."

So far, that's a pretty great story! Good legislation to protect public spaces, followed by a dose of citizen engagement and finally some swift action from the bureaucracy. But that message above, about the Toronto Hydro employees coming to disconnect the wires? That was thirteen years ago. And the billboards are still there! Despite our greatest efforts, we never found out what took place behind closed doors. Clearly the billboard company somehow outmanoeuvred city hall. All we were told was that "new information" prevented city staff from removing the signs—but they weren't able to explain what the new information was. We do know that no permit was ever produced, by the city or the company. The most likely scenario is that the billboard company's lawyers threatened the city with legal action and convinced them to back down. They probably argued that because the billboards had been there for so long, no one could ever prove or disprove whether a permit was issued decades ago, when the signs were first installed. This is ridiculous, of course, as the legal onus is on the sign company to keep records of its permits—not the city.

One day I'll get those two billboards taken down. But the amount of effort required to get the city to enforce its own bylaws is absurd, and this is what allows billboard companies to treat our public spaces like their own backyard. What cities desperately need is a simple public registry of every billboard, with information made available about any permits associated with each location. This is common for other industries: elevators display safety permits, bars post liquor licences, even hot dog vendors and transit buskers have permits on display. Those permits are made visible so that members of the public can be assured those businesses are operating within the law. Currently, we've got the worst possible approach to our sign laws: very little proactive enforcement, and a complaint-driven process that depends on citizens noticing if there's an illegal sign (which is impossible when there's no requirement for visible permits).

Meanwhile, the ad companies are also applying for—and securing—permits for new signs, often against the desires of nearby residents. The most important thing we can do to ease the flow of new billboards is simply to put decision-making power about our neighbourhoods into the hands of the people who actually live and work there. Democratize the streets. Remember that crazy proposal I mentioned earlier? For the massive video billboard suspended over the Don River? I remember stumbling upon the application while reading through a committee agenda at city hall and wondering how a project like that was moving forward. It occurred to me that maybe people simply didn't know it was happening. So I designed, printed and hand-delivered notices to dozens of households in the area to let residents know about the proposed monstrosity. When Jack Layton (the local councillor at the time) began receiving phone calls from concerned voters, he invited me to city hall to negotiate with the vice president of the advertising company. I had unexpectedly assumed a position of power, simply by acting as a conduit of information for ordinary citizens. The company offered to make the sign a little smaller and a little less bright, hoping I would be interested in a compromise. But I wasn't. I was polite, but there was no negotiation. In the end, on a shoestring budget, we completely defeated the multi-million-dollar proposal. All I had to do was let residents know what was happening at city hall and help them engage in the process. This, of course, is the job of government, and it's ridiculous that I had to spend my own time and money doing it for them.

Like any invasive species, billboards can be controlled. Illegal billboards should be removed. Highway billboards should be banned entirely, purely on the grounds of road safety. And the best way to regulate and minimize new signage is to make sure that citizens are aware of each new proposal and understand how to participate in the decision-making process. A truly democratic process that puts neighbourhoods in charge of their own spaces would spell the end of the entire outdoor advertising industry overnight.

CONCRETE CANVAS

Clearing the commercial clutter out of our public spaces is just the first step towards street neutrality. After all, the goal of decorporatizing the commons isn't to create a sterile or bland streetscape. Once we banish billboards, we can fill the void with community-driven expression. Traditional public art, which offers a counterbalance to commerce-driven imagery and messages, is a good start. Cities across North America are rapidly increasing the amount of public art on their streets, primarily by forcing developers to donate a small percentage of their construction costs to new public art installations. But as exciting as it is to see governments supporting the arts, many of these programs are top-down and feature commissioned artists who don't live in the community—or even the country. With no input from the actual public, these works often reflect the local community no more than a billboard would.

A better approach to public art is to get brushes into the hands of local artists. Indeed, a growing number of community-driven public art projects are doing just that, by securing government funding for local artists to leave their mark in their own community. The more local the art, and the artists, the more likely we are to see political content, cultural relevancy or nods to the history of the community. Glenna Boltuch Avila, former director of Los Angeles's CityWide Mural Program (and a mural artist herself), explains that community murals "are about people having an effect on their cities, taking responsibility for their visual and physical environment and leaving records of their lives and concerns." Like corporate billboards, collaborative community arts projects mark territory. Each local mural serves as a visual reminder that our streets are a collective space, that we're all shareholders and that we all have a connection to and a responsibility for our city and each other.

This message is especially powerful when we involve kids. Road murals (which I discussed in chapter 1) are perfect for children's participation because while kids love to paint, they're also kinda sloppy. If a knee-high artist puts too much paint on her brush while covering a wall, it drips down like a waterfall. But on a flat surface, a dripping brush is a small problem and a quick fix, which has allowed me to include kids of all ages in my road mural projects. An adult creates the design and sketches it on the road in chalk, and then the kids just have to paint inside the lines as best they can. It's even better when kids are producing the designs in the first place. The office I'm typing in right now is plastered from floor to ceiling with art made by my son, my nieces and nephews, and even my friends' kids. My fridge too, of course. And likely yours as well. Children's art is inspiring and therapeutic because kids' minds are playful, optimistic, imaginative and curious. So if kid art makes us happy in our homes, then why not in our neighbourhoods too?

A few years ago, I was walking in Seattle and was pleasantly shocked when I stumbled upon a bus shelter that was not only ad-free but also decorated by local kids! This wasn't a temporary installation, with art taped onto the shelters. The children's creation was built into the structure, as if it were a permanent fridge door!

A project of the King County Metro transit system, the Bus Shelter Mural Program has transformed more than nine hundred community spaces in the Seattle area. "Metro contributes panels and paint, and members of the community donate their artistic talent to create murals for Metro bus shelters," the county website explains. "Murals have been created by volunteers of all ages: students, scout troops, senior citizens, community groups and individual artists."

While Seattle transformed hundreds of bus shelters into miniature art galleries, the German city of Düsseldorf has taken transit art to a whole new level. When the city recently built a new subway line, it hired not only architects but artists as well. "Normally the construction part happens first and then the artists are commissioned," lead designer Heike Klussmann explained to the *Guardian* newspaper. "But here the architects, artists and engineers worked together from the beginning." Unlike the rapid transit stations in Vancouver, Edmonton, Calgary, Toronto, Ottawa and Montreal, Düsseldorf's U-Bahn line has no ads at all. When the new stations opened in 2016, the *Guardian*'s Giovanna Dunmall wrote, "What is perhaps most inspiring about the project is how the lack of adverts means people can be people, and not consumers."

In Toronto, meanwhile, our transit system has more and more ads all the time—inside vehicles, outside vehicles and even plastered on the walls, floors and turnstiles inside subways stations (a practice they literally call Station Domination). We're led to believe that these ads contribute significant revenue to the system, but the truth is it amounts to only about five cents per ride. I would happily pay an extra nickel to ride inside the country's largest art gallery.

When you see projects like Seattle's bus shelters or Düsseldorf's U-Bahn line, you realize that traditional advertising on transit systems and so-called Coordinated Street Furniture Programs not only cover our streets with hundreds of thousands of square feet of advertising, but also block the space from being used as a canvas for local artists, non-profits or community organizations. This is why we should treat outdoor advertisements as weeds, which by definition outcompete other species.

The most common form of visual community expression in any urban environment isn't actually painted murals but rather the classic grassroots paper poster that's taped, glued or stapled to a utility pole. These posters typically promote things like community meetings, local piano lessons, lost pets, concerts, yard sales, political protests or neighbourhood street parties. The opposite of billboards, the posters offer a window into a community and a reflection of the people who live there and what they're up to. Yet somehow, these valuable sheets of paper are often seen as visual pollution or clutter, and cities are constantly trying to control their presence—or even ban them completely.

Toronto City Council tried to ban postering in 2003, and I had the honour and pleasure of leading the Toronto Public Space Committee's campaign against the proposal. We organized public information sessions, press conferences and fundraisers, and we filled the city council chambers with angry residents defending their right to freedom of expression on their own streets. We won our battle, but we weren't the first. Our campaign was similar to many others that have been waged in city halls—and courtrooms—across Canada. In 1988, Ken Ramsden, Canada's postering hero, was fined by the city of Peterborough for putting up leaflets advertising his rock band, Reverend Ken and the Lost Followers. He decided to challenge the law in court, and he lost. So he took his case to provincial court, and lost again. Then, in 1993, he took it to the Supreme Court—and won. In a historic ruling, the court found that Peterborough's postering ban violated freedom of expression under the Canadian Charter of Rights and Freedoms. Two years later, Calgary implemented a similar ban, but the Supreme Court ruled against them too, basing the verdict on the Ramsden ruling. Community activist Chris Rickett then challenged anti-postering rules in Windsor (1996) and Stratford (1997), forcing both cities to back down. In 1998, the city of St. John's tried to enforce a poster ban, resulting in a public backlash that led to a brand-new postering law that stands to this day.

Twenty years later, corporate billboards are bigger and brighter than ever, but citizens are still battling with city halls for the right to put up a small piece of paper on their own streets. Cities should not only tolerate these posters but actively encourage them by creating spaces that are designed explicitly for community expression. Toronto has installed some outdoor boards for posters, but they're quite small and exclusively on commercial streets rather than residential ones. If you want something done right, you sometimes just have to do it yourself, and that's exactly what my neighbour John Keating did when he constructed a gorgeous two-metre-high outdoor community poster kiosk, complete with wooden trim and shingles. It was assembled in his backyard and then installed two blocks away, beside the sidewalk near our local high school. John's massive community message board is used heavily every week, with posters featuring local classes, services, meetings and events. Why isn't the city already providing these, in every neighbourhood? Even the city's indoor public spaces are poster-free. It's a sad reflection on our culture when our own libraries and community centres don't have neighbourhood message boards but every Starbucks does.

––––––––

Posters are wonderful, but why stop there? Rather than just creating spaces for static paper notices, we could also create opportunities for interactive visual content, like public whiteboards or chalkboards, encouraging people to share their thoughts—in the moment. Artist Candy Chang popularized this idea in 2011, when she painted an enormous chalkboard onto the side of an abandoned house in her New Orleans neighbourhood. Then she painted the following sentence, dozens of times, on the board:

"Before I die, I want to _____"

Small containers of chalk were attached to the wall, and the rest was up to her neighbours. The blank lines were quickly filled in, and then joined by even more answers scrawled above, below and between the stencilled sentences:

> Before I die, I want to abandon all insecurities. Before I die, I want to make the world a better place. Before I die, I want to experience unconditional love . . . live off the grid . . . be someone's cavalry . . . be completely myself . . . straddle the international dateline . . . plant a tree . . . see equality . . . get clean . . . be heard.

"Together, we've shown how powerful our public spaces can be if we're given the opportunity to have a voice and share more with one another," Chang says in her TED Talk. "Our shared spaces can better reflect what matters to us, as individuals and as a community, and with more ways to share our hopes, fears and stories, the people around us can not only help us make better places, they can help us lead better lives." Her idea was contagious, and there are now thousands of "Before I die . . ." walls across the world, in dozens of different languages.

Two years after Chang's experiment, Rebeka Rodriguez tried something similar but less structured in San Francisco. She transformed an alleyway simply by installing five chalkboards, without any prewritten sentences or blank lines to fill in. "I think we should have more conversations," Rodriguez told one local website, SFGate. "And we should have more places to have conversations." Many in the community were skeptical about her plan, and expected the boards to be filled with foolishness and obscenities. "I told Rebeka I didn't see how it was going to work," said a local security manager, Shawn Herman. "I was sure it was going to be a graffiti magnet. It's been a pleasant surprise. I was glad to be wrong this time." Another security guard, Matthew Wehner, told SFGate, "I've never seen a more tangible example of arts civilizing a community. What happened was not only surprising, it was downright shocking."

Chang and Rodriguez proved that humans are not only capable of contributing to thoughtful conversations in public spaces, but eager to do so. In my own neighbourhood, three years ago, someone placed a slick and glossy poster in the local subway station that read: "Hey Ladies, not getting any dates? Can't afford the high condo fees on your own? You are 30 and still not married? How is feminism working for you?" I'm not sure if the author was trying to create a discussion, but that's exactly what happened. Within days, another poster went up in response. This one read: "How is feminism working out for me? Just great, actually. Thanks to feminism, I can get an education, have a job and support myself financially, choose when and how to spend my money . . . vote and hold political office . . . leave a relationship if my partner is abusive. . . . Every day I am grateful for the freedom and opportunity I have as a result of the feminist movement." A third transit rider, Rosemary McManus, broadened the conversation by buying a large piece of yellow bristol board and writing, in large black letters, "How is feminism working for you?" She taped it up in the subway station, with the words "Please respond!" at the bottom and a plastic cup full of pens. Responses began to appear—feedback that was thoughtful, intelligent and constructive. It was perhaps the most honest expression of humanity I'd ever seen on the TTC.

The final item in our menu of ways to decorate our concrete canvas is street art. I'm not talking about official public installations authorized by the local planning authority, but rather the random bursts of expression that appear unexpectedly in public spaces. Yes, I'm talking about illegal art. Public attitudes about graffiti are complicated. No one wants a quick "tag" spray-painted on the front of his home, but at the same time, there is a growing appreciation of good street art—with or without a permit. Think of Banksy, who's earned international fame as a visual artist despite being a full-time vandal.

Playful and creative public space interventions that treat our cities like blank canvases can transform our streets into a twenty-four-hour unpredictable art gallery. There's a fine line between vandalism and urban beautification, of course, but I find that most public space artists try to respect private property and are thoughtful about their work. I've seen poetry taped up in bus shelters, knitted cozies on fire hydrants and trees, and scarves tied around utility poles with handwritten posters saying "Need a scarf? Take one!" Since the 1970s, one of my favourite artists, Rocky Dobey, has been creating copper etchings and bolting them onto street posts across Toronto. Much of his work is political, addressing issues such as poverty, police accountability, Indigenous rights and prison reform. Dobey and thousands before him have ensured that artistic expression isn't confined to white-walled galleries, but rather bleeds into unexpected places. And yet technically, all this art is illegal: Rocky's etchings, the hydrant cozies, the poetry, even the scarves.

Jordan Seiler, an artist, activist and one of my political heroes, uses existing advertisements as his canvas. In 2009, he organized a hundred volunteers to cover up billboards with white paint and then place art on top. By the numbers, the New York Street Advertising Takeover removed 120 ads, produced 2,000 square metres of public art and led to 9 arrests with 310 hours of cumulative jail time. In every single case, the charges were dismissed. Why? Because it turns out the ads were illegal in the first place! Seiler specifically targeted a company named NPA City Outdoor, which is notorious for violating city bylaws and abusing public spaces.

Back in 2002, I organized a similar event with the Toronto Public Space Committee called Art Attack. We invited people to a bar filled with large sheets of paper, crayons and markers. Participants created spontaneous works of art and then hit the streets to tape their masterpieces over existing ads. Was Art Attack illegal? Yes. Was it vandalism? I don't think so. The transit shelters weren't damaged, and even the ads were left unharmed, hanging quietly behind the newly installed pieces of art. By being careful not to damage any property, we were able to promote the event publicly and proudly. In fact, a television crew showed up at the bar and followed us onto the streets as we redecorated the urban landscape. (FYI, if you're interested in reclaiming ad space in your neighbourhood, Seiler fabricates and sells little "sculptures" that happen to be the exact shape and size as the metal keys that advertising companies use to open the display units on their transit shelters. They are available on his Public Access website.)

The ethics of street art comes down to personal judgment and discretion in regards to location, materials and permanence. Spray-painting over someone's storefront is not cool, but adding colour to a desolate alleyway is a generous act of urban beautification. Cementing stone tiles onto an ATM is probably a bad idea, but adding that same mosaic to a dull concrete utility pole is a mitzvah.

Banksy once described a dreamworld where someone like him would barely stand out: "Imagine a city where graffiti wasn't illegal, a city where everybody could draw whatever they liked. Where every street was awash with a million colours and little phrases. Where standing at a bus stop was never boring. A city that felt like a party where everyone was invited, not just the real estate agents and barons of big business." In this fantasy, everyone is a Banksy.

Guerrilla public art, whether executed on a large coordinated scale like Seiler's projects or in small, quiet injections like Dobey's, are bursts of voice that break through blandness, shaking pedestrians out of the predictable monotony of urban design. Each piece of street art is a gift, often anonymous, from someone who wanted to share something—with you. Enjoy it. And if you feel inclined, contribute your own masterpiece to the concrete canvas we live in. With a marker, some paint, mosaic tiles, copper or clay, you too can leave your mark and join the symphony of voices that make our streets interesting, alive and reflective of who we are.

———

"But what about Times Square?" you might be thinking. "Aren't there places where billboards, especially digital ones, can make a city feel vibrant and exciting?" Sure, but getting rid of commercial advertising doesn't mean you can't have a place like Times Square. Those same screens could simply be filled with more interesting content, actually created by local residents. In Toronto, for example, we have a knock-off of Times Square called Yonge-Dundas Square. It's surrounded by dozens of enormous video screens mounted on towers. The screens play ads twenty-four hours a day.

But just a few steps away, young artists are producing their own video projects at Ryerson University's Media Production program, which "challenges students to explore traditional and innovative media theory, platforms, and technologies in order to tell compelling stories and reach diverse audiences." A few blocks away lies George Brown College's School of Design, where you can "develop your talent and tap into your imagination so you can make your artistic mark," as well as OCAD University's new Campus for a Connected World, "an interdisciplinary, experimental zone for the development of creative digital solutions to today's urgent social, economic, technological and environmental challenges." Imagine if Yonge-Dundas Square was simply a constant live-feed of what kids at those three schools were producing each day. Now that's what I call a town square! Instead of a cesspool of offensive, patronizing, Anglo-centric, monocultural, hetero-normative, misogynist, body-shaming consumerist garbage, we'd have a town square that was interesting, unpredictable, inclusive, thought-provoking and representative of the people who call Toronto home.

———

Our public spaces serve as a great equalizer. In most parts of our lives, there's a clear economic hierarchy—physical reminders of who has more financial power than you do. No matter where you are in the income spectrum, you're always aware that someone else has more. Maybe you can afford a vacation to Mexico, but you still have to walk past the first-class passengers sipping their free wine as you board the plane. Maybe you can afford baseball season tickets, but as you strain to see the players from the upper bleachers, others are sitting right behind home plate. Whether it's the restaurants we can't afford to eat in or the cars we can't afford to buy, everything comes with a price tag or an entry fee that divides us into categories that are visible to all. But not in public space. We all cross the road at the same time, no matter what we've got in our wallets. The swing in the park, the path by the river, the bench on the sidewalk—none of these have admission fees, and therefore we all have equal access.

Public space is sacred, a place to recognize each other as equals. But billboards and ads on bus shelters, benches and garbage cans come with a cost. Those with the most economic power get the loudest voice, and we miss out on the community-driven messages, conversations and art projects that can bring our neighbourhoods alive and tell our stories. We've put a price tag on freedom of expression in the one place that is supposed to be economically neutral. Only by democratizing the visual environment can we begin to put the "public" back into public space.

If we truly want to treat public spaces as an equalizer, we need to find ways to create a culture of street neutrality, where anyone and everyone has the ability to legally and effectively express themselves and visually communicate with others. Because the degree to which residents feel a sense of collective ownership over our public spaces informs their willingness and desire to participate in the processes that shape our cities and neighbourhoods.

Why do we place such a high value on the democratic protection of a virtual space like the internet, yet at the same time seem so careless about an actual physical shared space? As writer Thor Benson noted, in regard to net neutrality, "There is no free expression when you have to pay extra to stand on the soap box." The same idea applies to our urban landscape, where our voices have been throttled to zero.

CHAPTER 9

SEEDS OF CHANGE

The two hundredth episode of *The Simpsons* features Homer, elected as Springfield's sanitation commissioner, recklessly dumping truckloads of garbage into an abandoned mine. The cave fills up quickly, but Homer's workers use bulldozers to squeeze more and more garbage inside until it finally erupts, burying the town in rivers of trash. The outrageous episode aired on April 26, 1998, and was immediately followed by an uncanny example of life imitating art. On June 19, just eight weeks after Homer's dystopian disaster premiered on television, the Ontario government approved a new mega-dump for Toronto's garbage—in an abandoned mine.

Located six hundred kilometres north of Toronto, the Adams Mine was carved out of the Canadian Shield over a period of three decades using explosives to extract iron ore. When the mine closed in 1990, the gargantuan pit left behind began to fill with water, transforming it into a lake as wide as thirty football fields and deep enough to submerge the Statue of Liberty standing on top of another Statue of Liberty. The proposed mega-dump called for millions of tonnes of garbage to be tossed directly into this lake each year, without any form of protective lining installed. Imagine millions of candy wrappers, light bulbs, diapers and paint cans— just thrown into a lake. The company behind the deal, Rail Cycle North, insisted that leachate (the toxic water found in all garbage dumps) would never leak out of the pit—even though the bedrock was highly fractured, and water was already flowing in and out through fissures. The absurd plan was guaranteed to poison the region's drinking water and agriculture for generations, but Rail Cycle North, promising jobs and money, was able to convince the Ontario government that intentionally creating a toxic lake was a good idea. With all the permits and approvals in place, only one thing stood in the way: ordinary people.

While Rail Cycle North's lobbyists were busy shaking hands with politicians and bureaucrats, another type of organizing was taking place. Environmentalists, farmers and Indigenous residents were holding meetings across the region and forming unprecedented alliances to fight the proposal. Sensing that their voices were being ignored by the powerbrokers in Toronto, these northerners slowly adapted their tactics to reflect the growing sense of urgency and determination. By the summer of 2000, the meetings had turned into rallies, the rallies into protests and the protests into blockades. Both access routes to the pit (the Adams Mine Road and the nearby rail line) were targets of militant occupations carried out by angry residents. These weren't lifelong activists; they were just ordinary people who got fed up. A retired schoolteacher. A legion volunteer. A rabbi. An RV salesman. "Unlikely radicals" is what local journalist and musician (and later MP) Charlie Angus called these residents, while proponents of the dump called them "environmental terrorists."

Back in Toronto, activists were beginning to organize through-out that summer as well. City councillor Jack Layton pulled together a small group of community leaders to draft a plan, and my friend and activist colleague Tooker Gomberg took me with him. I was twenty-five at the time, new to politics and eager to get involved. When tasks were being divided up, I offered to organize a rally—despite the fact that I had no experience doing that and no budget to work with. What I did have was a youthful, wide-eyed energy and I was ready to put that energy to good use. I booked a large hall, recruited key speakers from the North and printed thousands of flyers. On September 13, five hundred people showed up and listened intently to environmental activists, Toronto councillors, northern politicians and Chief Carol McBride of the Timiskaming First Nation. We collected donations and email addresses. The key message at the end of the rally was simple and straightforward: "Politics isn't a spectator sport. City council is going to make a decision in early October, and we need you inside the council chamber at city hall for the debate and the vote."

Meanwhile, the Toronto Environmental Alliance (TEA) sent teams of staff members and volunteers across the city to gather petition signatures and ask members of the public to phone their councillors. Our momentum was building, but our opponents had deep pockets and always seemed to have the upper hand. In the days leading up to the crucial vote, for example, Rail Cycle North spent tens of thousands of dollars on radio ads that began to play across

Toronto. The ads claimed that the Adams Mine dump was environmentally sound, and that northern residents supported the project—neither of which was true. We didn't have the resources to fight fire with fire, so I sent an email to hundreds of people who'd attended the rally and asked them to phone 1050 CHUM AM and request that the untruthful ad be removed from the air. Within hours, I got a message from the folks CHUM: "How can we stop all these phone calls?" Simple, I told them. All they had to do was pull the ad. They explained it was impossible to break the contract they had with Rail Cycle North, but they proposed a creative solution: I could record my own thirty-second ad and they would play it on air for pennies. This would at least level the playing field! I quickly wrote a short script and went into the CHUM studios, where one of their own DJs voiced the recording. Our ad went into on-air rotation the next day:

> Here are some facts about Toronto's garbage. The Adams
> Mine project is not a done deal yet. Rail Cycle North is not to
> be trusted. Experts have warned that the dump will pollute
> drinking water, and a recent poll says 77 percent of
> Timiskaming residents don't want it. There are other alterna-
> tives: safer dumps, composting and recycling. The Adams
> Mine project just doesn't make sense. Go to AdamsMine.com,
> find out more and then do something. Call or email your city
> councillor. Tell them you don't trust Rail Cycle North.

By the time city council finally began to debate the proposal, tensions were high. Executives and lobbyists from Rail Cycle North were in the council chamber to protect their multi-million-dollar invest-ment, but they were vastly outnumbered by hundreds of informed and assertive citizens who'd taken time off work to fight against cor-porate greed and government negligence. Most of the protesters were from Toronto, but a large contingent had travelled all the way from the North in rented school buses. Rail Cycle North had zero public support, but they had financial resources, environmental approvals and strong political connections at both city hall and the premier's office, and they were leveraging all these advantages to seal the deal. The odds were against us, and that's why I'll never forget the glorious moment when, a few weeks later, Jack Layton poured champagne into ten glasses which we raised to celebrate our improbable victory. The Adams Mine garbage dump was dead.

Two groups of citizens were responsible for this victory. First, the ordinary citizens who took the time to write letters, phone their representatives, attend rallies and, in some instances, physically block rail lines and highways. But these people could be effective only if they knew what was happening, when and where. That brings us to the second group: the organizers. Neither of these groups has any influence without the other. A political organizer is powerless without a long list of supporters, and those supporters are powerless if they aren't brought together into a unified effort. Activist leaders transform untapped human potential into collective voice by providing three resources: information, navigation and motivation. These are the ingredients that allow "unlikely radicals" to emerge from the general population.

> *Information:* There's an enormous toxic dump being proposed that will pollute the groundwater below thousands of hectares of towns, farmland and Indigenous territory.
>
> *Navigation:* The decision about whether to proceed with this dump will be made by Toronto city councillors, at city hall, in early October. The meeting is open to members of the public.
>
> *Motivation:* You can make a difference. Together, we can stop this reckless project.

During my two decades as an organizer, I've learned that people are more than happy to invest a little time and energy into democratic participation if they feel informed, are provided a clear and practical way to engage and are convinced that their investment will produce results. But here's the problem: there aren't many advocacy organizers out there! The non-profit sector—which includes groups of all sizes, from small grassroots activist campaigns to medium-sized organizations to large charities—is actually quite substantial and has billions of dollars in annual revenue. But how much of that revenue is being allocated to on-the-ground community organizing, using information, navigation and motivation to help ordinary people plug into the political process? Well, imagine the non-profit sector as a ten-slice pizza.

Half of its revenue comes directly from the government, as payments to groups that deliver public services. As they say, "Don't bite the hand that feeds you"—so you can be sure that those dollars aren't being spent on political organizing. That still leaves half a pizza, though. That portion is funded by philanthropists, foundations and members of the public who might be inclined to support advocacy efforts.

Most of these donations are directed to hospitals, schools, arts groups, religious groups and community sports. All worthy causes, but unlikely to be doing a lot of political organizing. If we subtract these groups, we've got less than a slice remaining.

These few bites are made up of groups whose core mandate is to address issues such as poverty, social justice and environmental protection. They can be roughly divided into two different approaches, upstream and downstream, based on a fable. A man standing near a river notices a child floating by, struggling to stay above water. The man jumps in the river and rescues the child, but within minutes, another child appears. Again, the man jumps in. More children appear, and other people begin helping with the growing rescue effort. At some point, a wise person suggests that they should walk upstream to figure out why all these kids are falling in the river.

Every issue we face has downstream and upstream solutions. One group might try to address homelessness by handing out sleeping bags or running a food bank. Those are downstream solutions because they're temporary fixes that don't really address the underlying causes of poverty. Another group might try to use education, navigation and motivation to achieve upstream solutions, such as redistribution of wealth, tenant protections or increased public spending on affordable housing. Upstream and downstream solutions are both important. As we work towards eliminating poverty, of course we need food banks, shelters and sleeping bags. The problem lies in the distribution of resources. While thousands of groups in Canada are pulling kids out of the water, very few are looking up the river. On the non-profit pizza, the groups focused on upstream advocacy are just a slice of tomato.

But we're not done yet, because upstream political advocacy doesn't necessarily include community organizing. Of the groups committed to shifting public policy, many practise behind-the-scenes lobbying rather than mobilizing the general public. This can be effective, but it doesn't empower ordinary people. Other groups may do organizing, but they use vague calls to action like "Vote for the environment." They're spreading motivation, but not much information or navigation. Effective community organizing requires precision and detail, where the call to action is something like this: "Please come to this important government meeting next Tuesday at 8 p.m. and sign up to speak. Read our FAQ to learn more about the issue, and don't forget to phone your city councillor. According to your postal code, your councillor is Sally Jones, and her number is . . ."

This is the kind of precise on-the-ground mobilizing that plugs ordinary people into the democratic process. It requires organizers who act as teachers, translators, guides and cheerleaders. These critical groups, the lifeblood of democracy, are incredibly obscure. On our pizza, they're just a single tomato seed.

Advocacy organizers carry out one of the most important functions in our democratic system: fostering an informed, engaged and politically mobilized population. Yet these groups receive only a shred of the vast resources available, leaving organizers as an obscure species lost in the shuffle of the non-profit landscape. And we wonder why most people are politically disengaged?

There are multiple reasons for this wildly disproportionate allocation of non-profit resources. One is the system's built-in resistance towards real change. Those who hold power and wealth will always be wary of any reform that fundamentally threatens the status quo, but they'll happily support a charity that's trying to plant some trees or feed kids. This general aversion towards upstream solutions, however, goes beyond the elites. Think of how much money people raise to help find a cure for cancer, compared to how much they give to advocacy groups battling corporate lobbyists to ban potential carcinogens from our food, makeup, toys and cleaning products. Everyone loves a philanthropist, but as soon as he starts to challenge root causes, he's often seen as a radical, a troublemaker or a complainer. The late Hélder Câmara, an activist archbishop from Brazil, famously summed up this discrepancy between our attitudes towards upstream and downstream organizing by saying, "When I give food to the poor, they call me a saint. When I ask why they are poor, they call me a communist."

This marginalization of upstream social change begins in our schools, where extracurricular programs about "making a difference" are exclusively framed in the context of charity. The kids learn about a particular cause, and then raise money for it (often with some sort of competitive angle). It's great that we teach kids about the importance of charity, but if we don't also expose them to upstream solutions or the groups fighting for those solutions, we're essentially teaching a form of defeatism: "Hey, we're stuck with poverty. We're stuck with pollution. So let's do some damage control!" That is the most disempowering and pessimistic way to teach kids about the role they can play in improving the world. What they need to know is that things like poverty and environmental degradation aren't static and are within our control. And they need to know that they have an opportunity to fix the problems they've inherited from their parents' generation—beyond band-aids. Instead, they're growing up thinking that social change and charity are synonymous.

But the biggest culprit of downstream dominance of the nonprofit sector is tax legislation. Although the words "non-profit" and "charity" are often used interchangeably, they're actually two distinct terms with very different legal meanings. Groups with charitable status are required to follow strict rules that limit their ability to do advocacy, while non-profit groups (without charitable status) can be much more innovative, politically vocal and effective when it comes to advocacy and community organizing. So why would any group choose to be a charity? Because charitable donations are tax-deductible. If you give a hundred dollars to a food bank, you can claim it as an income tax deduction. But if you give a hundred dollars to an advocacy group that's trying to reduce poverty, you can't claim it. This creates a financial incentive to avoid upstream solutions. Not surprisingly, charitable efforts attract much more financial support from philanthropists, draining potential resources away from the advocates who are trying to solve the root problems. This is a guaranteed recipe for a disengaged population and policy stagnation.

Over the years, Stephen Harper's Conservative government tightened the rules even further, directing the Canada Revenue Agency (CRA) to crack down on upstream political advocacy. When Oxfam Canada applied to renew its charitable status in 2014, the application was rejected by the CRA because Oxfam's stated goal is "to prevent and relieve poverty, vulnerability and suffering." The CRA forced the organization to change its mandate and claimed that "relieving poverty is charitable, but preventing it is not." Another group, Canadians for Nuclear Disarmament, had its charitable status revoked. A letter from the CRA explained why: "Much of the organization's activities and literature continues to be focused on nuclear disarmament and remains politically oriented. The organization's web site, under the heading 'get involved,' encourages readers to urge the prime minister, political party leaders and MP's to support a new international treaty banning nuclear weapons by way of a letter writing campaign."

This is the financial leash that governments can use to deter democratic participation: if you want a tax break, don't ask members of the public to get involved with democracy. Justin Trudeau's Liberal government has promised to make changes to Canada's tax laws to give charities more flexibility, and recently a group called Canada Without Poverty took the government to court and successfully argued that CRA's advocacy restrictions infringe upon the group's right to freedom of expression. So changes are likely coming, and that's a good thing.

But even if the government allows charities to expand their advocacy, we'll still have problems caused by confusion and fear. Under the existing rules, certain kinds of non-partisan advocacy are permitted, as long they account for less than 10 percent of a charity's resources. But because board members often don't understand these rules, they tend to take a risk-averse approach. "We have weak and confused sector organizations," explains charity law expert Mark Blumberg, who's calculated that more than 99 percent of charities conduct far fewer political activities than are allowed under the current rules. In fact, Blumberg estimates that the sector as a whole is spending only one-thousandth of its permitted threshold. So expanding the allowable activities might not make a huge difference. And even if the government removed *all* restrictions on non-partisan advocacy, there would still be a ban on partisan activity, which is also confusing because it's hard to define the word "partisan" when it comes to advocacy. I've been part of campaigns that were non-partisan, but at times we veered into grey areas. For example, we might put out a report card showing how each party's platform dealt with a certain issue. One party might get an A+, while another gets an F. Charitable groups would not be allowed to do this, or at least would be afraid of trying. Risk aversion will still rule the day. I can't tell you how many times I've sat in strategy meetings and heard great advocacy proposals shot down because of tax-related fear. "I don't think we're allowed to do that" is a song, stuck on replay, playing in the boardrooms of charities all across the country. So we end up with organizations that are scared to fight for real change and unable to be the sparks that our democracy so desperately needs.

So what can we do? To start, I propose a 5 percent diversion of all political, medical and social justice philanthropy away from charities and shift those resources to groups that know how to organize and aren't afraid to do it. Take a group like the Toronto Environmental Alliance (TEA), which has successfully remained one step ahead of corporate lobbyists by using trained organizers who strategically inform and mobilize citizens. TEA can do this work because it has explicitly chosen *not* to register as a charity. TEA's former executive director, Franz Hartmann, explains: "Our whole engagement model is premised on working with our supporters and inspiring them and giving them tools to effectively communicate with their elected officials. As soon as you become a charity, you're governed by CRA laws that regulate charities. By *not* being a charity, there is nothing stopping us from engaging people. No limits."

Most of Canada's best advocacy groups have made a similar decision. Look closely at their websites, and you'll notice a recurring disclaimer on their fundraising pages:

> Due to our political work, the Council of Canadians is not a
> registered charity. We are unable to provide charitable
> receipts for donations.

> To ensure our community's advocacy can be as effective as possible, Leadnow is not a charity, and donations are not eligible for a tax credit.

> Due to the hard-hitting nature of our campaigns, donations to Dogwood are not eligible for a charitable tax credit.

By choosing to be unburdened by the CRA's rules, these groups have greatly boosted their effectiveness—but they pay a price. Despite an impressive track record of community organizing and political victories, non-charitable advocacy groups are chronically underfunded and understaffed, and often struggle to pay their monthly bills. If we're ever going to turn the tide on issues like climate change and the wealth gap, these upstream groups will need a massive injection of resources so they can provide a counterbalance to private interest.

How would this 95/5 plan work? It could be implemented by donors, charities or foundations—or a combination of all three. Most donors don't even realize the critical difference between a charity and a non-profit, or the distinction between upstream and downstream approaches. I think most of these donors, if they knew, would happily redirect some of their money towards groups that are focused on community organizing—even if it meant a small reduction of their tax credits. Charitable groups themselves could assist in this diversion by advising their own donors to redirect a portion of their contributions:

> "Hello World Wildlife Fund! I'd like to donate $1,000 and get a tax receipt."

> "Well, thank you very much. We'd recommend giving us $950 and sending the remaining $50 to a group like the Toronto

Environmental Alliance. They can't give you a tax receipt, but because they're non-charitable, they can coordinate advocacy efforts in ways we can't."

We could also tap into community foundations that administer funds on behalf of wealthy individuals. Their donors typically have a specific issue they want to support (poverty, homelessness, mental health, etc.), but they often don't have a particular charity in mind. So the foundations end up acting as matchmaker. That's a perfect opportunity to say, "Thank you for your $400,000 donation. We'll happily take $380,000, give you a tax receipt and put that money to work on your behalf. We can also help you find a great advocacy group that could really use the remaining $20,000."

Disrupting the flow of philanthropy would be unbelievably transformative, providing a much-needed cash infusion to the most effective advocacy organizations and converting that lonely tomato seed into a juicy slice. It would also inoculate the sector against any restrictive CRA rules that may be implemented under future governments.

I know what you're thinking: Why would charities give up 5 percent of their revenue? I suppose they simply need to ask themselves if they want to be plucking kids from the river for eternity. As difficult as it might be for a food bank to give up 5 percent of its revenue, doing so would greatly increase the chances that one day the food bank wouldn't be needed anymore. And while this 95/5 diversion approach may seem radical, it's actually quite tame in comparison to other ideas that are being floated. For example, columnist Andrew Coyne has proposed that we get rid of the charitable tax credit altogether as a way to liberate the entire sector from government control. "As long as charities benefit from a special tax status," he writes, "governments will inevitably be involved in deciding what is charitable activity, and what is not—decisions that are arbitrary at best, and biased at worst."

Another twist is that charitable tax credits disproportionately benefit the wealthiest donors. At a time when more and more people are calling for higher taxes on the richest 1 percent, this is the group that gets the biggest tax breaks from charitable donations. Every time a donor gets a tax credit, it reduces government revenue, which means less public money for schools, employment programs, health care and so on. If the well-off really want to support a good cause, why do they need a tax credit? Or as Coyne puts it, "Why should millionaires be compensated for giving up something they would hardly miss?" On top of that, these tax credits for the rich are often subsiding the work of conservative advocacy groups that have successfully pushed for lower taxes and the dismantling of government programs. So we all end up paying for these anti-government efforts that work against our collective interests. "It's troubling to see tax expenditures amplifying the preferences of elite actors in public life," wrote David Callahan in his 2017 book, *The Givers*. "Most grant-making is done by wealthy individuals and foundations that are not representative of the broad spectrum of the public."

If we want to see real upstream changes in our lifetime, we must be bold enough to put all options on the table—even our revered charitable tax credits. At a minimum, a 5 percent diversion would kick-start a tidal wave of democratic participation.

THE AMBIGUOUS THIRD SECTOR

"Do non-profit organizations pay their employees?"
"How much does the founder of a non-profit make?"
"How do you make money if you own a non-profit?"

These are some of the most frequent questions asked on Google about non-profits, and they reveal a deep misunderstanding of the differences between the public sector (government), the private sector (businesses) and the so-called third sector (non-profits and charities). The stereotypes that drive this confusion are damaging to advocacy groups and contribute to their obscurity and marginalization. One of the biggest misconceptions is that no one gets paid in the non-profit sector. This comes partly from the misleading "non-profit" label itself, but also from another name for these groups—the voluntary sector. The truth is that most non-profits do have paid staff, with a wide range of salaries. Just like the private sector, some non-profit employees earn minimum wage, while others earn six-figure salaries, including the CEOs of the Ontario Society for the Prevention of Cruelty to Animals ($264,953 per year), the Red Cross ($321,299) and the Ontario Lung Association ($342,831). So while the organizations themselves can't technically earn a profit, their employees most definitely can.

Another stereotype divides the private and non-profit sectors based on their alleged goals: private companies are viewed as sleazy, greed-driven entities, while non-profits are angelic organizations trying to save the world. While that may have been partially true a hundred years ago, the lines between these two stereotypes are blurring more and more each day. In the private sector, companies are increasingly trying to project an image of social responsibility and pursuing a "triple bottom line" (a phrase coined in 1994 to describe a commitment to three measurements of success: economic, social and environmental). In addition, countless for-profit companies are embracing the "social enterprise" model, which combines an activist mandate with a market-driven revenue model. Meanwhile, there are supposed non-profits that don't serve any social justice or environmental purpose at all. The most prestigious and exclusive golf courses in Toronto, for example, with $60,000 initiation fees, are registered as non-profits. So if a for-profit can have an activist mandate, while a non-profit's core activity is destroying acres of natural habitat so a few dozen millionaires can drive around in motorized carts chatting about their latest mergers and acquisitions, then we clearly can't use goals as a defining distinction between these sectors.

The third stereotype is about revenue, asserting that corporations operate on a responsible and sustainable business model, while non-profits rely mostly on charitable handouts from foundations and governments. Reality is much messier. First, the biggest charitable handouts don't go to groups like the United Way, Red Cross or Oxfam. Rather they go to banks, oil companies and car manufacturers—each of which receive massive corporate welfare in the form of tax subsidies and taxpayer-funded corporate bailouts. Non-profits, on the other hand, are increasingly trying to reduce their dependency on handouts and philanthropy by creating decentralized revenue streams that include not only small donations or memberships but also market-based earned revenue from consulting fees, workshops and even product sales.

My own experience as both a small business owner and an advocacy entrepreneur has made me realize how similar these two worlds can be. Ten years ago, I was working on a project to create a new bicycle advocacy group in Toronto, and I travelled across North America on Greyhound buses visiting similar groups in Vancouver, Ottawa, New York City, Chicago, Portland, Seattle and San Francisco. One thing I quickly learned is that the more decentralized a group's funding was, the better. One had been sustaining itself from a single annual grant for years, but when the group's funder suddenly pulled out, there were no resources to move forward. The organizations that relied on thousands of donors, on the other hand, had more consistent funding and never had to worry about the cash flow suddenly drying up. A further advantage to decentralized funding is the freedom to advocate. The groups that received large grants from their city governments or foundations tended to focus primarily on uncontroversial programs like Bike Week or Bike to Work Day. But the groups that were actually fighting for—and winning—new government investments in bike infrastructure (new lanes, markings and parking) were funded primarily by cyclists themselves. So rather than applying for a grant from a foundation or the government, I put together a business plan that relied upon thousands of people paying an annual membership fee. When I was in my early twenties, I had owned a small business, renting industrial space in mid-Toronto to print custom T-shirts. I had to find and retain customers using effective marketing and customer service, and by delivering a quality product—all while keeping my costs low. A decade later, I was doing the same thing, but instead of selling screen-printed apparel, I was selling a safer city. Like a private-sector entrepreneur, I built a brand, put together an incredible team and went after dollars with a focus on creative marketing and creating buzz. We launched with a bang in May 2008 with a cover story in a weekly magazine and a public event in a downtown theatre that sold over a thousand tickets.

It's not as if there was no bike advocacy happening in Toronto up until that point. But existing initiatives were all based on the stereotypes of the non-profit sector. I was a member of a small group called Advocacy for Respect for Cyclists (ARC), for example. ARC was fun, dynamic and effective for its size, but the group had no funding and its capacity to organize fluctuated greatly depending on how much free time members had. I figured that in a city of three million people, someone should really be getting paid to organize cyclists into a powerful political voice. After all, there's a big difference between No advocacy and Yes advocacy. As difficult as it was to defeat the Adams Mine (a No campaign), it's much more difficult to build public support for things that don't yet exist. To win Yes victories, you really need paid staff—and that means earning revenue that is both substantial and stable.

Today, Cycle Toronto has three thousand members, $500,000 in annual revenue, eight staff members and $100,000 in assets. Jared Kolb, the executive director, appears in the mainstream media more than a hundred times each year, providing a much-needed counter-narrative to the anti-bike voices that used to dominate the news. As an upstream advocacy group, Cycle Toronto has twenty-eight thousand email subscribers, twenty-seven thousand social media followers, twenty-five local advocacy teams and more than two hundred regular active volunteers. It's a bleeding heart organization for sure, with a single goal of making our streets safer for those who choose to get around on two wheels. But rather than relying on traditional grants, Cycle Toronto has decentralized its revenue. Fifty percent comes directly from membership fees and small donations, and another 15 percent comes from earned revenue, including workshop fees, merchandise sales and valet bike parking, a service sold to large event organizers.

So let's sum this up: Non-profits can have good paying jobs or low-paying jobs. Same with the private sector. You can be saving the world, or not, in both sectors. Both groups earn revenue and can accumulate assets. Both often struggle to make ends meet, both seek new income streams and both strive for growth. You can have democratic control or top-down control in both. As both a small business owner in the 1990s and the manager of advocacy campaigns today, I have similar day-to-day tasks: balance the books, maintain a healthy revenue stream, keep my costs low and build a successful brand that resonates with my target audience.

THE DOUBLE BRAIN DRAIN

So what *is* the difference between these two sectors? Well, there are a few technical differences. For starters, non-profits—obviously—can't earn a profit. That doesn't mean they can't earn significant revenue and pay their staff well, but it does mean that if there's any money left over, they have to reinvest it in the organization. The thing is, that's exactly what most small companies do anyway: if they're lucky enough to have money left over after salaries (many don't), they often invest it back into the business. These are called retained earnings, and they mirror almost exactly how a non-profit would behave with its own surplus.

The real key difference between the private and non-profit sectors is ownership. To answer the question "How do you make money if you own a non-profit?": you *can't* own a non-profit. But as I've described above, you can indeed make money, as income. Imagine a kid with a lemonade stand who spends a dollar on lemons then brings in twenty dollars in revenue. Theoretically, if her stand was incorporated as a private company or a non-profit her short-term earning potential is nineteen dollars and her day-to-day operations are the same. The difference is that if the lemonade stand is structured as a non-profit, then she can't sell it to someone else. (Then again, only 5 to 20 percent of private companies that are listed for sale actually get bought by a new owner.)

I'm not suggesting that the differences aren't real. Private companies can attract capital investment precisely because of their ability to sell partial ownership (equity). And there are other differences that affect taxes, board transparency and government reporting. But the differences between these two sectors are much smaller than most people think.

Why is this important? And what does it have to do with democracy? My observation is that the almost arbitrary terms that divide organizations into two sectors, private and non-profit, are actually harmful to both groups. For-profits are marginalized through stereotypes that paint them as greedy and single-minded, while non-profits are marginalized by assumptions that the entire sector consists of low-income bleeding heart hippies who don't know how to manage a balance sheet. This binary lens feeds a bi-directional brain drain: those who are primarily driven by a commitment to environmental and social justice are likely to seek employment in the non-profit sector, while those with strong entrepreneurial and business skills are more likely to be drawn to the private sector. But we want bleeding heart hippies in corporate boardrooms, and we want clever MBAs in the world of social change and advocacy. We'd all benefit greatly from for-profit businesses paying more attention to their triple bottom line, and from non-profits taking an entrepreneurial approach to marketing, branding, revenue, investment and growth. Those are the skills that would allow advocacy groups to decentralize their revenue away from governments and large donors, and towards the more empowering and stable model of crowdsourced micro-donations from the general public, as well as market-based earned revenue.

Reversing the double brain drain would also trigger a much-needed boost of start-up mentality in the third sector. While the private sector is always evolving, with an entrepreneurial spirit that introduces new players who change the rules by disrupting the marketplace, the non-profit sector seems more static. It's often populated by the same groups we had a decade ago, doing the same work this year as they did last. This is partially the result of top-down funding models that tend to be risk-averse and dependent upon quick and measurable deliverables. Creativity is the primary casualty in these models because risk drives innovation, and focusing too much on quick results means that you're not investing in long-term research and development—as companies do. The obsession with measuring results also means that only certain types of outcomes are pursued. I was chatting with non-profit entrepreneur Geoff Cape recently, and he pointed out how silly it would be to use measurable impacts in other parts of life. "What's your performance metric as a parent?" he playfully asked. Just as we can't really quantify our children's happiness, confidence, creativity or empathy, it's a losing battle to try to quantify the degree to which a non-profit has inspired people, motivated them or given them hope.

"Most funders have no idea how advocacy works," one non-profit manager (who asked to remain anonymous) told me. "They've never been in the field." Her suggestion is that "before someone becomes a funder, they should have five years' experience in the advocacy world." That's not a bad idea, but the reality is that good advocacy will likely always fall through the cracks of traditional philanthropy models. This is why we need decentralized funding in the sector, and why we need to attract more business-minded people to the field of advocacy. Crowdsourced revenue will produce the strongest upstream advocacy, connecting ordinary people to the political process.

Don't get me wrong. I don't want to see our philanthropic foundations disappear. Despite the advantages of crowdsourced revenue, there are also crucial roles for large donors and foundations to play. Aside from the important downstream work they do, there are three main areas where they could leverage their wealth.

First, philanthropists could help upstream groups by supplying the hardest type of funding to find: start-up capital. While we're seeing rapid growth in areas like impact investing, social finance or community bonds—all of which invite investors to support worthy organizations or companies—very few of those dollars are going towards upstream advocacy. In the private sector, angel investors know that the odds of making money off any single bet is less than 50 percent. But the bets that do pay off usually pay off well, making up for the other losses. Foundations and large donors should take the same approach with seed stage venture philanthropy exclusively for advocacy groups. They need to take some risks and forget about their short-term deliverables. They need to recognize that if they invest money in ten disruptive start-up teams, nine of them might fail. But it's the tenth that changes the course of history.

Second, foundations and large donors could encourage innovation by letting go of the reins a little and decentralizing the distribution of their own funds. By taking the participatory budget model that I discussed in chapter 7 and applying it to their own philanthropy, these donors could transform themselves into crowd-granting agencies rather than a small group of decision-makers holding the purse strings.

Third, foundations could act as talent scouts for social change. Just as the worlds of music, sports, fashion and entertainment recruit new faces, foundations could have proactive scouts who are seeking new stars. Right now, the non-profit funding scene often feels like an insiders' game, with revenues being passed around among familiar faces. Outsiders often have no idea how to access potential funding opportunities—sometimes they don't even know they exist. So rather than waiting for some stranger to stumble upon and fill out a complicated grant application, foundations should have their ear to the ground. Every time a young person proves that she has the skills and the passion it takes to organize and mobilize her community towards political action and engagement, her phone should ring.

> "Hello, Sarah. I'm calling you from the Scout Foundation. We saw an article in the paper about the community garden you've recently started in your neighbourhood. It's fantastic."

"Thanks! It was just an abandoned parking lot before, and now it's a collaborative community space that has really brought people together. We had to do a lot of arm-twisting down at city hall to get permits and zoning changes!"

"Incredible. We know how much effort it must have taken to promote the project, get people to believe in it, work with the city's departments and manage your volunteers. That's why we'd like to give you five thousand dollars to support your work."

"Really? What do you want me to do with it?"

"That's up to you. Spend it any way you want. When you're done, tell us what you did. Then we might give you more! Thanks for all you do."

Just like our voting systems and parliament, the so-called third sector is based on rules, habits and terms that have barely been updated in centuries. At a bare minimum, the "non-profit" brand definitely needs to be retired. What could be less inspiring than a title that literally says nothing about what you do—while also implying that everyone involved is poor? Paul Alofs, former president of the Princess Margaret Hospital Foundation, once asked, "What other sector refers to itself by what it's not? Grocery stores don't call themselves 'not-furniture stores.'"

The past decade has seen some interesting efforts made at disrupting the traditional three-sector model, including the creation of new corporate structures that aim to serve as a hybrid between for-profit and non-profit. Depending on the country, state or province, these models take on different names, including social enterprise, community interest companies, social purpose corporations and low-profit corporation. Another exciting development is the independent "B-Corp" designation, whose motto is "measure what matters." B-Corp offers certification to "companies [that] meet rigorous standards of social and environmental performance, accountability, and transparency." Rather than focusing on whether there is share capital (i.e., ownership), B-Corp uses a series of metrics such as employee benefits, environmental standards, democratic governance, transparency, ethical procurement standards and CEO–worker income disparity to move beyond the profit/non-profit binary rut. These developments are a step forward, but the emphasis so far has been almost exclusively on reforming the private sector to make it more compassionate, rather than reforming the non-profit sector to make it more sustainable and innovative.

I've spent two decades as a tomato seed organizer, focused primarily on three topics: sustainable transportation, visual communication in public spaces and electoral reform. (Poetically: bikes, billboards and ballots.) People have asked why I've scattered myself across these seemingly disconnected topics, but there's a common thread. In each case, I'm trying to give voice and power to an underdog, a group that's being systemically excluded by a dominant force. Roads designed exclusively for cars, invasive corporate signs and a cartel of prehistoric political parties—each of these suffocates other voices. In each case, there are elite forces at work maintaining the status quo. And in each case, those forces can be overpowered only by effective political advocacy. This is why the under-resourcing of advocacy groups is a threat to democracy. With a weak and underfunded sector that suffers from risk aversion, damaging stereotypes and top-down revenue flow, our potential to organize is stifled. With so few community organizers on the non-profit pizza, we're missing out on our greatest resource: people power.

If you visit the Adams Mine today, you'll find a gorgeous deep lake without a single diaper or paint can in it. An environmental disaster was avoided because of one thing: people who were

CHAPTER 10

END OF HEROES

In a quiet meadow by the Thames River in 1215, King John of England reluctantly met with a group of rebellious barons who'd grown tired of his tyrannical leadership. Weeks earlier, these mutineers had declared war on the monarch and seized London. But on this spring day, they offered a truce: peace and loyalty in exchange for unprecedented limitations on the king's power. They handed John a list of demands written on sheepskin, a document that came to be known as the Magna Carta—or the Great Charter. It was one of the most important turning points in the history of Western democracy. Truth be told, the document was by no means a manifesto for the people—it was a manifesto for a small handful of rich men. But it was a crack in the armour. While the Magna Carta didn't mark the end of dictatorial monarchy, it was the beginning of the end.

While chapter 6 was about the tone of leadership, this chapter is about the shape of leadership—the shape of power. Hierarchy can look like a pyramid, with a single person acting unilaterally at the top, or it can be rounded, with collaborative decision-making. The Magna Carta rounded the pointy tip of power ever so slightly, giving limited powers to a council of twenty-five barons. Over time, more people rose up to oppose the monarch's authority and the shape of power became even more rounded. Singular control was gradually replaced by councils and parliaments—groups of people who would talk and listen in order to make decisions. Indeed, the word "parliament" comes from the French *parler*, "to speak." But kings and queens desperately clung to power as their authority slowly slipped away. Really, really slowly. The word "parliament" wasn't introduced for another twenty years after the Magna Carta, and it took thirty more years before anyone other than knights and barons were allowed to join the legislature. A further seventy-five years passed before the "commons" met separately from the nobility, and two hundred more before the House of Commons was given its own meeting space. But still the monarchs grasped at power. Almost four hundred years after the Great Charter, King James I claimed to have God-given authority to rule unilaterally, declaring, "The state of monarchy is the supremest thing upon earth. For kings are not only God's lieutenants upon earth, and sit upon God's throne, but even by God himself they are called gods."

But it was too late. Britain's parliamentarians had tasted power, and they wanted more. During the 1640s, the legislature vigorously challenged the power of King Charles I, first by declaring war and then by dropping a two-handed axe on his neck. But still it took another forty years until the Glorious Revolution finally affirmed the authority of Parliament. Even then, the monarch still retained a royal veto, but that sole remaining power was increasingly viewed as ceremonial and was last used in 1708. At that point, the transition was complete. Not a transition to democracy (less than 5 percent of the population was allowed to vote), but a transition of shape, from pointy (unilateral decisions) to rounded (deliberative decisions).

Having finally severed the king's powers (and his head), Britons had a strong cultural resistance to concentrating power in the hands of a single person. The idea of a prime minister was evolving, but the position was considered "first among equals," rather than one man above the legislature. Political leaders, including prime ministers themselves, emphasized the supremacy of the deliberative parliament and strongly condemned any suggestion that there should be a single leader in charge. "According to our constitution we can have no sole and prime minister," declared senior parliamentarian Samuel Sandys. Prime Minister George Grenville called his own position "an odious title."

Meanwhile, the American colonies were also developing rounded power structures, with very little decision-making authority given to single leaders. Historian Richard Beeman wrote that "most of the newly independent states, reacting to the excesses of the colonial governors, adopted constitutions that denied their elected governors a veto power." Benjamin Franklin, the president of Philadelphia at the time, "was nothing more than the chair of a body of nearly equal councillors," Beeman explained. Imagine: toppled kings, invisible prime ministers and powerless presidents. Even well into the nineteenth century, there was strong resistance to pointy power on both sides of the Atlantic, as illustrated by this 1829 quote from the House of Commons dismissing the role of a prime minister: "Nothing could be more mischievous or unconstitutional than to recognize by act of parliament the existence of such an office."

But that was the peak of anti-pointiness and the pendulum started to swing back. In Britain, elections began to revolve around party leaders rather than local candidates or platforms, and cultural acceptance of the role of a prime minster grew, even though there was no official job description. This created confusion, as two powers seemed to coexist: a rounded Parliament and a pointy prime minister. Who was actually in charge? Prime Minister Arthur Balfour explained, in 1904: "The PM has no salary as PM, has no statutory duties as PM, his name occurs in no Acts of Parliament, and though holding the most important place in the constitutional hierarchy, he has no place which is recognized by the laws of this country. This is a strange paradox."

Just as the monarchs had seen their power slowly slip away, now it was elected legislators who saw their power gradually erode. By the time I was born, the rounded nature of British government was almost gone (as documented in Richard Crossman's *The Myth of Cabinet Government*), and it has now been all but obliterated (described in Michael Foley's *The Rise of the British Presidency*). "Caucus revolts" do indeed happen occasionally in the United Kingdom (such as the recent Brexit debacle), but these are incredibly rare and are typically short-lived moments that result in the transfer of unitary leadership from one person to another. The shape of power remains the same.

The transformation here in Canada has been even more dramatic, beginning with Pierre Trudeau's reforms that concentrated power in the Prime Minister's Office. Donald Savoie's 1999 book *Governing from the Centre: The Concentration of Power in Canadian Politics* describes a thirty-year process that saw our House of Commons mutate from round to pointy. Stephen Harper himself has described Canada's modern parliament as a "benign dictatorship."

Please keep in mind that the word "monarch" doesn't mean unelected. It simply means "to rule alone"—from the Greek *monos* and *arkhein*. Today, prime ministers seem to rule alone. Over a period of eight centuries, from the Magna Carta to the present, the shape of power slowly shifted from pointy to round, before rapidly shifting back. If we could accurately map this journey, it would look something like this:

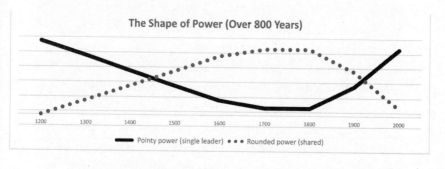

The Shape of Power (Over 800 Years)

— Pointy power (single leader) • • • Rounded power (shared)

In academic terms, those last two hundred years represent a shift from "legislative" power (parliaments, congresses, councils) to "executive" power (prime ministers, governors, presidents, mayors). This reversal happened even though our modern political systems were designed explicitly to decentralize government and prevent one person from gaining too much authority. While we've come to see our mayors, presidents and prime ministers as being at the top of our political pyramid, nothing could be further from how executive power was originally proposed three centuries ago. In fact, the term "executive," which we now associate with all senior levels of power and decision-making, was actually coined to represent the exact opposite: someone who "executes" decisions made by someone else. It was supposed to be a managerial role, implementing the will of the supreme body: the rounded and deliberative legislature.

John Locke, one of the earliest theorists on this topic, published *The Second Treatise of Government* in 1689—just one year after England's Glorious Revolution. In it, he describes three branches of government: one with "legislative or supreme power," another whose role is "only in the execution of such laws," and a third of judicial courts consisting of "indifferent and upright judges." Locke was clear that "there can be but one supreme power, which is the legislative." Political philosopher Charles Montesquieu, another pioneer who emphasized the importance of separating the three branches of government, described the legislative branch as the decision-making body representing "the general will of the state" and the executive branch as the managerial force overseeing "the execution of that general will."

Yet here we are, with a political culture that revolves entirely around the executive branch. The weakening influence of the Canadian House of Commons has been swift, dramatic and carefully documented by experts such as Donald Savoie. This transformation in Canadian legislative power, from round to pointy, is often described as a shift towards "presidential" power—a reference to the American system, which is dominated by whoever sits in the Oval Office. But this too represents a gross misunderstanding. Believe it or not, the American president was originally intended to have a negligible role in decision-making. Having successfully overthrown the British monarchy, the last thing America's founding fathers wanted was to create a position that could place too much power in the hands of one person. And unlike the British, who built a system that evolved slowly over time, the fifty-five American leaders who gathered in Philadelphia to draft their constitution in 1787 had the rare opportunity to create a new democracy from scratch. Roger Sherman, the representative from Connecticut, channelled both Locke and Montesquieu, declaring that the legislature—not the executive—was "the depository of the supreme will of the society," and that the president's role should be "nothing more than an institution for carrying the will of the Legislature into effect."

So they agreed almost unanimously on one thing: they didn't want an elected president, because once elected, he would likely behave, as North Carolina's Hugh Williamson put it, as an "elective King, and feel the spirit of one." But they were also committed to Montesquieu's concept of separation of powers, and that made them equally reluctant to adopt the British model, which featured an executive branch (prime minister and cabinet) chosen by—and from within—the legislative branch (Parliament).

For months, America's founders debated. They agreed to have term limits as one mechanism to prevent pointy power from taking hold, but they still couldn't figure out how the president would be chosen. Of the four major models presented to the convention, none supported an elected president. On June 2, they voted 8–2 in favour of giving Congress the power to choose the president, and then reconfirmed that decision on June 26, in a 7–3 vote. But then they changed their minds—repeatedly. Their fear of creating a managerial position that might grow over time into a unilateral monarch was strong. In the end, they rejected both models; there would be no elected president nor an executive chosen by the Senate or the House of Representatives. Instead, they drafted an interesting compromise: the American people would elect a *third* legislature, which would have only one task: choose a president. Under this plan, no one would run for president—candidates would run for the Electoral College, and that group would get together to appoint a president of their choosing.

It was a clever plan, but it didn't work. Within a couple of elections, candidates for the Electoral College had become proxies for political parties, pre-committed to voting for a particular presidential candidate. And thus the third legislature had no real decision-making power at all. Being elected to the Electoral College was supposed to be a high honour that invited members to participate in analysis and deliberation. Instead, today's pledged candidates represent a complete subversion of what the college was designed to do. Even the courts have described members as "voluntary party lackeys and intellectual nonentities."

So while we tend to think of the American president as a powerful figure chosen by the people, the founding fathers actually bent over backwards to ensure that he would not be elected, or even seen as an elected leader, and would not gain legislative power. And just like the word "executive" originally meant the opposite of how we use it today, a "president" was supposed to be someone who "presides" over the execution of the decisions made by the legislative branch: a managerial role, not one of influential power. Yet today's American presidents talk and act as kings, routinely signing unilateral executive orders, which were never supposed to be used in a legislative manner. In fact, executive orders were barely supposed to be used at all. The first ten presidents respected this intention, issuing an average of only one executive order per year! But the most recent ten presidents have issued an average of fifty per year. Donald Trump, in his first few months in office, was issuing a new executive order every three days.

If Locke, Montesquieu or the founding fathers saw today's presidents and prime ministers, they would be in absolute disbelief. Despite their strongest efforts to ensure that the executive branch played an invisible managerial role, we've culturally and politically reverted to that most ancient model of democracy, the great leader. How did this happen? The uncomfortable answer is this: deep down, we want it. There's a beautiful simplicity to pointy power, and a certain comfort that's woven into our cultural DNA. Moses, Jesus, Churchill, Guevara, Skywalker, Potter— there's no human narrative as common as the single hero, most often male, protecting his people. The idea that someone is in charge, watching over us, appeals to our deepest evolutionary instincts. When Locke was writing about legislative power, he addressed our addiction to singular leadership, pointing out that as young children, we become used to authoritarian structures in our homes, and therefore "it was no wonder that they should naturally run into that form of government, which from their infancy they had been all accustomed to; and by which, by experience, they had found both easy and safe."

But while parental dominance may be an appropriate approach for raising toddlers, the mainstream political application of pointy power among adults is tragic. Our search for heroes shifts attention from policy to personality and creates a permanent culture of political spectacle and disengagement. It overshadows both the rounded legislative body and the general population. That's how the hero narrative works: Moses splits the sea and everyone else just walks through. In modern terms, that means putting all your faith in a political saviour who promises to fix everything. Your hero might be Justin Trudeau or Doug Ford, Bernie Sanders or Donald Trump, but in each case, your role is the same: help him get elected, and he'll take care of the rest. Meaningful participatory politics and the single-hero model can't co-exist, however, because when we hoist up individual saviours, we make everyone else feel small in comparison.

Compounding the problem, pop culture often presents the saviour model alongside a prophecy plot: a protagonist who's told he's the chosen one. This recurring fable further distorts the true nature of leadership, which is having the courage to take action without invitation. It also helps explain why we so often elect the sons of former leaders: it fits the fairy tale of heroic destiny. Data scientist Seth Stephens-Davidowitz has calculated that sons of politicians are almost nine thousand times more likely to get elected to Congress than the average American. As this book is going to print, my prime minister is the son of a prime minister, my premier is the son of a parliamentarian, his brother was my mayor, and his nephew is on city council, which also includes five other political sons. Not surprisingly, this pattern is almost exclusively male. While 117 MPs have sat in Canada's House of Commons as brothers, not a single MP has ever seen his or her sister elected.

The last eight hundred years have seen steady improvements in so many areas of democracy, including human rights, freedom of the press and expansion of the right to vote, but the shape of power is stuck in the Dark Ages. Today's governments are deeply centralized and dominated by individual leaders, who are often the sons of former leaders. The average voter is disengaged, cynical and often feels voiceless in the face of policies that seem to favour the elite. In so many ways, it begins to look strangely familiar.

———

The executive branch, which was supposed to act as a check against legislative tyranny, has become the tyranny itself. It wasn't a violent takeover but rather a gradual overshadowing of the rounded bodies. While all citizens can easily name their premier, prime minister, mayor, president or governor, very few know the names of their city councillors or local members of Parliament or Congress,

let alone their representative in the Electoral College. It's as if our rounded legislatures don't even exist. This is what we've learned: when we create an elected deliberative legislative body in addition to an executive structure that revolves around a single leader who is elected (or even perceived to be elected), the executive will eventually usurp and hijack the legislative. This can be summed up with a simple six-word rule: a single leader annihilates the group. Let's call this SLAG, for short. It doesn't mean that all single leaders are tyrannical. A mayor or a president can very well play a constructive role that encourages both participation and consensus. But the trend towards top-down, centralized control is undeniable and almost universal. SLAG is the greatest threat to democracy and the primary cause of our reversion to pointy power. SLAG happens in governments at all levels, but it also leads to pointy power structures far beyond our parliaments and councils. Every organization we create, no matter how complex the structure, tends to have one solitary commander in chief at the tip of the hierarchical pyramid. Political parties have a single leader. Non-profit boards are required to choose a senior executive. And we even push kids towards this single-leader-at-the-top model, asking them to elect their own student council president. Why? Is there a practical reason why every decision-making body or organization needs a single leader, or is it just a cultural remnant of our centuries-old relationship to a biblical and medieval version of leadership and power? To answer this, let's start by looking at the four reasons that Locke and Montesquieu believed we should have an executive branch in the first place.

The first motivation was purely administrative. If a legislature makes a decision, someone has to make sure it gets carried out. Locke wrote, "There is no need that the legislative should be always in being, not having always business to do. Therefore it is necessary there should be a power always in being, which should see to the execution of the laws that are made." Second was the idea of checks and balances: making sure that one part of the government couldn't seize unilateral power and become tyrannical. "There would be an end of everything, were the same man of the same body, to exercise those three powers, that of enacting laws, that of executing the public resolutions, and of trying the causes of individuals," Montesquieu warned. "To prevent this abuse, it is necessary from the very nature of things, that power should be a check to power." The third reason for having an executive was to deal with unexpected things that may come up and require urgent decisions, or to address things that "legislators may not be able to foresee," explained Locke. This was the origin of those executive orders, which were to be used only in times "where the law has given no direction, till the legislative can be conveniently assembled to provide for it." Lastly, a single executive leader could serve as a spokesperson, representing a country on the international stage.

All four motivations seem reasonable for the time they were written, but so much has changed in the past three hundred years. Philosophers of the sixteenth century could never have foreseen today's army of professional civil servants, who are "always in being" and "see to the execution of the laws." And the idea that "power should be a check to power" was created before any of our modern checks on power arose, including independent journalism. Daily newspapers were uncommon (and those that did exist were highly censored by the state), and the first radio news broadcast was still two hundred years away. In other words, no one was really watching the politicians. If the legislative members tried to seize all power by changing the rules in their own favour, it could be days before anyone even heard about it, so it made sense to have competing branches of government internally acting as watchdogs. Today, every legislative session is being live-tweeted and the slightest political scandal is shared instantly with millions—an enormous check and balance that Locke and Montesquieu could not have imagined in their wildest dreams.

So if we know that an executive structure will almost always usurp a deliberative legislature, and we also know that the reasons for creating the executive in the first place seem less credible now than they may have three centuries ago, then it's worth asking: Does government really need three branches? What would happen if we did some pruning and got rid of the executive branch? Does Parliament need a prime minister? Does Congress really need a president? And why does every city council need a mayor? What would happen if we allowed these bodies to collectively lead? For example, a city council could make decisions on its own and then hire a non-political general manager to execute the plans. I'm not the first to propose this. In fact, this rounded form of municipal government is called a council–manager system, and it's technically being used in thousands of cities across North America. America's National Civic League has a Model City Charter that "rejects the separation of powers concept with powers divided between the council and an elected chief executive." Instead, the charter proposes that "all powers be vested in the council and that the administration of the city's operations be by a city manager appointed by and serving at the pleasure of the council." But sadly, even this model charter can't let go of the hero model and leaves the door open for a "non-executive mayor" whose role is mostly ceremonial, while "the city manager shall be the chief executive of the city." These "weak mayor" models often undermine their own goals by maintaining a singular leadership position.

Technically, Toronto's governance system is supposed to be a weak mayor with a powerful council. But almost every policy discussion I've ever seen revolves around the mayor, known officially as His Worship. That's SLAG in action. There was a short period in 2014 when Toronto had no mayor at all, however, and we got an accidental glimpse of what a SLAG-free government might feel like. Rob Ford was the sitting mayor but became increasingly marginalized at city hall after a series of embarrassing scandals. Councillors began to lead collaboratively without him—an accidental experiment in leaderless government. Council stripped the mayor of most of his powers, as well as his budget. And when Ford went to rehab for two months, we literally had no mayor. As a community activist, I noticed a big difference during those strange years. Before and after Ford, it was absolutely necessary to secure the support of the mayor's office in order to get any proposal approved by council. But during the Ford years, I was able to win significant political victories both with and without the mayor's support. The councillors were in charge—as they should be but rarely are. If a rounded model can work for a city council, could it maybe work for a legislature too? Can we prune all of our executive branches, eliminating all mayors, presidents and prime ministers? Luckily, we don't need to be that drastic—at least not right away. We can put away our pruning shears while still actively undoing the past two hundred years of political regression. This is how:

ROTATION AND DILUTION

SLAG happens when a single leader is elected, or perceived to be elected. Both the British and the American systems try to avoid this problem—the former by asking the legislature to choose the prime minister, and the latter by creating the Electoral College to choose a president. Yet both have reverted to the same "elective monarchy" they were designed to avoid. So how should an executive be chosen? The simplest answer is that our elected legislators should just take turns. The shape is no less pointy on any given day, but it serves as a power-sharing approach. More importantly, at election time, no candidates are running for mayor or positioning themselves to be prime minister. The focus of the electorate and the media shifts to all the local candidates, painting a picture of collective leadership. This approach is already being used in some American cities, where city councillors take turns sitting in the mayor's chair. When a council, congress or parliament appoints a temporary leader, that person can fulfill all four of the original motivations for an executive branch—without depriving the legislators of their power and influence.

We can also alter our pointy pyramids of hierarchy by taking the position of commander in chief and sharing it a little. Rather than having one leader at the top, how about diluting that power among two or three people, transforming the sharp tip of power into a small plateau? Could a party have two leaders? Could a city have two mayors? Could a nation have three presidents? There are a few examples that prove that co-leadership, while rare, is indeed viable. In Canada, the provincial party Québec Solidaire has had two co-leaders (one male, one female) since its founding in 2006. The New Zealand Green Party has also had two co-leaders, going all the way back to 1995. In 2016, Caroline Lucas and Jonathan Bartley both announced they were going to run for leader of the UK's Green Party—as a team. Three months later, 86 percent of membership had voted for the combo, making them the first co-leaders of a national British party, which they described as a job-share arrangement. The private sector too has seen experiments with co-leadership, mostly within small start-ups but also at a handful of larger companies, such as Whole Foods, Smucker's, Citigroup and Oracle.

Believe it or not, shared executive leadership at the national level came very close to happening in no other place than the United States of America. During those drawn-out debates among the founding fathers about how to restrict executive power, both Edmund Randolph (Governor of Virginia) and Hugh Williamson (representing North Carolina) proposed that the country should have three presidents rather than one. Randolph prophetically warned that a sole executive would serve as "the foetus of monarchy" and would lead them back towards the "executive tyranny" they'd just overthrown. It was an awkward debate because George Washington was in the room and everyone knew he was most likely to become president if a single position was created. And that's just what the founding fathers voted for, on June 4, 1787. The vote was 7–3, with New York, Delaware and Maryland voting against (plus further dissent within the Virginia delegation). Historian Richard Beeman suggested that "had Washington been absent, it is entirely possible that the framers of the constitution would have created a multiple executive." In other words, the most common form of executive power in the modern world may have been designed by fluke, due to a moment of awkward peer pressure.

The path forward here is to start locally, with municipal governments, school boards and even student councils, slowly disrupting the cultural norm that expects a static single leader to rule over each legislative body. Using dilution and rotation, and some occasional pruning, we can give decision-making power back to our legislatures, where it belongs. But then again, our legislatures too are composed of heroes, with each parliamentarian, councillor or member of congress having won a local election. While a rotating, diluted or pruned government would offer a more collaborative approach to decision-making, we also need to think about what kinds of people currently end up in those seats.

The traditional model of singular leadership, amplified by the aggressive nature of our elections, tends to attract candidates who are extroverted and often overly confident. Introverts, who make up more than 25 percent of the general population, tend to be better listeners and more thoughtful in their deliberation. Yet under our current system, how would a quiet, mild-mannered policy genius ever find herself participating in a deliberative legislative body? We also know that our elections tend to elevate people who don't reflect the diversity of the general population. They are more likely to be male, white, wealthy and part of a political family. While we've seen some progress on this front, the data is still dismal.

So as long as we have elections of any kind, we're likely to have legislatures full of extrovert leaders who can't relate to the diverse populations they represent. That brings us to the ultimate democratic teardown.

END OF ELECTIONS

In 1973, Princeton economics professor Burton Malkiel triggered outrage by writing this sentence in a book: "A blindfolded monkey throwing darts at a newspaper's financial pages could select a portfolio that would do just as well as one carefully selected by experts." Creative journalists around the world put Malkiel's theory to the test, beginning with a chimpanzee named Raven, whose portfolio gained 213 percent in one year, ranking her the twenty-second-best money manager in America and outperforming more than six thousand Wall Street experts. Adam the monkey was next. He drew red circles around stocks listed in the *Chicago Sun-Times* from 2003 to 2006, and managed to beat the market average every year. Three years later, a Russian chimp named Lusha chose investments using a set of cubes. Her portfolio outperformed 94 percent of her country's investment funds, growing 300 percent in one year. Finally, as part of an experiment conducted by the *Observer* newspaper in England in 2012, a cat named Orlando chose a portfolio that outperformed the stock picks of three professional fund managers.

These stories inevitably inspired endless witty headlines across the world: "Any Monkey Can Beat the Market," and "Wall Street Chumps Lose Out to Chimp." Academics investigated these four-legged investors in an effort to understand how randomness could beat out high-paid professionals. Essentially, it seems to boil down to two things. First, the average growth of the market is so strong over time that your safest bet is to gamble on a large number of stocks (the more the better), putting your faith in the collective average rather than gambling on a few risky items. The second factor is hidden gems. While so-called experts tend to bet on high-profile, large-value stocks, it's often the overlooked "small-cap" stocks that outperform them.

Is there something we can learn here for our democracy? Maybe instead of electing our government, we could just ask Lusha and Raven to pick a bunch of people to lead us. Perhaps we too would discover that our collective wisdom is stronger than our hand-picked politicians, and that across Canada, there are valuable small-cap citizens: hidden gems that are consistently overlooked in our general elections.

Does that sound crazy to you? Letting random people make important decisions? It's not crazy at all. In fact, we already do this all the time in court, with juries composed of random people who typically have no background whatsoever in the judicial system. We put people's fate and future into the hands of these randomly selected barbers, plumbers, writers, teachers and construction workers. If we're comfortable doing this in our courts, then why not in our city halls or legislatures? This is actually how democracy was originally practised, back in ancient Greece. Instead of ballot boxes, the Athenians used a *kleroterion*, a strange machine carved out of solid rock and full of hundreds of small slots, each filled with a small token bearing someone's name. White and black balls fell randomly through a pipe and dictated which tokens were chosen— just like those bouncy ball machines used to pick winning lottery numbers! If your name was chosen, you were now a politician. This system of random democracy is called sortition (or sometimes lottocracy or demarchy). Some city-states in Italy used randomly selected city councils from the twelfth to the eighteenth century, while next door in Switzerland, sortition was used to elect mayors for almost two hundred years (1640 to 1837). In the Indian village of Uttaramerur, leaders were chosen randomly—by children! More recently, a string of academic proposals have recommended sortition for Iraq, England, the US and Canada.

The benefits of sortition would be enormous. First, it would immediately level the playing field. We all know politics is an insiders game that disproportionately rewards those who have family connections, unconditional partisan loyalty, personal wealth and public notoriety. The average Canadian would never dream of running for government, even if he had good ideas and a passion for policy. He simply wouldn't know where to start. With sortition, there would be no insiders and no political heroes: we'd all have an equal chance of sitting in a council seat or in Parliament. From gender to ethnicity to economic background, our governments would—for the first time— be representative of our country's diversity. And without expensive election campaigns, the role of big money and the influence of campaign contributions would evaporate. Political parties would also disappear, along with their whips and other mechanisms of controlling legislators, which would actually get us closer to the original design of our political system. (Political parties are not mentioned at all in the Canadian Constitution, and the names of political parties didn't even appear on ballots until the 1960s.) With sortition, each member of government would be completely independent, not owing any favours to financial supporters, party leaders or strategists.

After spending twelve years in the Nova Scotia legislature as an MLA, including three years as minister of finance, Graham Steele wrote, "I love the idea if I were an independent MLA of listening to everyone and then making up my own mind on the issues of the day in a way that makes the most sense for my constituents. Sitting as an independent would be liberating. The final decision on every vote would be mine, guided only by my conscience and my constituents." Yet while independent politicians were once common in Canada, only two MPs have entered our national Parliament as independents in the past three decades. Sortition would deliver an entire legislature of independents.

Random selection would also likely provide an enormous amount of political stability. With partisan elections, we often see wild policy swings between left and right. New programs are created, then dismantled, then created again. With sortition, we'd probably plot a steadier course because each new government would represent the average views of the same population. Lastly, sortition could help rebuild faith in democracy by bringing politics closer to the people. Parliament would cease being viewed as a distant, disconnected club of the elite and would be recognized as a group of ordinary people. Everyone would know someone who'd served in it. Maybe your mechanic, your co-worker or your cousin.

I know what you're probably thinking: Random selection might work for juries, but are ordinary people truly smart enough to be involved with high-level decision-making? And would they actually listen to each other, or would they simply bring their preformed opinions to the table and argue? It's easy to hold a cynical view about the wisdom of the average voter, but we have evidence that perhaps our cynicism is misplaced. In fact, Canada happens to be home to some of the largest sortition experiments in the world, and the results may shock you. These projects are based on the bold premise that random ordinary people, in the right environment, will happily and productively participate in thoughtful and meaningful political dialogue that produces high-quality policy proposals and recommendations. The journey began in British Columbia in 2004, with the randomly selected Citizens' Assembly on Electoral Reform (discussed briefly in chapters 3 and 7). This historic and unprecedented assembly was put together with an emphasis on geographic, economic and cultural diversity, and was then led through four stages that stretched over eleven months. First, they learned about the topic from experts, followed by public consultations to hear from other ordinary citizens as well as interest groups. Then they discussed their opinions and debated the options, for weeks. Finally, the members voted on various proposals and delivered a detailed report recommending a proportional voting system.

The BC Citizens' Assembly is regarded worldwide as proof that random citizens are capable of discussing and resolving complex political topics. In fact the model has been replicated throughout Canada and across the world. The most interesting spin-off is a Toronto company called MASS LBP (for "led by people"), which creates smaller versions of the citizens' assembly called citizens' reference panels. Here's how it works: Governments approach MASS with a problem—let's say, about health policy, income inequality or regional transportation. MASS then mails out invitations to thousands of randomly selected addresses, asking people to participate in a discussion. Unlike focus groups or public polling, the citizens' reference panels don't invite people to share what they think they already know. They dare them to absorb more information, to practise listening and to learn how to think together with others, slowly and carefully, in a collective process for the common good.

It's a radical premise: policy being developed by random strangers with no experience or training in the field. But it's working. So far, over a period of ten years, MASS has been contracted to coordinate dozens of reference panels involving more than a thousand randomly selected people who have cumulatively spent more than thirty thousand hours deliberating on important policy issues and offering recommendations that aren't tainted by partisan grudges, special interests or lack of information. By changing both the tone and the shape of leadership, MASS provides the one thing that governments have proven incapable of providing themselves: a thoughtful conversation.

While we're not about to cancel all elections in Canada and replace them with stone *kleroterions*, we can still play around with the idea of random selection. Why not start experimenting locally in our schools? One organization, called Democracy in Practice, has done just that, replacing elected student leaders with randomly selected representatives in four schools in Bolivia. Co-founder Adam Cronkright explains: "Student government can empower students to deliberate, decide, and act on important issues that affect them and their school communities. But unfortunately, around the world, student governments tend to be modelled after adult governments, with campaigns, candidates, elections, presidents and vice presidents. This model heavily advantages the most ambitious, the most popular, and the most charismatic students. This creates real inequalities between students when it comes to civic skill development, and it incorrectly teaches young people this idea that there are a select few natural-born leaders, and that for the rest of us participating in a democracy simply means casting an occasional vote for who you think is the best and brightest among those few."

While the project is currently based only in schools, the long-term goals are much bolder. The organizers proclaim that "underlying many of today's social, economic, and environmental problems are approaches to democracy that are exclusive, unrepresentative, and ineffective," and they propose that the way forward for reform—at all levels of government—is to "think beyond elections and develop fundamentally better ways to do democracy." They consider their school projects to be laboratories of democratic innovation, proving that inclusive and diverse democracy truly works and that everyone has the capacity to lead.

The next step could be local school boards. Or for those who feel that random selection is less democratic or accountable than an ordinary election, how about trying sortition for Canada's Senate? It's not elected anyway! Canadians are currently stuck with an archaic Senate filled with people who were hand-picked by prime ministers. It's the worst of all worlds: unelected, unrepresentative and unaccountable. With public support for Senate at an all-time low, what a great opportunity to try something new! Across the Atlantic, this idea has already been proposed in Anthony Barnett and Peter Carty's book *The Athenian Option: Radical Reform for the House of Lords*.

In today's democracy, we're all expected to act like stockbrokers. At election time, we look at the options available, weigh the pros and cons of each and then take that information to the voting booth, where we place our votes as best we can. But the field has already been narrowed by the parties, which have nominated their candidates. Essentially, our ballots are a list of pre-selected large-cap candidates: ambitious community leaders, successful business owners, celebrities or those born into political families. What about the millions of small-cap citizens, the ones you've never heard of, who might excel in government if given the chance?

No matter how much we tinker with electoral systems or campaign finance reform, elections will always be an exercise in choosing heroes. But leadership comes in many shapes and sizes, and doesn't always appear as a smooth-talking saviour. Shifting to sortition would require us to overcome our mistrust of each other and our collective cynicism of human capacity. It would finally introduce real diversity in government and would represent the greatest single vote of confidence we could ever make towards our friends, our families, our neighbours and ourselves. And that brings us to the final section of this chapter: a look at how we've allowed our cultural preference for pointy leadership to distort our view of what a hero truly is, and who can be one.

A HOUSE OF MIRRORS

One of my favourite books as a child, *What Do People Do All Day?* by Richard Scarry, was full of intricate illustrations of cities and homes with all their hidden machinery exposed. It revealed the complex and fascinating world that lies hidden beneath our pavement and inside our own walls. I've also been lucky enough to live in a couple of industrial lofts where most of the pipes and wires were exposed—just like in Scarry's books. I like seeing the guts of my home. Not only is it easier to fix things, but it also feels good to be aware of the physical networks that we depend on. Knowledge is power.

But we hide not only our physical systems, we conceal other networks too. Behind every hero is a team, a movement, a history—all obscured by the hero's individual tale. The movement for independence in India began long before Gandhi arrived, and scientists were building magnificent light bulbs while Thomas Edison was in diapers. Every time we take an extraordinary person and make him or her *the* story, we erase the other players and perpetuate a distorted model of leadership that is unrealistic and unattainable. It's a house of mirrors that turns history into a spectacle of celebrity, and in doing so, it makes leadership seem foreign and distant.

We do this at the micro local level too. If you pay close attention, you'll begin to notice examples all around you of collective efforts being distorted into stories of individuals. Rather than celebrating collective participation and the small contributions of regular people, we predictably put a few people up on pedestals—in all sectors and fields—and celebrate them as gurus, whiz kids and heroes. We love our top forty under forty lists. The twenty-five most influential people. Person of the year. Top ten activists. Even as a small-scale community organizer, I've experienced the artificial pedestal. When I'm trying to get media coverage for a political project, I often end up as part of a story that focuses on me rather than the issue I'm working on or the team I'm working with. Fourteen years ago, I started to push back against the trend. *Eye Weekly*, a free newspaper in Toronto, was writing a feature about the Toronto Public Space Committee—a project I'd created six years earlier. They wanted to put my face on the front page, but I wasn't comfortable being the sole representative of a team of talented and passionate volunteers.

I proposed a group photo, but they insisted that their covers always featured either one person or a very small group (such as a rock band). I wanted the whole team—more than a dozen people—to be featured. They threatened to cancel the entire article, but I took a risk and dug in my heels. It was a standoff.

I fought hard because I truly believed my colleagues deserved credit for their work. But my motivation wasn't entirely selfless—there were strategic reasons as well. The Public Space Committee was always seeking new volunteers to help with our cause, and I knew that thousands of people would see the *Eye* cover. A photo of me on my own might lead someone to think, "Good for him," but a group photo could allow a reader to imagine herself in the picture as well and to wonder, "How do I join that group?" A story of a singular heroic effort is an invitation to applaud. But a story of a collective effort is an invitation to participate. In the end, we worked out a compromise: a group photo with seventeen people, with my face larger than anyone else's.

Pointy yet round. Over the following years, I've repeated that same negotiation process with other media outlets and secured group photos in publications including *Toronto Life*, the *National Post* and the *Toronto Star*.

This approach could be applied to politics as well, especially at the local level. Every city councillor has full-time staff members who help with policy development and constituency issues. When these candidates run for office, why not put the faces of their whole team on their leaflets and lawn signs saying "Vote for Us"? It's not only more honest—it's more interesting. But subverting photos is easy. The harder challenge is to liberate voices that aren't physically obscured, but rather subtly silenced through environmental design. For example, how many times have you been in a meeting where a few overly confident people dominate the conversation while the rest remain quiet? This common scenario creates the illusion that most of the room is content to sit passively without being heard. More likely, they feel uncomfortable speaking out because the physical room and the meeting itself are designed to promote hierarchy. The next time you walk into a public meeting or a workshop where all the seats are arranged in rows facing a single podium, politely interrupt the proceedings and propose that they be rearranged in a circle. It's such a small and simple act, but it will completely transform the room and encourage higher levels of participation. Another easy tactic to create rounded power in a room and encourage less confident voices to speak out is to get each person accustomed to hearing his or her own voice out loud. A simple go-around will do. Ask people to introduce themselves and perhaps answer some kind of ice-breaking question. If I'm hosting a meeting, I'll also occasionally ask, "Is there anyone who hasn't spoken yet who wants to say anything?" These may seem like small details, but they're subversive because they break down our traditional models of participation, which tend to revolve around a few loud voices.

Speaking of loud voices, I should point out here that there are two victims when it comes to podiums and artificial hierarchy: those who are excluded, and those who are placed upon the pedestals. Rates of depression and burnout are high among those who are politically active because the pressures of being a leader in a hero-obsessed culture are enormous. As a young teenage activist, I became friends with a quirky fellow named Tooker Gomberg, and he served as a role model and mentor. Two decades older than me, he was an inspiration because he revealed the possibility of being middle-aged without cynicism and without apathy. He believed in people and in the power of creative protest. And he seemed fearless. I watched him deliver passionate speeches, hurling facts and inspiration through microphones and megaphones. I watched in awe when he lit a match to an enormous papier mâché model of the earth, and when he was handcuffed as a result of civil disobedience. I watched in admiration when he ran for mayor of Toronto in 2000, finishing second with more than fifty thousand votes. And I sat in numb silence on March 4, 2004, when I heard that he was missing and his bicycle had been found abandoned on Halifax's colossal Macdonald Bridge. Tooker was crushed by the weight of his own expectations and perceived failures, and fuelled by the unintended cruelness of our cultural hero fixation. We expect too little of the masses, and we expect too much of our leaders. Both are incredibly dangerous.

I often feel these pressures too, and it's frightening. I've had two nervous breakdowns, both of which were debilitating and required medical attention. I'm trying to learn how to reduce my own expectations and to be led by honest and humble goals. It's difficult, because the house of mirrors constantly produces unhealthy expectations about success, volume of work and perfection. In 2010, when I was invited to deliver a talk about apathy at TEDx Toronto, I spent days rehearsing the seven-minute presentation because every TED Talk I'd ever seen seemed smooth and flawless. When I finally walked in front of the audience, I was terrified that I might stumble or forget my lines. A TEDx Talk is like a tattoo, I felt. I wanted it to be perfect. And sure enough, it wasn't. Less than two minutes into the presentation, one of my slides loaded improperly with misplaced and jumbled words, which caused me to stumble and forced me to provide an unscripted explanation to the audience. Sixty seconds later, my mental hard drive crashed and my mind went blank. I knew I had a line I was supposed to deliver before I switched to the next slide, but I couldn't find it in my brain. In front of hundreds of people, I just stood there and stared helplessly at the PowerPoint screen, hoping something would somehow trigger my memory. As the clock ticked, I had to decide how many seconds I could afford to let slip away. After eight seconds—during which I expressed myself with three interspersed sounds, "so . . . um . . . uh . . ."—I gave up and confessed that I'd forgotten a sentence. I laughed and told the audience, "It'll come back to me later." (It didn't.) Thankfully, the rest of the presentation went smoothly. Ten days later, the video went online and my blemished tattoo was visible for all to see. I regretted not practising more, but I was okay with it. After all, my presentation specifically mentioned how we need to see heroism as something that is not perfect or glamorous. How appropriate, then, that my speech was neither.

What happened next was unexpected and revealing. Six months after my TEDx presentation in Toronto, the folks down at TED headquarters in New York got in touch and told me they liked it and wanted to put it on the main TED website—without the *x*. I would essentially have a full-fledged TED Talk, despite having never spoken at an international TED conference. I would seem much more important than I truly am. This was great news! A few weeks later, my video appeared on TED.com, but it was a little different than my original presentation: there were no jumbled fonts and no forgotten lines. Instead, they'd replaced my damaged slide and deleted the embarrassing ums and uhs. On one hand, I was thankful that the TED folks had taken the time to make me look like I'd practised more. On the other hand, it didn't feel right. I suddenly realized why all TED Talks seem so smooth, and it occurred to me that this was a huge disservice to the public, just as airbrushed fashion models can feed our insecurities about our own bodies. So many intelligent people with lots to say are terrified of public speaking, even in front of small groups. But our insecurities are merely a consequence of our expectations, or what we imagine other people's expectations to be. So every time we try to make leadership look more perfect than it truly is, we're actually scaring people away from even trying. Allowing leadership to be messy and clumsy would make life easier for those on the pedestals, but more importantly, it would encourage more people to take on leadership roles. And that's revolutionary, because real change happens when leadership becomes contagious.

Focusing on heroes rather than teams and then airbrushing those heroes to perfection amplifies the exclusive nature of leadership and power. We urgently need to push back against the celebrification of political heroes because while there's no societal damage to hiding the pipes and wires in our homes, there is a true consequence to plastering over the realities of leadership.

When I recently joined all four of Canada's major political parties, the most curious thing I received in the mail was a glossy wall calendar from the Conservative Party. The cover featured party leader Andrew Scheer, standing alone in front of the House of Commons. No party members or volunteers or staffers or even elected members of the Conservative caucus to be seen. Just Scheer. On the inside cover: a photo of Scheer. Again, alone. Then each month has a photo of Scheer—sitting alone at his desk, standing alone on a hill overlooking the ocean, being showered by confetti. Month after month, the calendar is a tribute to one man. (Imagine your dad making a calendar for your whole family but filling it with photos only of himself.) One exception in the Conservative calendar is the June photo, which does show members of the caucus standing in the legislature. But while Scheer is in clearest focus, the other thirty people (all clapping and cheering wildly for their leader) are mostly blurry. This is an organization with 97 members of Parliament, 241 recent former candidates, dozens of full-time staff members and 338 local riding associations that coordinate thousands of volunteers. But in the calendar, they're all invisible. This is SLAG. Hero culture, by constructing exaggerated pedestals, makes everyone else invisible.

Bottom line: hero-based politics is not only archaic and lazy, but the narrowness of our pointy executive structures disempowers anyone who isn't in the top position and minimizes opportunities for collective bodies to discuss, listen, learn and compromise. If our goal is to create a culture of participation, not only politically but in our communities, schools and workplaces, then we need to topple these pedestals. Challenging this cultural relationship to leadership is one of the most important journeys we can embark upon. So if you want to see real change, don't get distracted by which saviour might win the next election. Instead, look at the big picture: How is power shared in our society? What shape should our political processes have? How do we create political spaces that are inclusive and participatory? How do we dethrone the elite and open the doors for ordinary people to participate meaningfully? And ultimately, how do we help people find—and have faith in— their own voices? Canada's citizens' assemblies and MASS LBP's reference panels have proven what ordinary people are capable of when they are asked to lead. Imagine a world where we tap into those same human qualities and skills, but on an exponentially larger scale.

We're stuck in a rut. Despite centuries of political evolution, our pointy political structures remain unchallenged. We may have stripped our kings of their automatic hereditary power, but we never really let go, culturally, of the idea of a single great leader.

The rigid gospels of hierarchy and executive power are holding us back and perpetuating SLAG. But the irony is that while we cling to traditions that were formed more than a century ago, we've forgotten that people like Locke and Montesquieu, or those barons who handed King John that piece of sheepskin, weren't traditionalists. They were the rebels and innovators of their time. They would cringe at the knowledge that we now adhere to their words with religious fervour. These are people who challenged existing structures by proposing ideas that shattered the status quo. They would want us to do the same. Executive rotation and dilution, a little pruning, smashing our house of mirrors and experimenting with a little randomness—all of these are ingredients for a new kind of revolution that continues our species' long journey towards collective empowerment.

When Donald Trump was elected president with substantially fewer votes than Hillary Clinton, a chorus of voices called for the elimination of the Electoral College. I say to them: don't limit your imaginations. We can move our democracy forward only by shifting our attention away from who sits at the top of the pyramid. We need to change the shape of power itself. If America's founding fathers were alive today and were invited to fix our broken democracy, they wouldn't get rid of the Electoral College. They'd get rid of the presidency.

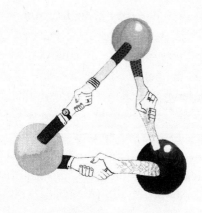

CHAPTER 11

CLOSE TO HOME

We spend most of our lives adapting to other people's expectations and rules, first as children, then as students and finally as employees. You could easily go through your entire life without ever being asked, "Hey, do you think we could be running this place better?" From crib to grave, we're often simply following orders, which is really a form of mass infantilization of the general public. It's also a leading cause of cynicism and apathy because if we don't have opportunities to exercise our democratic muscles on a daily basis, then we're not developing the skills and confidence required to participate in political activity.

You can't run a marathon if you're out of shape. The result is a political culture dominated by a small group of hyper-engaged insiders, while the average person is increasingly tuning out. What a colossal waste of talent and creativity.

The cure for being out of shape politically is to create opportunities for meaningful decision-making in the places where we spend most of our waking hours: our schools, workplaces and neighbourhoods. Incorporating democracy into your daily life would allow you to strengthen your voice, develop skills of collective action, learn about the needs and realities of others and take control of your surroundings. This teardown begins in our classrooms.

FREE-RANGE SCHOOLS

Every school has a hidden curriculum. I don't mean a secret agenda developed behind closed doors, but simply the things we absorb in the classroom as a side effect. During our school years, we're developing habits and values that are deeply affected by the school's environment. These side effects can have more impact on a student's future than the actual course content. Our relationship to power and authority is formed in these early years, when we're exposed for the first time in our lives to the concept of leadership and hierarchy outside of our homes.

Yet what pops into your mind when you hear the words "principal's office"? Let me guess: trouble, detention, shame, discipline, fear. What a tragedy that we teach kids at such a young age that authority is something to be avoided, and that interacting with leaders is primarily a consequence of bad behaviour. Essentially, we're teaching political apathy. Schools can help kids learn to believe in themselves and find their voice, or the hidden curriculum can teach them to be obedient, avoid authority and lose faith in their own ideas. If we want to help kids find their voice, we need them to know that their ideas have value and there are ways to make their voice heard by those in power. Imagine if the principal was introduced on the first day of school not as someone to avoid but as someone who's there to listen, whose office is always open and who's open to feedback and new ideas. Why not have monthly school assemblies where the principal and teachers get on stage and invite students to ask questions or propose ideas? Or maybe the principal could visit each classroom and ask, "Hey, do you think we could be running this place better?" Or better yet, what if schools themselves were somewhat democratic and students had partial control over the curriculum, conflict resolution or even the school budget or staffing decisions? To most people, the idea of a democratic school probably sounds absurd. It's one thing to imagine a principal who listens to students—but actually sharing power and using trust rather than threats to maximize a student's education? Insanity! And yet, this is the premise behind the democratic schools movement, a small but thriving slice of the modern education sector. Democratic schools are a minor subset of the alternative school community, and they come in different shapes and sizes. But they're all designed around one simple principle: learning doesn't have to be forced.

Jefferson County Open School (JCOS) is a democratic school located in a suburb near Denver. From the outside, it looks like any regular school, but the learning environment inside bears little resemblance to what most of us would expect. Instead of desks, they have group tables and couches. The staff members are called advisers and are known by their first names. There are no report cards or grades or credits. Instead, the students set their own expectations and goals, and then work together with their peers to achieve those goals, assisted by the staff advisers.

North Star Teens, based in a small town near Springfield, Massachusetts, operates on a different model. While JCOS avoids grades and report cards, the school still has to participate in the annual statewide standardized tests in order to receive public funding. North Star is different because technically it's not a school at all. It's called a "self-directed learning centre," and its motto is "Learning is natural, school is optional." In other words, if you decide to go to North Star, you aren't switching schools—you're dropping out. In a local TEDx Talk, co-founder and executive director Ken Danford proudly declares: "I've helped more than five hundred teens stop going to school." He was a public school teacher himself, but he became disenchanted with his job because the students always seemed unhappy, stressed or bored. "No one wanted to be there," he explains. A turning point for him came when a student told him: "School makes me miserable. But of all my teachers, you make me the least miserable." That was flattering—sort of. But, Danford notes, "being the least misery-inducing adult in a teen's life did not make me feel like I was maximizing my career." So he and fellow teacher Joshua Hornick resigned their jobs and invited their students to "resign with us." "If we build it they will come," was their plan, says Danford. "And they did. Talented kids. Bored kids. Depressed kids. Inspired kids."

That was 1996, and since then the North Star model has been replicated across the United States and recently entered Canada with the opening of Ottawa's Compass Centre for Self-Directed Learning in 2013. I spoke with Abby Karos, Compass's executive director and co-founder, to find out what inspired her to start Canada's first educational centre for dropouts. "It's absolute madness," she told me, "that we expect kids to go out and be productive members of society, and to care about democracy, when for twelve years, for most of their waking hours, they're not taught how to make decisions, how to figure out who they are, and how to get where they want to go." She said she considers our public school system to be a form of industrial schooling that robs kids of their creativity, their confidence and their freedom. "At Compass, we're giving kids their time back," she explained. This all sounded quite wonderful to me, but I couldn't help thinking it was perhaps naïve. What do these students do with all that freedom? I imagined classrooms full of teenagers playing video games all day. I needed to witness these democratic schools for myself and meet the students. So I journeyed from Colorado to New Hampshire to Eastern Ontario, visiting JCOS, North Star and Compass.

My first observation at all three locations was that the students seemed to really enjoy being there. I could see it in their faces, and they confirmed it during my interviews. "This feels like home," Taylor told me at JCOS. "I hate breaks [and] I hate summer vacations, because I'd rather be here." That reminded me of Danford's TEDx presentation, when he said: "Imagine a world where teens are living for today, and not just for weekends and vacations. How about waking up excited, taking risks? How about looking forward to Mondays?" Okay, it's great to see teens who are happy and "living for today," but are they actually learning anything? Without fear of punishment, poor grades or detention—why would they be motivated to study? The answer seems to be that they want to learn. And when they're put in democratic control of that learning, they actually get excited about it. This may sound like some kind of utopian experiment, but I can tell you that the teens I met were incredibly smart, eloquent, engaged—and learning a lot.

At their own direction, they were studying topics as diverse as creative writing, Spanish, piano, yoga, quantum physics and costuming. (The costuming class is taught by Emme, one of the teens at North Star. Teens teaching teens seems to be a normal thing at democratic schools). Most importantly, the students I spoke to feel that they're retaining what they learn, because they're exploring topics that genuinely interest them. "By sixth grade, you've got basic math, basic reading and a conceptual understanding of science. After that, we're just memorizing facts for tests, and then forgetting all of it," explained Phoebe, a young North Star member. "But here, you're only in a class because you want to be there. When you want to learn something, you're going to be inevitably more successful than being forced to memorize something." Her friend Persephone added, "I'm not just learning it for the test—I'm learning it for myself." Karos described the curriculum at Compass as a buffet of learning as opposed to a prearranged sit-down menu. The kids choose their own food, eat as much as they want when they want and often cook for each other.

One question still lingered in my head: What about university? As a teen I was told, hundreds of times, that if my grades were low, I wouldn't get into university. But if the kids at North Star and Compass weren't getting any credits or diplomas, surely there was no way they could ever go to college or university, right? "There's a myth," Danford told me, "that if you don't graduate from high school, you'll be doomed. It's not true. We see our kids get into first-rate universities without high school diplomas. There is nothing you can do with a high school diploma that you can't do without one."

Sure enough, the data seems to support that view. Most North Star members indeed go on to post-secondary school. In fact, universities these days are actively recruiting kids who have been home-schooled precisely because typical schools don't teach kids how to be independent thinkers. "It's a huge advantage in a lot of ways," said Carlo Ricci, a professor at the Schulich School of

Education at Nipissing University. "What universities expect students to do is become self-directed learners. Home-schoolers are fantastic at this. It's an easier transition from home-schooling to post-secondary than it would be going from a mainstream school."

Self-direction and autonomy are exactly what democratic schools are all about. At North Star, the kids spend only two to four days per week in the building—the choice is left up to each teen. On their off days, they're either learning things like dance, snowboarding or theatre, or they have part-time jobs, such as working at a daycare or organizing kids' birthday parties. Rather than wasting their free time on video games, these teens were making smart decisions and in many ways seemed to be growing up faster than their peers at traditional schools. When I was chatting with my friend Annahid Dashtgard about the lack of emotional intelligence in political spaces (see chapter 6), she pointed out that ideally these skills would be developed early in life. "How do we teach our kids about self-awareness? How to notice who's included, who's excluded? How to really build inclusive environments and how to recognize different forms of power?" At the three schools I visited, they seemed to have achieved just that. During a group interview at North Star, a teen named Nolan was speaking when a thought jumped into my head. I opened my mouth and interrupted him mid-sentence. It's a bad habit I have, of speaking over others when the thoughts in my head become louder than the words I'm supposed to be listening to. But one of Nolan's friends put her hand up, looked at him and said, "Nolan, were you done answering?" She had the awareness to notice he'd been cut off, the empathy to care about it, the motivation to ask him directly about it and the confidence to override my leadership, allowing him to finish. Those are fairly mature traits that I wouldn't necessarily expect from someone her age. In fact, I've

As someone who clearly remembers being terrified of bullies in junior high, I find the idea of a safe educational environment appealing. But what I witnessed at the democratic schools goes much deeper than safety and comfort. In fact, I can't help wondering if the lack of bullying is the most revolutionary outcome of these experiments. If we're to imagine that teen social hierarchies, peer pressure and bullying are the precursors to the aggressive and adversarial politics that adults practise, perhaps these schools are planting the seeds of a democratic revolution. Because all the things these kids are learning in their hidden curriculum—how to listen, empathize, respect and collaborate—are the exact same things that are almost non-existent in our modern political structures.

The driving force behind this revolution can be summed up in one simple word: trust. Instead of the infantilization I described earlier, these kids were being treated with deep and genuine respect. "In the same way that democracy is about trusting that everyday citizens will make good choices and will elect people that they think will represent them well," Karos explained, "this is about trusting that kids actually want to learn, and that they want to succeed, and that they don't need to be forced." One of the most revealing moments of my JCOS visit was something I noticed about Principal Scott Bain during a small group discussion with him, a staff adviser and five students. But it wasn't Bain's words that struck me—it was his silence. Throughout the hour, he barely said a word. I'd travelled thousands of kilometres to learn about his school, but rather than sharing his own thoughts, he sat quietly and let the kids speak for themselves. It wasn't until the very end of the hour that he contributed a few comments. "The school trusts kids to make real decisions," he said, and he described how kids today grow up in a culture where the most complicated decision they have to make is whether to drink Coke or Pepsi. "Part of what our school is teaching them is that you can actually be trusted to make real decisions about your education, and therefore you take on the ownership. Because people have to be trusted to govern themselves, and they're not afforded that trust in most educational settings." The trust at JCOS runs so deep that students even sit on the hiring committee.

JCOS, despite being a democratic school, curiously refrains from the one democratic activity that most schools do have: elections! Instead of voting for a student council, they have a student leadership group that anyone can join and which makes real decisions that affect the whole school body. They've discarded competitive democracy entirely and replaced it with an opportunity for any student to build collaboration skills and experience participatory decision-making. When a nearby school sent letters to all the regional student councils, inviting their presidents to a Katy Perry concert, the students at JCOS weren't sure what to do. How does a round school fit into a pointy world? They ultimately decided to pull a name out of a hat to select which student would pretend to be their president. What a great example of how they've subverted the hidden curriculum!

Persephone from North Star told me that a learning environment based on trust "makes you feel like you matter and you're not just a student or a number, you're actually a person who has opinions and you can transform those opinions into action." I can't help linking those thoughts to the #MeToo movement, which has finally exposed sexual misconduct as a normalized and widespread phenomenon too often swept under the rug. Because #MeToo isn't really about sexual consent—it's about power. More specifically, it's about people abusing power by making others feel small and then being immune to consequence because they're operating in a culture of fear. It's that fear of power that allowed these abuses to go on for so long, unchallenged. If we're not teaching our children, as part of the hidden curriculum, how to directly challenge power and why power sometimes needs to be challenged, then we shouldn't be surprised to find ourselves living in a culture where adults fear authority and become enablers of physical and emotional violence. This is the biggest failure of our traditional education system: it teaches, encourages and rewards obedience, without providing any context. It's our moral duty to raise fiercely independent children. Not just for their safety, but to allow them to flourish in every way they can. Only then can democracy tap into our collective skills and capacities.

Simply put, we'll never have a healthy democracy if we don't fix our schools. So many things that I've written about in this book— the tone of power, the shape of power, the alienating nature of elections—are things that begin in school. But JCOS, North Star and Compass prove that we don't have to settle for the status quo, that our teenage years don't have to represent the beginning of lifelong cynicism, resentment and disengagement, and that we can empower kids to believe in themselves and discover their own skills and motivations. Karos described the Compass approach as offering both "freedom of choice" and "freedom of movement," which sparked a strange thought in my mind: How many people buy free-range eggs because they feel guilty about chickens being trapped in a box, but then send their kids to a school that forces them to sit in a chair for six hours a day? We should probably treat our kids at least as well as we do our poultry.

To be clear, fully democratic schools may not be for everyone. Some teens need or want structure and maybe even some rules. But all kids deserve access to a variety of education models so they can choose the approach that feels most comfortable to them. Sadly, we're moving backwards, not forwards. Just before this book went to print, I heard the news that Compass Teens had closed their doors. There was no shortage of teens who wanted to be there, but there was a shortage of money to pay the bills. This is so tragic because all the teens I spoke with all wished they could share their experiences with more kids their age. "It would be great for people to know this is an option," Emme told me at North Star. "I left school because it wasn't a good environment for my mental health. I had no idea this was an option, and that I could feel good about my own choices. We're normal kids, growing our own voices."

YOU'RE NOT THE BOSS OF ME

For the past fifteen years, I've kept a small cardboard box filled with ceramic tiles on a shelf in my office. The box is labelled "FaSinPat," short for the Spanish phrase *Fábrica Sin Patrones*, a factory without bosses. The tiles were a souvenir from a 2003 visit to Argentina, where I served on a film crew for six months. Two years earlier, the Argentinian economy had collapsed, and panicked factory owners had pulled their investments and capital out of the country. Overnight, businesses were shut down, putting thousands of people out of work. But rather than simply accept their fate, some of these workers did the unthinkable: they broke open the factory doors and simply went back to their jobs—without permission and without a boss. Activist journalists Naomi Klein and Avi Lewis were co-directing a documentary film about these occupied factories and had invited me to join their team.

For half a year, we filmed workers as they tried to break into their own workplaces, we filmed as they turned their abandoned machinery back on, and we filmed meetings where every employee had an equal vote. Technically, these workers were trespassing—and teams of police officers would occasionally try to evict them. But the workers, along with hundreds of neighbours and family members, would literally fight back. Our cameras rolled as young men used slingshots to defend their tile factory and as seamstresses of all ages stood arm in arm, breathing in tear gas as they blocked riot police from entering their suit factory. It was one of the most interesting, unpredictable and inspiring experiences of my life (and at times, the most dangerous). And it got me thinking about workplace democracy.

Most of us spend at least a third of our waking hours at work. Just like our schools, our workplaces can help us develop democratic skills or they can contribute to a sense of disempowerment, apathy or lack of confidence. A company based on top-down layers of authority and with no mechanisms for innovative ideas or feedback to flow up the chain will inevitably result in a demoralized and unproductive workforce. There's a lot of talk these days about employee engagement and employee voice systems that strive to boost workplace morale and crowdsource creative solutions. One organization, WorldBlu, even offers an international certification standard to recognize "world-class freedom-centered (rather than fear-based) organizations and leaders." Labour unions can play an important role too, giving employees a platform to meaningfully communicate and effectively negotiate with management in relation to wages, benefits and work conditions. (Not surprisingly, studies show that unionized workers are significantly more likely than non-unionized workers to participate in political activities outside the workplace, such as voting, attending meetings or joining a party.) But while a unionized workplace creates and leverages negotiating power on issues such as wages and benefits, it still maintains a top-down relationship with owners and perpetuates an "us versus them" dynamic. The most democratic workplaces are those where the employees aren't simply negotiating with or feeling heard by the boss—they *are* the boss.

The good news is that you don't have to travel to Argentina to find a factory without bosses. Canada and the US both have companies that are owned and democratically controlled by the workers. This is a legal structure called a worker cooperative, or co-op. This is not to be confused with companies that offer their workers stock options or voting shares, which allocate democratic power based on quantity of ownership. In a co-op, each worker has one single vote—a level playing field for everyone. That doesn't mean they have no hierarchy or managers, however. It simply means that the workers themselves set the direction and policies of the company, and that the managers are democratically accountable to the workers, not the other way around. The workers, as owners, are collectively in charge. The bad news is that co-ops in North America are incredibly rare. According to the Canadian Worker Cooperative Federation (CWCF), there were only 346 worker-owned co-ops in Canada as of 2006, employing just 13,209 people—a very tiny fraction of the country's labour force.

If co-ops give workers more power and more voice, why are there so few of them? The answer is complex. First, there are simply cultural norms that stand in the way. By the time we're adults, structures based on obedience and discipline have been completely normalized for us. If we don't develop habits of cooperation and collaboration as youth, we're unlikely to seek those models as adults. Second, most entrepreneurs believe that top-down hierarchy is a good business model in terms of efficiency, effective management and profit. But there's evidence showing that co-ops are actually good for business. As co-owners, employees are much more invested in the outcome. And as engaged workers, they are more likely to offer constructive ideas and feedback. For both of these reasons, a co-op business will likely see less turnover and higher rates of loyalty, pride and innovation. In fact, according to the CWCF, worker-owned co-ops have a higher success rate than other small businesses. Another obstacle stunting the spread of co-ops is simply a general lack of public awareness. MBA programs, for example, don't touch the mechanics and benefits of democratic workplace models. As the CWCF points out, "When one considers that in Canada the worker co-op model is generally not taught in elementary schools, high schools, or universities, and that most working people do not have experience in running a business or understanding of worker co-op principles, it is not surprising that the number of worker co-ops in Canada is low."

For the few outliers who do attempt to create co-ops, additional barriers are placed in their way. A friend of mine recently started a cooperatively owned board game cafe and described how the government makes it easy to register a traditional business (a twenty-minute process that can be done online) but hasn't modernized the process to register a cooperative—which can take weeks and can be done only by mail. Those trying to create traditional top-down start-up companies have access to more resources, more training and more capital than those who are trying to create a co-op. Not surprisingly, countries that invest in, promote and support the creation of co-ops have a much higher number of cooperative workplaces. In Italy, for example, support for cooperatives is enshrined in their constitution and includes tax incentives and capital investment, as well as support with research, education and training. As a result, Italy has more than seven thousand worker co-ops. Quebec also offers tax credits, along with technical support and sources of capital, leading to growth of worker co-ops at double the rate seen in other provinces. Community-driven support networks have sprung up, like the Canadian Alternative Investment Co-op (a $6 million fund created by the faith community) and the Toronto-based Carrot Cache. But institutional support from government has been slow and under-resourced.

As you can see, the whole system seems to be rigged against the creation of new co-ops. Fortunately, starting a co-op from scratch isn't the only path towards democratic workplaces. During my six months in Argentina, the workers we filmed weren't starting new companies but reclaiming existing workplaces and transforming them into collective structures. In North America, similar transformations are beginning to happen, a process called conversion. Inspired by the occupied factories in Argentina, Brendan Martin co-founded an organization called The Working World, with the goal of helping workers legally take over their own factories or offices. "We put finance in the hands of working people without making them put down collateral," he explains. The Working World has assisted with the creation of more than two hundred democratic co-ops across North and South America, has loaned more than $4 million and can boast of a 98 percent repayment rate. But Martin isn't the first to try this. The Italian government, for example, has a special conversion fund that helps workers purchase companies from their employers. The newest player in this field is Project Equity, whose goal is to convince retiring business owners to sell their companies to the workers rather than to another private owner. The plan is based on . . . well, old people. According to their research, 60 percent of US business owners plan to sell their companies over the next decade. In other words, as the baby boomers move into their golden years, we're on the verge of an unprecedented opportunity to convert hundreds of thousands of businesses to a democratic ownership model—an economic teardown.

My time in Argentina proved to me that worker-controlled companies can function successfully within a free market. But rather
than waiting for North American workers to arm themselves with
slingshots, we can simply foster the right conditions for co-op conversion and creation, including tax incentives, access to loans and
a modernized MBA curriculum. Nothing would be more transfor-
mational for our political culture than to have a citizenry that
spends forty hours each week in a democratic space.

MOLECULES AND MAPLE SYRUP

Twenty years ago, I launched the Downtown De-Fence Project,
which offers free fence removal to any homeowner. The idea was
born after my friends and I moved into a small rental house in
downtown Toronto and noticed that most of our neighbours' front
yards were surrounded by chain-link fences. It seemed odd and
unpleasant to have metallic barriers separating each property,
so I simply offered to take them down—free of charge. I printed a
hundred leaflets, dropped them in people's mailboxes, and sure
enough my phone started to ring with requests for chain-link
removal. I bought a metal grinder, a hacksaw and some bolt cut-
ters, and I began to recruit volunteers to join the de-fencing team.
The project grew, more leaflets were printed, and one by one we've
liberated dozens of lawns across the city.

Two decades later, I'm still receiving requests for fence removals.
The aesthetic impact of opening up a caged lawn makes the project
worth my time and energy. But it's not really about beauty—it's
about community. While we live in a time of unprecedented online
connectedness, we also live in a time of unprecedented social dis-
connectedness, IRL. While most of us know the names of our next-
door neighbours, it's not unusual to have no relationship with them

beyond an occasional hello. Our televisions, laptops and tablets keep us busy inside our homes. I remember standing at the end of my street a few years ago, watching firefighters battle a burning rooftop, and chatting with others who'd gathered. As flames lit the evening sky and we introduced ourselves and shared stories about the neighbourhood, it occurred to me that I'd never met any of these people before. Why did it take a disaster to bring us together? I was quite embarrassed to realize that although I'd been researching a book about how to increase citizen engagement, I barely knew my own neighbours. This phenomenon, of people living close to each other yet being socially disconnected, is often called the atomization of society, and it ties directly to the theme of democracy because those in power benefit greatly when we retreat into our homes. When neighbours know each other, they are more likely to be informed, engaged and organized. Their voices become stronger. If political action requires collaborative effort, then atomization is a recipe for apathy and for centralized power in the hands of the few.

Following the burning roof incident, I decided to get more involved with my community. I joined the Regal Heights Residents' Association, a small but active group of local neighbours. Shortly afterwards, I was invited to join the executive committee, where I currently serve as the membership director. Our group organizes events that are political in nature, such as all-candidates debates during elections, and also takes on humanitarian causes including helping a Syrian refugee couple and their five children as they adapt to a new life in Canada. We also coordinate a range of community-building activities for the sole purpose of creating stronger connections between neighbours and improving our shared physical spaces. We host a pumpkin-carving event, a Canada Day parade and a biannual street party that transforms our quiet residential roadway into a festival grounds complete with live music, sports, face-painting and a sit-down dinner in the middle of the street. We get involved in local planning issues as well, such as a recent development application that proposed to knock down two affordable rental homes and replace them with luxury townhomes. The proposal included replacing a dozen trees with an underground parking garage. We worked closely with a coalition of neighbours and tenants, and successfully saved both the trees and the rental units.

But while the Regal Heights Residents' Association has much to be proud of, the truth is that our neighbourhood suffers from the same problem as society at large: very few of the local residents are actually involved. More than two thousand people live in our community, but only a few dozen attend our annual meetings. I wouldn't be surprised to find out that most of our neighbours don't even know that the group exists. For the most part, Regal Heights is atomized. As our membership director, I see this as a failure. But it's also an incredible opportunity, because any scientist will tell you that under the right conditions, atoms eagerly create bonds with other atoms to form stable molecules.

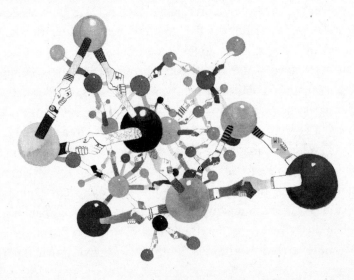

So I recently embarked on a research adventure to learn about ways to improve the conditions for neighbourhood molecular bonding. My research led me to two places: Los Angeles, which has a network of 96 neighbourhood councils (NCs), and Edmonton, with its century-old system of 157 community leagues. These two models are different than the "bite-sized" planning boards and borough councils I discussed in chapter 2, because neither is seen as a separate lower-tier of government. Instead, they're simply platforms for grassroots neighbourhood volunteers to collaborate. They're molecule-makers. Also, they're hyper-local. While each community board in New York represents roughly 150,000 residents and Montreal's borough councils represent 90,000 on average, Los Angeles has one NC for every 41,000 residents and Edmonton has one community league per every 6,000 residents. So while NYC and Montreal help put the "local" back into local government, the models I looked at in LA and Edmonton were even smaller, operating on the scale of a small village.

The Los Angeles system first caught my attention when I stumbled upon a photo of a municipal office with an unusual sign on the glass door: "Department of Neighborhood Empowerment." Some online digging revealed the history and details of LA's neighbourhood councils (created in 1999, they've since grown into one of the largest of their kind). But once again, I wanted to see for myself how these experiments were impacting real people. So when I read that LA's citywide NC elections were coming up, I impulsively bought a plane ticket and tweeted about my spontaneous research trip. Within minutes, I'd received an email from Stephen Box, the director of outreach and communications for the Department of Neighborhood Empowerment (recently rebranded as EmpowerLA). "I saw your tweet," he wrote. "Would love to connect. You can join us at city hall. There's a desk for you, if you'd like. Do you need a place to stay?" A few weeks later, I was staying in Stephen's home and commuting with him each morning to the EmpowerLA offices at city hall.

During my week-long visit, I dropped in on neighbourhood council meetings, regional summits and local elections and interviewed dozens of NC volunteers. The most common word I heard was "voice." "Los Angeles is too big for city council to understand the issues of each neighbourhood," I was told. "But the NCs give people a voice." This political influence was also described as "power in numbers" and "a platform to stand on." Another common theme was that NCs served as a bridge between people and government, with information flowing both ways. City hall "can channel through us," one resident told me, while the NCs serve as the "eyes and ears" of the community. (The city's planning department, for example, consults directly with NCs as part of every development application.) The third theme was education, in terms of both learning how municipal decision-making works and also developing new leadership skills.

I heard these same three themes mentioned when I travelled to Edmonton to learn about its community leagues, one of the oldest neighbourhood empowerment structures in North America. I met Julie Kusiek, who became active in her community league through an advocacy campaign to save the local swimming pool and then went on to create a grassroots project that turned urban planning in Edmonton upside down. Two major roads in Kusiek's neighbourhood were scheduled for reconstruction, and the traditional process would be top-down, with the city's planners and engineers drafting a plan before consulting citizens. "No matter how good of an engineer you are, you don't have the lived local experience that you might need to make the best decision possible," Kusiek told me. "By having local community members share their local diverse experience, you'll get a much better understanding of what the needs are, the fears are, to make a decision that's going to work very well for everybody." So through her community league, she and her team approached the city with their own wish list, which included major improvements for cyclists and pedestrians. The initial response from city staff was dismissive, but the community league continued to push, and eventually their proposals were incorporated into the final plan, an unprecedented example of community-led urban planning. "Community leagues have become a really practical way to give a home to advocacy projects," Kusiek told me. "They create a sense of community ownership over the problem and over the solution."

One thing that really stood out for me in LA is that neighbourhood councils offer free and automatic membership to anyone who lives or works in the area, including non-citizens. Some NCs even offer voting rights to anyone over the age of twelve. Here in Toronto, most neighbourhood groups charge an annual membership fee, in the range of ten to twenty-five dollars a year. As the membership director of my local group, I can tell you it's an administrative headache to maintain an accurate database of members, to collect money and to repeatedly remind those who haven't paid. I also feel that paying creates two tiers of residents in the neighbourhood: members and non-members. So I recently proposed that the Regal Heights Residents' Association get rid of our membership list entirely. Under our new system, we've extended membership to the whole neighbourhood, which allows us to focus on outreach, programs and events rather than tracking our accounts receivable.

There was some concern in my neighbourhood about losing the revenue from paid memberships. But to be honest, we weren't really pulling in very much: around six hundred dollars per year. While it's possible to do community organizing on a low budget like that, neighbourhood groups are more likely to become insular rather than participatory without consistent and substantial funding. That's because effective and inclusive organizing requires resources. For example, one of the questions I asked neighbourhood leaders in both LA and Edmonton was, "How did you first get involved with your local council/league?" The most common answer? "I got a newsletter at my front door." It's so easy to forget in this digital age that the best way to reach people often still involves handing out pieces of paper. But graphic design and full-colour printing isn't cheap. Neither is distribution! In my neighbourhood, we'll deliver leaflets door to door by hand, but we can't get inside the multi-residential buildings in our area—which means we're inadvertently excluding roughly 20 percent of the neighbourhood. To reach those doors, we'd have to pay for postal service. So it's no surprise that our membership is dominated by those living in single-family homes, with tenants grossly underrepresented. It's nice to be grassroots, but having money in the bank opens so many doors to inclusion. For example, one neighbourhood council in LA has translators at each meeting, complete with UN-style headsets, so everyone in the room can participate equally. That ain't cheap.

In my neighbourhood, we've now replaced mandatory membership fees with an annual voluntary crowdfunding drive. It's more inclusive and less work for us, and surprisingly, we've actually quadrupled our revenue. Win, win, win. But it's still not enough to do the kind of outreach that I'd like to see. Also, when groups rely on lower-income communities. Libraries, community centres, schools and government buildings tend to have meeting rooms available for public use, but rental fees, insurance, security requirements and endless paperwork all contribute to a system that is unnecessarily complicated and often inaccessible. When members of my residents' group once tried to book a single room in our local high school for a public meeting, they were asked to pay a $75 booking fee, a $23 application fee and $23 for insurance—just for a simple two-hour meeting inside a building we've already paid for with our tax dollars! When we tried to book the auditorium at the same school for an all-candidates election debate, we were told that we'd have to pay for two police officers, each at $60 per hour, for a minimum of four hours. The total bill, including the police, was $1,700. City hall has meeting spaces, but first residents must get a councillor to officially sponsor their event, which reminds me of high school, where every student club required a staff sponsor before it was recognized as an official group. Why do adult citizens need a stamp of approval from a politician to use a public space? The building doesn't belong to city council—it belongs to *us*.

The best way to stifle public participation is to limit access to public meeting spaces. This problem doesn't exist in Edmonton because each community has its own league hall—a physical building that is owned and run by local residents. An added bonus is that each league hall provides a free location to install a billboard. But rather than selling cars, burgers or Botox, these community signs promote neighbourhood engagement. Masood Makarechian, past president of the Edmonton Federation of Community Leagues (EFCL), told me that he first got involved in his local league simply because he saw an announcement about the annual general meeting on the community league sign.

Neighbourhoods need dedicated spaces like Edmonton's league halls, or if that's not possible, existing public buildings need to open their doors physically, financially and administratively. Ideally, our libraries, community centres and city halls could get together and create one central online booking portal—an Airbnb for neighbourhood meetings. You'd just type in your preferred date, time, location, number of people, and any special needs (video projector, smartboard, microphone) and you'd get a list of available spaces, which you could then book directly from the website. Access to funds and space are part of the conditions required to create bonds between atomized neighbours—and to create empowered communities.

The final ingredient in the battle against community atomization is a central body that supports molecular formation across a city. Toronto has dozens of residents' associations, but for the most part, they rarely speak to each other. That means they aren't sharing resources, learning from each other or amplifying their political voice by coordinating advocacy efforts. This isn't the case in Los Angeles, where EmpowerLA helps organize the annual Congress of Neighbourhoods, monthly Leadership Academy workshops, the Civic University, the Civic Youth Leadership Academy and the annual Empower LA Awards. With a substantial budget and twenty-four staff, Empower LA offers each region its own advocate, who attends NC meetings and offers administrative support and training. Edmonton's Federation of Community Leagues (which operates at arm's length from the city bureaucracy) also facilitates collaboration through events such the annual Community League Day and the Community League Showcase, which brings people together for a huge party to celebrate innovative ideas from across the city. (I dropped in on their 2015 showcase and saw hundreds of residents

You're probably thinking, "What the heck does any of this have to do with democracy? We started out talking about elections, legislatures and political parties, and now we're talking about maple syrup?" But the answer is that any activity that brings atoms together is a miniature revolution. When communities are atomized, they have no power and no voice. When they begin to collaborate, even on projects that may seem trivial, it triggers a snowball effect that is infinite in its possibilities. It's also really important to design small and simple entry points to community collaboration (like boiling sap), to attract new participants who might feel intimidated by larger projects. Lastly, I've learned the importance of creating projects that have tangible results. Community activism can be incredibly demoralizing at times because it's quite common to invest enormous amounts of energy into a project without seeing any immediate results. If you're only doing that, people will burn out, give up and tune out. But the simplest things, such as a road mural or bottles of homemade maple syrup, feed people's sense of optimism because they can see (and even taste) the tangible results of their efforts. That kind of community-building is both addictive and contagious, and it's almost guaranteed to serve as a gateway to further connections and deeper engagement.

But while small and playful projects are necessary, the real magic happens when a community tries to collaborate on complex decisions or permanent alterations to a neighbourhood. Last year, for example, a few neighbours and I redesigned a local intersection, using only chalk and leaves, to make the space safer for pedestrians.

Our "before and after" photo unexpectedly went viral on social media, became a worldwide news story and even won an award from an American blog about urbanism. It was fun, and everyone liked the story. It was also harmless, because our installation was temporary. But then we started working with the city's transportation department to design a permanent makeover—and everything changed. I'm now in the middle of intense discussions and negotiations with my neighbours. Some are concerned about losing parking; others are concerned about snow removal or garbage pickup or drainage. Some are angry. What started out as a fun project has turned into a very messy process. In some ways, it's a nightmare. But I'm also excited, because this is what community-building is really all about. How do people learn how to work together on a complex issue, express their needs, build trust and work towards consensus, when previously they hadn't even known each other's names? Most residents' groups tend to focus on two categories of activities: opposing bad development proposals and organizing events that temporarily alter the streetscape, such as a block party. These are important, but neither requires in-depth dialogue. It's the difficult collaborations—when carried out slowly, carefully and thoughtfully—that are the most fruitful and build the strongest molecular bonds.

When we allow ourselves to become atomized, our neighbour-hoods serve as dormant reservoirs of untapped energy. But when we create structured, accessible and democratic neighbourhood organizations, supported financially and administratively by the local government, we end up with communities that are more dynamic, inclusive, safe and strong. Participation at the micro-local level breathes life into neighbourhoods, while also serving as a stepping stone for deeper political engagement. "I've never been a political person," I was told by someone who now serves as the vice president of the neighbourhood council. In Edmonton and Los Angeles, I heard that neighbourhood groups "bring the community together," "turn top-down into collaboration," and "give people power to get involved and make them feel part of the city family." "Family" is not a word we often hear used to describe urban neighbourhoods. Jesse Martinez, a volunteer with the Mission Hills Neighborhood Council, described his participation as a life-changing experience. "It's lit a fire under me. It's been said that

CONCLUSION

UNRIGGED

It's a popular political joke, that while we can barely get people to participate in elections once every four years, *American Idol* can attract millions of voters every week. But let's reverse the environmental factors and see what happens. Imagine *American Idol* with only two or three contestants in the first episode, singing the same songs as the last season. The contestants don't sing very well, and most of them seem to be there only because their dads were once singers. The rules are convoluted and viewers are told that an unpopular contestant might win because of the way votes are tabulated. The singers spend most of their time on stage making fun of each other, instead of singing. Lastly, on the evening of the finale, viewers are asked to leave their homes and line up for hours to cast a vote at a polling station. Under these circumstances, *American Idol* votes would plummet from millions to zero.

Our actions are shaped by our environment. A process can be designed to be open, inclusive, inviting and participatory, or it can be rigged. Now let's do the reverse exercise: If we can rig *American Idol* to reduce participation to zero, can we do the opposite for politics? Imagine a kid named Sarah: She grows up in a democratic school that encourages her to find her own voice, to challenge authority and to learn how to be an effective communicator and leader. She walks to school each day passing murals, posters and billboards featuring local art and messages from community groups. She lives in a neighbourhood with an active residents' association that brings people of all ages together to collaborate on projects. She starts voting at age sixteen, gets randomly selected to sit on her campus Students' Association and is invited to join a political party that is inclusive, democratic and part of a coalition government. Sarah gets a job in a democratic workplace and learns how to participate in collective decision-making. She gets an invitation to attend a participatory budget town hall in her neighbourhood, where she can vote directly on how her tax dollars are spent. The invitation is bright and colourful. The meeting is at a convenient nearby location, at a convenient time, with free food and childcare. The event is casual, without any political jargon, and the politicians in attendance seem diverse, inter-generational and relatable. At election time, Sarah gets a booklet at her door, listing all of the candidates with photos and short descriptions of their platforms. All the candidates knock on her door, because with a proportional system using a ranked ballot they know that every single vote will count, even if they are only ranked second or third. There are no negative campaigns, there's a wide variety of candidates to choose from, and there is no risk of vote splitting. On election day, every candidate's team leaves a flyer at her door, reminding her to vote. After dinner, Sarah flips through the booklet one last time and looks at one of the leaflets that were dropped at her door. "Don't forget," it says, "You can vote on your computer, tablet or smartphone!"

Just as our *American Idol* turnout went from millions to zero, simply by changing the environmental factors, Sarah's likelihood of voting goes from unlikely to 100 percent. But most importantly, she's not going to see election night as the end of the process, but rather the beginning. She knows that democracy isn't just about voting, it's about how she interacts with the system between elections. She knows that her voice matters, that she deserves to be heard, and that she can make a difference and help shape the world around her.

Those who've decided to tune out politics today are simply responding, rationally, to a political culture dominated by toxic partisanship, elite condescension, privatized avenues of community expression, broken voting systems that perpetuate stale monopolies, and a culture steeped in disempowering models of celebrity hero worship. Who can blame them? Our lives are busy and stressful. We make difficult decisions each day about how to spend our time, energy, money and attention. And those decisions are made based on a rainbow of factors that can either encourage or discourage engagement.

In the introduction, I asked: "If you gave a group of people hockey sticks but no rink and no puck, would you really be surprised if they eventually put down their sticks and walked away?" But we need more than pucks and nets, because people don't just randomly become hockey players in the first place. They grow up surrounded by hockey culture and they begin to learn skills at a young age. Democracy is no different. Without a familiar culture, without training and without massive investment in democratic architecture, average people won't become players and the political world will remain an isolated domain of the establishment.

For the record, I'm not unappreciative of the many things we should be grateful for, including the right to vote, freedom of the press, or human rights enforced by independent courts. There are many populations around the world still struggling for these basic liberties and protections. But those basics are just a starting point, a foundation to build upon. So let's build. Only by transforming our existing political culture from being alienating, divisive and disheartening to something that feels meaningful, authentic and engaging can we turn things around.

The good news is that every single obstacle, every disincentive and every barrier, can be dismantled and reversed. That's the task that faces us. But first we need to crack open the doors of change by letting go of tradition. More than any other aspect of society, our democracy is steeped in ritual that subverts any effort towards reform. "Chains of office" get draped around the necks of mayors who are known as "Your Worship." Four-foot-long silver maces lie like holy objects in council chambers and legislatures across the country, despite originating from weapons that were used like clubs to bash people's faces. There's nothing wrong with celebrating a little history, but when tradition becomes the core aesthetic of our parliaments, we've chained ourselves to the past. Outside of government, these kinds of rituals would be laughed at. Imagine a CEO or board chair wearing a chain of office around her neck, carrying a silver mace with her to each board meeting or expecting everyone to bow when she entered the room. Our obsession with political tradition clouds our ability to envision change. So while Apple updates the iPhone operating system every few months, we've been unable to upgrade our own democracy. We just do it the same way over and over, ignoring the bugs, breakdowns and deficiencies.

We can break this cycle. Just as every generation laughs at the clothes, dance moves and social norms of their parents' generation, I can easily imagine a day when we'll all look back and laugh at a young, unrecognizable democracy, one that failed to engage, failed to inspire, used broken voting systems, covered its public spaces with commercial garbage, taught our kids how to be obedient, designed our government systems in ways that were both inconvenient and inhospitable and tolerated infantile, partisan bickering as though it were somehow legitimate political dialogue.

All we have to do is raise our expectations, and then begin walking towards that vision.

Let me confess, there are moments I doubt my core thesis and I worry that maybe our political dysfunction is just the inevitable result of human nature. But then I remind myself of the citizens' reference panels organized by MASS LBP, described in chapter 10. MASS overturns the assumption that innovation and wisdom come primarily from experts, academics and political elites. Instead, they seek wisdom from the most unexpected of sources: randomly selected political outsiders who are tasked with creating rich and thoughtful policy recommendations. MASS rejects the cynical view of human nature that assumes people would rather watch TV or lie on a beach than participate in political discourse that could improve their lives and the lives of others. MASS treats people not as consumers or voters but as thinkers, asking them to contribute the things that we are so rarely invited to share: our personal thoughts and our abilities to be reasonable, intelligent, empathetic and creative beings. By abandoning the low expectations we have of our neighbours—of each other—the MASS experiment reveals who we truly are. By creating environments of informed, inclusive and civil discourse, these randomly selected panels give us a glimpse of what's possible, politically, if we dare ourselves to imagine.

I'm calling for nothing less than a political awakening. A spiritual transformation that places our unconditional collective faith and trust not only in our neighbours, our family and our friends— but in ourselves. It's a cultural transformation that places public participation at the core of its method, because anything less is an abandonment of opportunity.

The stakes are high and there's no time to waste. Our species' relationship to the planet today can only be described as cancerous. The concentration of wealth and power is grotesque. Divisive forces are intentionally sowing fear and hatred. And the growing levels of cynicism and disengagement threaten any hope of meaningful change. But the future of our species doesn't need to look like an impending train wreck. We're capable of so much more.

YOUR TURN: A CALL TO ACTION

None of the changes proposed in this book will happen on their own. And any effort towards reform will be blocked and viciously fought at every step by those who benefit from the status quo. But, with your help, we most definitely can build a new future.

I don't expect you to agree with all my proposals, or even half of them. But here's my pitch: pick one, and nudge it forward. How, you ask? Let's start with a few simple activist tips: First, don't expect change to look or feel like a revolution. I hope I've convinced you by now that our task is not to seek a political sledgehammer, but rather to embark on a surgical teardown of our political ecosystem. We're not smashing the state—we're saving it. Second, you don't need to run for office. I was once being interviewed along with a fellow activist, Desmond Cole, and the journalist asked us both why we decided to work as community organizers, rather than run for office and work "on the inside." Before I could formulate an answer, Des challenged her premise: "Why does being unelected mean that we're on the 'outside'?" Bingo. We're all political players, with different roles, inside or outside our legislatures. In fact, politicians have less power than you may think because they are constantly constrained by the goalposts of public opinion. You can have a much larger impact by moving those goalposts! Third, you will inevitably encounter seemingly endless set backs that will fill you with disillusionment. And you will feel anger at times. That's all ok. Take that rage and turn it into fuel. All around us, we're witnessing dangerous leaders take advantage of people's anger, by offering false promises based on fear and hatred. The challenge of positive politics is not to dismiss or suppress this rage, but to artfully re-channel people's anger into something constructive. Fourth, there are no rules to activism, and no proper path. It's a constantly evolving process that requires new learning at every step and the ability to adapt to changing external factors. As long as you're trying your best to be informed, inclusive and effective, you'll be moving us all forward.

Lastly, activists come in infinite shapes and sizes, and you just need to figure out what works for you. Some people choose grand solo performances, like Doris Haddock, who walked five thousand kilometres across the United States to advocate for campaign finance reform. Known as "Granny D," she was eighty-eight years old when she departed California and ninety when she arrived in Washington to the cheers of thousands of supporters. Or Doug Hughes, who personally delivered 535 letters—one for each member of Congress—asking them to get big money out of politics. That's not so unusual, except for the fact that his delivery route included flying a tiny single-seat gyrocopter through restricted airspace and landing on the lawn of the Capitol Building. He was arrested and sentenced to four months in prison. Or Sheldon Bergson, who was so disappointed to learn that Canadian ballots don't include a "None of the Above" option, that he legally changed his name to None of the Above and ran for Parliament. (Actually, he knew that ballots showed the last name first, and he also wanted to appear at the bottom of each ballot, so he changed his name to Above Znoneofthe.)

While my heart fills with limitless admiration for activists like Bergson or Granny D, this is obviously not the path forward for most people. Not even close. I can't stress this enough: You don't have to be an activist superhero to make change happen. You just need to invest a little bit of your time and find a way to plug into a group or a movement that speaks to your values and concerns. If no group exists, then consider starting one. It's hard work, but it's really fun and you won't be doing it alone.

Some of the ideas I've proposed require government action, some can be implemented by groups or neighbourhoods without any need for government approval, and some of these ideas are micro-reforms that you or I can do in our daily lives. Create a community chalkboard in your neighbourhood. Work with your local school board to review their mind-numbing civics curriculum. Join a political party and then find ways to gently boost their inclusiveness and authenticity. Propose reform inside your own workplace, giving you and your co-workers more voice. Start a neighbourhood association. Then, if you're feeling motivated for more, join (or start) a campaign to lower the voting age, to create a lower tier of neighbourhood government, or to modernize our voting systems. If you're a philanthropist, or work for a non-profit foundation, consider diverting 5 percent of your funds towards non-charitable advocacy efforts. Or if you're part of any type of organization that has a singular position of senior leadership at the top (a chair, principal or president), try to find the courage to challenge this archaic model by proposing a little dilution, rotation or random selection. Or just tear down a chain link fence or make some maple syrup with your neighbours.

Regardless of which path appeals to you, this is the most important thing: Don't wait for permission or a personalized invitation. You have to invite yourself. This is your chance to find your political voice and declare war on cynicism. By tearing down the structures, assumptions and traditions that stand in our way, we can unleash our collective wisdom, love and imagination. And *that* would truly be a revolution.

ACKNOWLEDGMENTS

Despite only one person's name appearing on the cover, this book has hundreds of fingerprints on it. Six years ago, Teardown was a fantasy and I truly had no clue where to start. It was my friend Peter MacLeod who suggested I'd need an editor and introduced me to Michelle Macaleese who then told me I needed an agent and introduced me to Rick Broadhead who informed me that I needed a book proposal. Rick took an enormous leap of faith by joining the project and has been acting as my cheerleader, advocate and advisor for half a decade. I could never have navigated this path without him. Our first proposal was (rightfully) rejected by every publisher in Toronto but one editor, Kate Cassaday, took the time to offer honest feedback and advice. Based on her suggestions, I re-wrote the proposal and in 2014 four publishers offered to produce the book. I want to thank all of them, because it was such a huge confidence boost for me as a first-time author: Tim Rostron and Lynn Henry at Doubleday, Jenny Bradshaw and Doug Pepper at McClelland & Stewart, Amanda Lewis and Anne Collins at Knopf and Nick Garrison at Penguin. I chose Nick, and he has suffered the consequences since. Throughout endless delays, major re-writes and at least six different book titles, Nick has remained a steady and grounded collaborator and advisor. I delivered a bloated manuscript with 100 long-winded chapters, and he showed me how to turn it into a book.

Two others complete the core Teardown team: Marlena Zuber filled our pages with enchanted drawings and Zack Medow joined the project early on, as our research director. Zack and I installed a floor-to-ceiling corkboard in his living room and mapped out not only the book but also an ambitious research tour that took me to 23 cities in 6 provinces and 7 states and resulted in 127 interviews. A few interviewees in particular were extraordinarily generous with their time and thoughtfulness: Mark Coffin, Duff Connacher, Andrew Coyne, Annahid Dashtgard, Danny Graham, Alex Norris, Julia Pope and Graham Steele. Special thanks go to the teachers who welcomed me into their schools: Abby Karos (Compass teens), Loran Diehl Saito and Ken Danford (North Star), Scott Bain and Roberta Page (JCOS), Jody Danchuk (City Hall School Calgary) and Linda Hut (City Hall School Edmonton). And, of course, the dozens of kids who openly shared their time and thoughts.

During my travels, many couches and guestrooms were generously shared, making my trips more affordable and less lonely. I was sheltered by Kyle Bailey, Stephen and Enci Box, Andrea Curtis, Don Darnell, Jean-Sébastien Dufresne, Linda Hut, Keith Poore, Emma Pullman, Heather Smith, Rob Richie and Cynthia Terrell, Cara Brown McCormick and Colum Grove-White. Also, thanks to Wendy Katherine, Naomi Klein and Avi Lewis for lending their entire homes for writing retreats. Most of *Teardown* however, was written and edited at Stella's Lunchbox café and I want to thank the staff for tolerating my daily rent-free presence: Brunetta, Caterina, Helen, Jamie, Lexi, Matt and Tony.

Colum Grove White and Shelley Craig helped me battle procrastination and doubt, by offering much-needed weekly harassment. The final draft was polished by Les Bowser who proposed hundreds of clever edits and then by Janice Weaver—who proposed thousands. Finally, the digital words were transformed into an actual book and distributed across Canada by the great folks at Penguin Random House including David Ross, Scott Loomer,

Paisley McNab, Sharon Klein, Rachel Wharton and Pat Perry. The glorious design is the work of Andrew Roberts and Five Seventeen.

I'd be a fool not to mention the children in my life. Not only do they provide a steady stream of joy and purpose, but their curious minds fill me with so much hope for the future. Adam, Ahmed, Anika, Asher, Audrey, Caelen, Charlotte, Colin, Eddie, Elica, Ella, Elsa, Emmet, Eric, Esmé, Felix, Forest, Hamza, Imogen, Jack, Jacob, Jayden, Jess, Joel, Léa, Mawada, Mila, Muraid, Nina, Olie, Oona, Polly, Quays, River, Rouaa, Ruby, Santiago, Seth, Simon, Squigles, Stella, Stokely, Toma, Winnie and Zoe.

I'm very grateful to the people who kept me employed, fed and housed during the six years it took to produce this work: Theresa Beenken, Christy de Couto and the entire team at National Speakers Bureau, Ana Skinner and Jehad Aliweiwi at the Laidlaw Foundation, Alan Broadbent and Elizabeth McIsaac at the Maytree Foundation, Sharon Avery and Julia Howell at the Toronto Foundation, Kathryn and Jeff Dennler, Rudyard Griffiths and Peter MacLeod.

I'd also like to briefly acknowledge my privilege. I happen to be part of a demographic that wields an unreasonable amount of political power and almost entirely saturates the publishing world. Privilege alone doesn't get you through every door, but it ensures those doors are unlocked. I mention this because it's a reality inseparable from the theme of the book. Our democracy can only be healed if we conquer the biases that amplify some voices above others.

Lastly, an avalanche of love and gratitude for my partner Pauline Craig. Her infinite patience and unwavering support allowed me to complete this journey.

My apologies to anyone I've carelessly overlooked. Any errors in this book are mine alone. And thank *you*, for reading.

IMAGE CREDITS

INDEX